Revisiting Modality

Issues in Hispanic and Lusophone Linguistics (IHLL)
ISSN 2213-3887

IHLL aims to provide a single home for the highest quality monographs and edited volumes pertaining to Hispanic and Lusophone linguistics. In an effort to be as inclusive as possible, the series includes volumes that represent the many sub-fields and paradigms of linguistics that do high quality research targeting Iberian Romance languages. IHLL considers proposals that focus on formal syntax, semantics, morphology, phonetics/phonology, pragmatics from any established research paradigm, as well as psycholinguistics, language acquisition, historical linguistics, applied linguistics and sociolinguistics. The editorial board is comprised of experts in all of the aforementioned fields.

For an overview of all books published in this series, please see *benjamins.com/catalog/ihll*

Editors

Patrícia Amaral
Indiana University

Megan Solon
Indiana University

Editorial Board

Jennifer Cabrelli
University of Illinois at Chicago

Sonia Colina
University of Arizona

João Costa
Universidade Nova de Lisboa

Inês Duarte
Universidade de Lisboa

Daniel Erker
Boston University

Timothy L. Face
University of Minnesota

Sónia Frota
Universidade de Lisboa

Ángel J. Gallego
Universitat Autònoma de Barcelona

María del Pilar García Mayo
Universidad del País Vasco

Anna Gavarró
Universitat Autònoma de Barcelona

Michael Iverson
Indiana University

Matthew Kanwit
University of Pittsburgh

Juana M. Liceras
University of Ottawa

John M. Lipski
Pennsylvania State University

Gillian Lord
University of Florida

Jairo Nunes
Universidade de São Paulo

Acrisio Pires
University of Michigan, Ann Arbor

Pilar Prieto
Universitat Pompeu Fabra

Jason Rothman
UiT The Arctic University and Universidad Nebrija

Liliana Sánchez
Rutgers University

Ana Lúcia Santos
Universidade de Lisboa

Scott A. Schwenter
Ohio State University

Naomi Lapidus Shin
University of New Mexico

Carmen Silva-Corvalán
University of Southern California

Miquel Simonet
University of Arizona

Juan Uriagereka
University of Maryland

Elena Valenzuela
University of Ottawa

Bill VanPatten
Michigan State University

Volume 40

Revisiting Modality. A corpus-based study of epistemic adverbs in Galician
by Vítor Míguez

Revisiting Modality
A corpus-based study
of epistemic adverbs in Galician

Vítor Míguez
Instituto da Lingua Galega / University of Santiago de Compostela

John Benjamins Publishing Company
Amsterdam / Philadelphia

The paper used in this publication meets the minimum requirements of the American National Standard for Information Sciences – Permanence of Paper for Printed Library Materials, ANSI z39.48-1984.

DOI 10.1075/ihll.40

Cataloging-in-Publication Data available from Library of Congress:
LCCN 2024006904 (PRINT) / 2024006905 (E-BOOK)

ISBN 978 90 272 1473 7 (HB)
ISBN 978 90 272 4698 1 (E-BOOK)

© 2024 – John Benjamins B.V.
No part of this book may be reproduced in any form, by print, photoprint, microfilm, or any other means, without written permission from the publisher.

John Benjamins Publishing Company · https://benjamins.com

Table of contents

Acknowledgments	IX
Abbreviations	XI
List of figures	XIII
List of tables	XV
Table of listings	XVII

PART I. Preliminaries

CHAPTER 1. Introduction — 2
1.1 Scope and main goals 2
1.2 Outline of the book 3
1.3 From *modus* to modality 4
1.4 Modality in Galician linguistics 7

PART II. Theoretical background

CHAPTER 2. The concept of modality — 12
2.1 Modal taxonomies 12
    2.1.1 The traditional classes of modality 12
    2.1.2 Other proposals for the organization of modality 15
        2.1.2.1 Dynamic and deontic modality beyond the traditional view 15
        2.1.2.2 Alternative divisions of modal space 17
        2.1.2.3 Boulomaic modality: A neglected modal class 19
    2.1.3 Galician approaches to modality and the modals 20
2.2 Theories of modality 29
    2.2.1 Possible worlds semantics 30
    2.2.2 The factuality approach 33
    2.2.3 Modality as force dynamics 36
2.3 The typological perspective on modality 38
2.4 Critical summary 41

CHAPTER 3. Functionalist approaches to modality   44
3.1   Functional grammar models   44
   3.1.1   Functional Grammar   45
   3.1.2   Role and Reference Grammar   48
   3.1.3   Functional Procedural Grammar and the paradigmatic approach   49
3.2   Systemic Functional Grammar   55
3.3   Discourse-functional and interactional approaches   56

CHAPTER 4. Modality and neighboring categories   59
4.1   Modality and TAME   59
   4.1.1   Tense   60
   4.1.2   Aspect   63
   4.1.3   Mood   64
   4.1.4   Evidentiality   67
4.2   Modality and discourse strategy   74
   4.2.1   Mitigation   75
   4.2.2   Concession   77
   4.2.3   Strengthening   79
4.3   Modality and (inter)subjectivity   81

CHAPTER 5. Modality revisited: The Galician system   85
5.1   A revision of modality and modal categories   85
5.2   The expression of modal categories in Galician   88

PART III. A focus on epistemic adverbs
CHAPTER 6. Corpus and method   102
6.1   Epistemic modality as expressed by adverbs   102
6.2   Galician epistemic adverbs   104
   6.2.1   *Certamente* and *seguramente*   106
   6.2.2   *Probablemente* and *posiblemente*   107
   6.2.3   *Quizais* and *se cadra*   108
6.3   Corpus design   109
6.4   Variables   110
   6.4.1   The adverbial phrase   111
   6.4.2   The verb phrase   111
   6.4.3   The clause   113
   6.4.4   Beyond the clause   116
   6.4.5   The extra-linguistic context   117
   6.4.6   Summary of variables   118
6.5   Statistical approach   120

CHAPTER 7. Epistemic adverbs: Syntagmatic and paradigmatic properties   **121**
7.1 Variables and hypotheses   121
7.2 Univariate and bivariate results   123
    7.2.1 A general picture   123
    7.2.2 Adverb modifiers   126
    7.2.3 A note on mood   128
7.3 Multivariate results: Logistic regression   130
    7.3.1 The pairwise approach   132
    7.3.2 The one vs. rest approach   137
7.4 Summary and discussion   138
    7.4.1 How epistemic adverbs are alike   139
    7.4.2 How epistemic adverbs differ from one another   142

CHAPTER 8. Epistemic adverbs: A pragmatic approach   **146**
8.1 Variables and hypotheses   147
8.2 Pragmatic analysis   148
    8.2.1 Modal uses   149
    8.2.2 Discourse-oriented uses   154
        8.2.2.1 Mitigation   154
        8.2.2.2 Strengthening   157
        8.2.2.3 Tendency   162
    8.2.3 Other uses   164
    8.2.4 Results   166
8.3 Adverb meaning and co-occurrence with (near-)epistemic expressions   167
8.4 Adverb meaning and position   176
8.5 Adverb meaning and orality   181
8.6 Summary and discussion   182
    8.6.1 Main findings   182
    8.6.2 Diachronic implications   185

PART IV. **Conclusion**

CHAPTER 9. General summary and discussion   **194**
9.1 Theoretical findings and implications   194
9.2 Empirical findings and implications   196
9.3 Future lines of research   199

Bibliography   **201**

Appendixes
A. Appendix of tables ... 218

B. Appendix of listings ... 224

Acknowledgments

The present monograph is a revised version of my PhD dissertation entitled *Aproximación á modalidade epistémica en galego: o dominio adverbial*, submitted and defended in 2021 at the University of Santiago de Compostela.

First of all, I would like to thank my supervisor, Francisco Cidrás, for providing me with his insight, frankness, and friendship along the way. I am also much indebted to Jan Nuyts and Bert Cornillie for opening their doors to me as a visiting PhD student, and for generously sharing their time and knowledge with me. The other members of the jury, Johannes Kabatek and María José López Couso, offered valuable feedback and advice as well. Furthermore, I acknowledge the help of two anonymous reviewers, whose comments and suggestions have greatly improved the final version of this book.

Funding by the Xunta de Galicia and the European Social Fund (ED481A-2017/23) allowed me to join the Instituto da Lingua Galega as a PhD fellow, where I carried out most of the research published in this book. Thanks to my colleagues at the Instituto da Lingua Galega and the many international visitors we had over the years for creating a friendly and stimulating working environment. Special thanks go out to Maruxa Álvarez de la Granja, who provided me with great opportunities and advice.

Finally, the unconditional support of my parents, my brother, and my partner, Claudia, mean more than I can put into words. They bear most responsibility for this book coming into existence.

Abbreviations

CORGA	*Corpus de Referencia do Galego Actual [4.0]* (Centro Ramón Piñeiro para a investigación en humanidades, 2022)
FG	Functional Grammar
FPG	Functional Procedural Grammar
IND	Indicative mood
LP	Left Periphery
MLR	Multinomial Logistic Regression
RP	Right Periphery
RRG	Role and Reference Grammar
SBJV	Subjunctive mood
SFG	Systemic Functional Grammar
SoA	State of Affairs
TAM(E)	Tense-Aspect-Mood(-Evidentiality)
TILG	*Tesouro Informatizado da Lingua Galega [4.1]* (Santamarina et al., 2018)
TMILG	*Tesouro Medieval Informatizado da Lingua Galega* (Varela Barreiro, 2007)
WALS	*The world atlas of language structures online* (Dryer & Haspelmath, 2013)

List of figures

3.1	Layers and operators in FG	46
5.1	Semantic structure of deontic and affective modality	90
5.2	Semantic structure of epistemic modality	93
5.3	Semantic structure of inferential modality	96
7.1	Mood distribution across adverbs	129

List of tables

3.1	Modal categories in FG	47
3.2	Determining factors in the use of epistemic expressions	52
3.3	Syntactic patterns of epistemic expression types	54
4.1	Verbal mood in Galician	66
6.1	Summary of variables	118
7.1	Summary of bivariate results	123
7.2	Position distribution by clause type	126
7.3	Summary of the MLR model for *certamente*	133
7.4	Summary of the MLR model for *seguramente*	134
7.5	Summary of the MLR model for *posiblemente*	135
7.6	Summary of the MLR model for *quizais*	135
7.7	Summary of the MLR model for *se cadra*	136
7.8	Estimates of the MLR model (one vs. rest approach)	138
7.9	Bivariate results for DISTANCE and POSITION	141
8.1	Absolute frequency of uses by adverb	166
8.2	Results for MEANING. Conservative count	167
8.3	Results for MEANING. Progressive count	167
8.4	MEANING by POSITION. Conservative count	180
8.5	MEANING by POSITION. Progressive count	180
8.6	MEANING by MEDIUM. Conservative count	181
8.7	MEANING by MEDIUM. Progressive count	182
A.1	Frequency of VERB lemmas in the dataset	218
A.2	Mood share by adverb	222
A.3	Mood share by adverb. Pre-verbal position only	223
A.4	*p*-values for the MLR model (one vs. rest approach)	223

Table of listings

B.1 Summary of the morpho-syntactic MLR model. Pairwise approach — 224
B.2 Summary of the morpho-syntactic MLR model. One vs. rest approach — 225
B.3 Summary of the lexico-semantic MLR model. Pairwise approach — 226
B.4 Summary of the lexico-semantic MLR model. One vs. rest approach — 228
B.5 Summary of the final MLR model. Pairwise approach — 229
B.6 Summary of the final MLR model. One vs. rest approach — 231

PART I

Preliminaries

CHAPTER 1

Introduction

1.1 Scope and main goals

This book revisits the notion of modality from the perspective of Galician, an understudied language (see §1.4). Although Galician linguistics has made significant breakthroughs in the past 50 years, especially in dialectology and lexicography, there remain some areas where there is still a lot of work to be done. The complex and vast field of modality is one such area, and the purpose of this book is to explore this linguistic domain in Galician.

Modality has been traditionally linked to the meanings of possibility and necessity expressed through the auxiliary verbs *can* and *must* and their equivalents in other languages, such as *poder* and *deber (de)* in Galician. This linguistic domain has become very popular in the past decades, and a plethora of scholarly research has been devoted to examining it from very different perspectives. Nevertheless, modality has systematically been a slippery slope for linguists. Its theoretical study is characterized by a continued revision of its definition and divisions, and its practical applications by the permanent search for new descriptions and analyses.

The purpose of this book is both descriptive and theoretical. The descriptive goal is to provide a general picture of the Galician modal system and a detailed account of epistemic adverbs, including their syntactic, semantic, and pragmatic properties. On the basis of corpus data from Present-Day Galician the book will study how speakers/writers use modal expressions for various purposes, and how epistemic adverbs differ from one another. The theoretical goal is to contribute to the discussion about the nature of modality. In the search for a coherent framework for describing modal categories in Galician this book will examine the main traditional approaches to modality and the relations between modality and nearby categories such as mood, evidentiality, and mitigation. In doing so it will show how the traditional views on modality are problematic, and provide a more coherent approach to modal categories.

The implications of both the theoretical and the descriptive results are manifold. On the theoretical side, the study of languages like Galician, with a weak tradition of modal studies, offers an opportunity to revisit well-established but problematic conceptions of modal categories. An important conclusion of this book is that the traditional notion of modality is not a coherent one and must not be considered a basic category of analysis, but a supercategory encompassing different types of attitudinal judgments. In this view, the general concept of modality is sidelined in favor of the conceptually simple and coherent notions of deontic modality, affective modality, epistemic modality, and inferential modality. The description of the Galician modal system starts from a narrow definition of these conceptual domains and takes on a broad perspective on their formal realization, thus providing a global perspective of modal categories in the language under a novel framework. On the descriptive side, the book focuses on epistemic adverbs, which have been regarded as neutral devices to express epistemic modality, but stand out for their quantity and variety. Combining a quantitative and a qualitative perspective, the book shows that adverbs make up a rich semantic scale, and establishes several factors that condition their occurrence in discourse, challenging previous conceptions of this grammatical domain.

1.2 Outline of the book

This introductory chapter is followed by eight chapters, which are divided into two main parts (Parts II and III) plus a concluding part (Part IV) that offers a general summary and discussion of the most important results. Part II focuses on the theory, surveying the main approaches to modality and neighboring categories. This will provide the necessary theoretical background for the analysis in Part III, which examines six epistemic adverbs from both a formal and a functional perspective using a statistical method.

The opening chapter of Part II (Chapter 2) introduces the concept of modality as has been traditionally understood under the influence of logic, and examines specifically linguistic approaches from various schools (formal, functional, cognitive, and typological). Chapter 3 zooms in on the functionalist approaches to modality, which study the notion in the context of qualifications of States of Affairs (SoAs) and pay attention to its role in interaction. These ideas will be instrumental in revisiting the notion of modality and in studying modal devices from a pragmatic perspective later in the book. Chapter 4 discusses the relations between modality and neighboring categories such as tense, mood, evidentiality, mitigation, and (inter)subjectivity. Establishing the boundaries of modality is challenging but crucial in trying to obtain a basic grasp of the notion. Chapter 5 synthesizes many of the previously discussed ideas into an alternative framework for the study of modality, and illustrates this proposal with Galician data, providing a general picture of the modal system of the language.

Part III focuses on epistemic adverbs. It starts with a chapter (Chapter 6) that presents the corpus and method used in the study, offering an overview of the semantic properties and historical development of the adverbs under examination and elaborating on the empirical basis for the survey. Chapter 7 reports and discusses the results of the corpus study, whereas in Chapter 8 a careful pragmatic analysis of the data samples is conducted. Focused, respectively, on the formal and the functional dimension of the adverbs, these chapters complement each other, and provide answers to many of the questions raised in Part II. Chapter 9 concludes the book by offering a general summary of the main theoretical and empirical findings and identifying potential avenues for further research.

The remainder of this chapter offers an overview of the history of modality (§1.3) and an account of modal work in Galician linguistics (§1.4). This will provide the necessary context for discussing the concept of modality, the Galician modal system, and epistemic adverbs in Parts II and III.

1.3 From *modus* to modality

For most of its history, modality has been a notion confined to the realm of logic. In its relatively recent treatment within linguistics we can still see traces that reveal this past. These traces are very evident in handbooks of semantics, a discipline strongly grounded in philosophical research, such as the ones by Leech (1970), Lyons (1977), Kearns (2011), and García Murga (2014), or in monographs on modality, such as Portner's (2009). These works assume the tenets of propositional logic, and take on a formal approach, materialized in an interest in matters such as the truth conditions of a modalized proposition, the interchangeability of modal operators through negation, or the formal characterization of counterfactuals. The formal approach to semantics also takes from logic the model of possible worlds and the tendency to limit its analysis to modal auxiliaries or equivalent expressions, explained in light of the notions of possibility and necessity.

This influence of logic on linguistics can also be seen in works more distant from philosophy, such as Palmer's (1979, 1986), who recognizes the importance of the philosopher von Wright (1951) when determining the types of modality. More or less explicitly, the ideas of logic about modality are present in most linguistic works on the subject. This is natural, given the history of the notion of modality, but it can be problematic when it predisposes grammatical works to operate with criteria that are foreign to them. In this sense, the influence of logic resulted in a habit strongly rooted in early linguistic work on modality: the almost exclusive attention to modal verbs.

Even though the term *modality* enjoys a very widespread use today, in other historical periods this was not the case. During Antiquity and the Middle Ages, the closely related term *modus* (the Latin equivalent of *mood*) was in much more prominent use. In the various meanings given to *modus*, we can detect the origins of the modern notion of modality. Latin *modus* means 'measure, manner'. Its first appearance as an expression for linguistic description dates from the 1st century CE in the work of the rhetorician and pedagogue Quintilian, who detects a tendency to make mistakes related to verbal categories, including the *modus* (van der Auwera & Zamorano Aguilar, 2016, p. 11). This author takes the concept from the influential Greek work *Tékhne grammatiké* 'Art of grammar' by Dionysius Thrax (2nd century BC), where the term *énklisis* 'inclination, deviation' is used to designate one of the eight attributes of the verb (cf. Robins, 2000, pp. 71–72). This verbal attribute corresponds to what we know today as the morphological category of mood, which in Galician distinguishes between the indicative, the subjunctive, and the imperative.

This usage is the one that prevails in grammatical and philosophical treatises over the centuries, but van der Auwera and Zamorano Aguilar (2016, pp. 12, 17) identify two other meanings of the term *modus*. On the one hand, the one with more ancient origins goes back to the work of Protagoras, a pre-Socratic philosopher of the 5th century BCE. In his view, statements could be desiderative, interrogative, assertive, or imperative, and this linguistic dimension was later labeled *modus*. On the other hand, the origins of the most recent meaning can be found in the work of Boethius, a philosopher of the 5th and 6th centuries, who, based on Aristotle, noted that the content of a proposition could be qualified as necessary, possible, impossible, or contingent. These characterizations of the proposition were called *modi* and correspond to a good extent with the modern semantic concept of modality.

Thus, three meanings of the Latin word *modus*[1] are attested in the linguistic and philosophical treatises from the Middle Ages onward, without it being clear in many cases what should be understood when the term is used. This is a consequence of a certain proximity between the three notions conveyed by the term *modus*: for example, an order (Protagoric notion) is expressed through the morphological category of the imperative (Dionysian notion) and involves the qualification of the expression as necessary (Boethian notion). Three concepts of

---

1. During the 13th and 14th centuries "speculative grammars" were produced within the framework of scholastic philosophy. Such works *speculated* about the relationship between language, mind, and reality. In this context, the term *modus* acquires a new meaning: the *modi* are the properties of things with reference to their existence (*modi essendi*), as apprehended by the mind (*modi intelligendi*), or as expressed by language (*modi significandi*). The great importance of this concept meant that the followers of this school were known as *modistae* 'Modists' (cf. Robins, 2000, pp. 118–138). Nonetheless, this use of *modus* corresponds to a specific theoretical school that was limited in time, and had little influence on the current understanding of mood and modality.

modern linguistics can be glimpsed in the polysemy of the term *modus*: illocutionary moods or sentence types, the verbal category of mood, and the semantic category of modality.[2] The latter, that is, the modern successor of the Boethian notion, is the one that focuses the interest of the rest of this book. From here on, unless otherwise indicated, *modality* refers to this semantic concept.

Kant, in his *Kritik der reinen Vernuft* 'Critique of Pure Reason' (1781), was the first to use the term *modality* (*Modalität*, in the German original) in the same vein in which Boethius used *modus*, that is to say, in reference to the necessity or possibility of a proposition (van der Auwera & Zamorano Aguilar, 2016, p. 21). The distinction between necessity and possibility is a conspicuous philosophical issue, studied by scholars since Greek Antiquity, with Aristotle as a prominent figure. The use of *modality* to refer to this area of logic, initiated by Kant, was consolidated until it replaced the term *mood*. As a consequence, today modal logic is the formal study of modalities, understood as expressions used to qualify the truth of a proposition, such as *possibly* and *necessarily* (cf. Garson, 2018). Since philosophers start from natural language in their analysis (e.g., Carnap, 1947; von Wright, 1951), it was a matter of time before the subject attracted the attention of linguists, but this did not happen until well into the 20th century: in this connection, one must highlight the works of Halliday (1970a), Leech (1970, 1981), Lyons (1977), Palmer (1979, 1986), and Coates (1983), which accord a privileged place to English modal auxiliaries such as *must* and *may*, examining them in the light of the concept of modality.

However, there exist previous works worth mentioning, such as Bally's (1932/1965), who understands modality in terms of the *modus/dictum* distinction and exerted a great deal of influence on Spanish linguistics (see Jiménez Juliá, 1989). According to Bally (1932/1965, pp. 35–52), *modus* is the result of a thought operation (such as believing) carried out by a thinking subject (the speaker) on a representation (what is intended to enunciate or *dictum*). Although Bally's (1932/1965) proposal was widely recognized, the dominant way of doing linguistics today is that of the Anglo-Saxon sphere, and the categories applied to the English language

---

2. The terminological confusion created by the polysemy of Latin *modus* remains largely in force, and continues to determine scientific habits and practices. A good example can be found in *The Oxford handbook of modality and mood* (Nuyts & van der Auwera, 2016), where three notions of a different nature are dealt with using only two terminological labels (see §4.1.3): *mood* is used for either sentence types or the distinction between the indicative and the subjunctive, whereas *modality* refers to semantic notions related to necessity and possibility. A similar example of overlapping designations comes from Galician linguistics. In the Galician grammatical tradition the term *modo* 'mood' is systematically identified with the morphological category of the verb and its semantics, whereas *modalidade* 'modality' is used to refer either to sentence types (*modalidades da oración*) or to the semantics of non-factuality.

prevail. Just like in the past the morphological perspective dominated the field of modality as a consequence of the central place of Greek and Latin in grammatical theory, nowadays the category of auxiliary verbs, as the epitome of modality, concentrates the efforts of linguistics as far as modal studies are concerned.

In recent decades, the concept of modality has been on the rise, and in the past ten years alone numerous monographs have been published devoted to its study from various perspectives (e.g., Abraham, 2020; Arregui et al., 2017; Hilpert et al., 2021; Kehayov, 2017), as well as several handbooks focused on modality and related categories (Haßler, 2022; Nuyts & van der Auwera, 2016). However, in Galician linguistics modality has rarely been used as a notion for linguistic analysis.

1.4 Modality in Galician linguistics

Galician is a language with an irregular history. It was a prominent Romance variety in west Iberia during the Late Middle Ages, but has been in a diglossic situation where Spanish has the upper hand since the 16th century. As a consequence, Galician linguistics did not fully develop until the last quarter of the 20th century. Grammar studies in particular were in a very poor state, which according to Cidrás and Dubert-García (2017, pp. 113–114) may be explained by the secondary role of grammar in the Galician nationalist program, in addition to the lack of legal and social recognition of the language and its age-old exclusion from university studies and the academic world in general. This state of neglect began to be remedied in the 1960s, with the inclusion of Galician studies in the university curricula and, especially, with the foundation of the Instituto da Lingua Galega (Institute of the Galician Language or ILG) at the University of Santiago de Compostela in 1971, which has since developed an intense research activity in many linguistic areas. Today, Galician is taught and researched in the three Galician universities.[3]

Álvarez (2019, pp. 99–106) points out the existence of a period of expansion in which Galician linguistics has been in a permanent process of construction. This period spans over the past 50 years, and is shaped by four main concerns: (i) the priority of spoken language in linguistic fieldwork and description, (ii) the study of the Galician written tradition and the development of resources from it, (iii) the development of a Galician standard variety, and (iv) the dissemination of research results in different fronts. The lines of research at the ILG have favored lexicography and dialectology as a result of the necessity of developing the standard variety, so that grammar studies have not been the most privileged. How-

---

3. Álvarez (2019) and Regueira (2022) offer updated overviews of the development of Galician linguistics.

ever, since the birth of the ILG grammar studies have had a notable presence and continuity, even if not as part of major dialectal and lexicographical projects such as the *Atlas Lingüístico Galego* 'Galician Language Atlas' or the *Tesouros Informatizados da Lingua* 'Computerized Thesauri of the Language' (Cidrás & Dubert-García, 2017, p. 115).

The first modern grammar of Galician was published in 1986, authored by Álvarez, Regueira, and Monteagudo.[4] This *Gramática galega* 'Galician grammar' became obsolete barely a decade after its publication, with the release of the *Gramáticas da lingua galega* 'Grammars of the Galician language' by Freixeiro Mato, from 1998 to 2003 (four volumes, with a second edition in 2006), and by Álvarez and Xove, in 2002, which have been the works of reference of the past two decades. This is a good illustration of the breakthroughs made during the 1990s in the area of Galician grammar. Nevertheless, we must accept that grammatical studies were not a priority at the dawn of modern Galician linguistics, which explains why our grammatical tradition has the form of a "short and winding river," as Cidrás and Dubert-García (2017) put it. What remains of this section is an overview of the main contributions to modality in Galician linguistics. Later in the book I will offer a more in depth review of Galician approaches to modal verbs (§ 2.1.3), tense (§ 4.1.1), verbal mood (§ 4.1.3), and epistemic adverbs (§ 6.2).

Modality has very little consistency as a theoretical concept in Galician grammar. In the reference works by Freixeiro Mato (2000/2006a) and Álvarez and Xove (2002) one can detect traces of modality in the treatment of verbal periphrases and mood, adverbs, and textual markers. However, there is no separate treatment of modality as a category of analysis, largely because these works are organized around formal rather than functional categories. This tendency to start from formal categories in the analysis is dominant in studies on modality at a general level, and is verified in Galician approaches to this domain.

One of the first sets of linguistic forms to receive particular attention outside of a reference grammar, in line with its importance in the conception of the category of modality, is that of modal auxiliaries. Rojo (1974) offers the first thourough account of Galician verbal periphrases, whereas Montero Küpper (1999) explores the correspondences between Galician and German modal auxiliaries, and identifies a series of epistemic and deontic values for *deber (de)* 'must', *poder* 'can/may', *haber (de)* 'have to', and *ter que* 'have to'. However, the most important contribution in this regard is by Álvarez and Xove (2002), as they put forward a comprehensive proposal in both the formal and semantic details of this area of grammar which accounts for the behavior of modal auxiliaries, uses concepts such as neces-

---

4. Prior to that, the most notable contributions to Galician grammatical studies are the works by Saco Arce (1868) and Carballo Calero (1966).

sity, possibility, and obligation, and differentiates between the modalization of the assertion and the modalization of the event. Nevertheless, it is surprising how little and late attention has been given to modal auxiliaries in Galician linguistics outside of reference grammars, especially when compared to their centrality in the study of modality in other languages.

In contrast with this is the rather strong attention paid to the markers *disque* 'it is said, they say' and *seica* 'it is said, apparently, as it seems', which are widely used, and, not being found in Standard Peninsular Spanish,[5] have a clear emblematic value. These markers were studied by Rosales Sequeiros (2000) from Relevance Theory, by Sousa (2012) from a grammaticalization perspective, by Cidrás (2016) from a constructionalization point of view, and by González-Vázquez (2021) from a pragmatic angle. The interest on these linguistic devices is twofold. On the one hand, the works of Sousa (2012) and Cidrás (2016) show the diachronic interest raised by these forms and their evolutionary pattern, which simplifies biclausal constructions ('verb + complement': *disque* '(he/she/it) says that'; *seica* '(I) know that') through the grammaticalization of the verb of the original main sentence, a well-known cross-linguistic phenomenon (Harris & Campbell, 1995, Chapter 7). On the other hand, Rosales Sequeiros (2000) and González-Vázquez (2021) provide some insights into the semantics and pragmatics of *disque* and *seica*. In particular, González-Vázquez (2021) points out that *seica*, besides conveying a wide range of evidential meanings (inferential, reportative, quotative), plays a role in interaction, functioning as a device related to positive and negative politeness, mirativity, and shared knowledge. A recent review of the literature dealing with *disque* and *seica* and an illustration of their main linguistic features can be found in González Vázquez (2022).

If the emblematic character and the peculiarities of the diachronic evolution offer an explanation for the relatively high attention paid to *disque* and *seica*, these same factors make the almost total omission of the marker *se cadra* 'perhaps' in Galician grammatical studies quite striking. The first individualized study of this epistemic device is by Rodríguez-Espiñeira (2019), who actually focuses on the Spanish calque *si cuadra*, but inevitably studies the origin and evolution of the Galician form. This work is a very relevant contribution to Galician grammar, as it reveals the recent emergence of this epistemic marker from a conditional clause denoting a casual event, in line with the development of other expressions of possibility from the notion of happenstance, such as English *perhaps* (< *per* 'for, by' + *hap* 'occurrence, chance') (see López-Couso & Méndez-Naya, 2021, 2023).

---

5. Cognate forms of *disque* are found in Asturian, American Spanish, Brazilian Portuguese, and Sicilian (Cruschina & Remberger, 2008; Sousa, 2012).

Closing the list of works that deal with particular linguistic forms is the paper by Loureiro-Porto (2014) on necessity and impersonality in English and Galician, which contrasts Galician *cómpre* 'it is necessary' or 'it is convenient' with *need* and other English expressions. This work is a very original contribution, insofar as it studies in detail an expression completely forgotten in Galician grammars, and draws attention to its systematic exclusion from the list of modal auxiliaries.

Finally, the works by García Represas (2000, 2001) take on a function-to-form approach to modality. They start from notions such as doubt, necessity, and obligation, and explore their linguistic expression in Galician. These works are very different from the previous ones inasmuch as they try to provide a comprehensive picture of the possibilities of the language to express particular meanings, thus paying attention to a variety of formal devices, rather than focusing on particular expression types. They pioneer the discussion of interesting but complicated issues that will be dealt with later in this book, such as the precise meaning of the modal future or the semantic shift from possibility to probability, but they do so in a very short space and using very few examples as evidence, resulting in analyses that often raise more questions than they provide answers.

From this general review, one can conclude that the study of modality in Galician still has a long way to go. Many expressions, such as modal auxiliaries, have yet to be examined in depth, and a general account of modality is missing. As illustrated above (§ 1.3), modality has become a hot topic in contemporary linguistics, and the past half century has witnessed the appearance of a huge amount of work on this subject from the most diverse perspectives. Modern Galician linguistics got off the ground during the same period in which modality began to establish itself as a research topic in other linguistic traditions. The relatively recent linguistic interest on modality, together with the internal factors that limited the development of Galician grammatical studies, may explain the late treatment of modal units and, in general, the low consistency of modality as a research topic in Galician linguistics. During the past 50 years there have been remarkable advances in the knowledge of many different aspects of Galician, but the systematic study of some relevant areas of grammar, such as modality, is still an outstanding task.

PART II

Theoretical background

CHAPTER 2

The concept of modality

Both the definition of modality and the classification of its types involve numerous difficulties and disagreements. Rigorous characterizations of the notion are scarce. Nonetheless, the taxonomic proposals are almost as abundant as the authors who study modality. For this reason, I will begin by reviewing those categories that are typically treated under the umbrella of modality (§ 2.1) and deal later with the proposals for their definition and theoretical treatment (§ 2.2). Additionally, the insights on the concept of modality that can be gained from linguistic typology will be explored in § 2.3. The chapter concludes with a critical summary of the problems faced by the most popular approaches to modality, and advances how modality is to be conceived of in this book (§ 2.4).

2.1 Modal taxonomies

The characterization of modality is often limited to listing the set of more specific notions included under the label. There is considerable agreement regarding the elements that make up the core of the category, which are recognized by the majority of authors. This traditional classification of modality is illustrated in § 2.1.1. The discrepancies are found, essentially, in the organization of modal space and the status of the most peripheral notions, and have resulted in an abundance of taxonomic proposals, the most relevant of which are presented in the second part of the section (§ 2.1.2).

2.1.1 The traditional classes of modality

The three basic types of modality distinguished in the logical tradition are alethic (from Greek *alétheia* 'truth'), relating to the modes of truth, deontic (from Greek *déon* 'obligation, duty'), relating to the modes of obligation, and epistemic (from Greek *epistéme* 'knowledge'), relating to the modes of knowledge (von Wright, 1951, pp. 1–4). The first class has received the most attention in the logical tradition, where key concepts for the characterization of modal categories are necessity and possibility. For example, if a proposition is true in any circumstance, it is said to be necessarily true (e.g., *The diameter of a circle must pass through its center*). If it is not necessarily false, it is said to be possibly true (e.g., *A person may be older than their uncle*). This type of modality is also called logical modality (Carnap, 1947, pp. 173–177; Kearns, 2011, pp. 79–84; von Wright, 1951, p. 28).

However, in linguistics, alethic modality is scarcely used. Palmer (1986, p. 11) points out the difficulty of distinguishing alethic modality from epistemic modality when he states that "there is no distinction between … what is logically true and what the speaker believes, as a matter of fact, to be true." Nevertheless, examples like the above can be epistemically modalized (e.g., *The diameter of a circle must probably pass through its center*), pointing to a greater proximity of alethic modality to non-epistemic types of modality, which can also fall under the scope of epistemic modality. Alethic modality is rarely used in linguistics because the utterances that express it are infrequent (Narrog, 2012, p. 7), and can probably be assimilated to a class of non-epistemic modality, such as dynamic modality (see §2.1.2.1).

In linguistics, the traditional classes of modality are dynamic, deontic, and epistemic (Nuyts, 2006, pp. 2–6). All of them had already been proposed in the framework of modal logic by von Wright (1951), who grants the last two a place equal to that of alethic modality. Dynamic modality is mentioned by von Wright (1951, p. 28), but only in a brief note. The following series of examples illustrate, respectively, dynamic, deontic, and epistemic modality, using the Galician modal auxiliaries *deber (de)* 'must' and *poder* 'can/may'.[1]

(1) Dynamic modality
    a. Esa rapaza *pode* nadar dez quilómetros seguidos.
       'That girl can swim ten kilometers in a row.'
    b. *Debo* saír de aquí canto antes.
       'I must get out of here as soon as possible.'

(2) Deontic modality
    a. Xa *podes* marchar.
       'You can go now.'
    b. O neno *debía* volver antes das 11.
       'The boy had to be back by 11.'

(3) Epistemic modality
    a. A inacción do goberno *puido* causar esta desfeita.
       'The government's inaction may have caused this mess.'
    b. A acusada *debe de* estar ocultándolles información.
       'The accused must be withholding information from them.'

---

1. Throughout the book all translations from Galician are mine, unless stated otherwise.

Dynamic modality ascribes an ability or capacity (1a) or a necessity (1b) to the first participant of a SoA. Palmer (2001, pp. 76–79) distinguishes two types of dynamic possibility (abilitive and volitive), corresponding to the English auxiliaries *can* and *will*. Dynamic necessity is expressed using modal *must*, albeit these cases are rare, according to the author (cf. Palmer, 1990, pp. 113–132). Van der Auwera and Plungian (1998), in turn, distinguish between participant-internal dynamic modality, which would correspond to the typical reading of (1), and participant-external dynamic modality. The latter is represented in examples such as those in (4), where it is the external circumstances, rather than the internal properties of the participant, that make the SoA possible or necessary.

(4) a. Agora que despexaron o curso do río, esa rapaza *pode* nadar dez quilómetros seguidos.
 'Now that they cleared up the course of the river, that girl can swim ten kilometers in a row.'
 b. Para chegar a tempo á competición de natación, *debo* saír de aquí canto antes.
 'In order to arrive in time to the swimming contest, I must get out of here as soon as possible.'

Deontic modality is traditionally defined in terms of permission (2a) and obligation (2b), understood as indications of the possibility or necessity of the SoA in relation to a moral code. This apparently clear and strict definition hides some internal diversity. In this connection, Palmer (2001, pp. 70–72) argues that the most common type of deontics is that of directives, which constitute a class of speech acts whose purpose is to get the interlocutor to carry out a certain action. From this perspective, (2a) can be interpreted as a directive, but (2b) cannot. In addition, Palmer (2001, pp. 72–73) distinguishes another type of deontics that he calls commissives, linked to speech acts in which the speaker commits themselves to perform some action. Under this label Palmer (2001, p. 72) covers uses of the English auxiliary *shall*, such as *John shall have the book tomorrow* or *You shall do as you are told*.

Epistemic modality is often defined either as an evaluation of the probabilities that an SoA has happened/happens/will happen or as the expression of the speaker's commitment to their message. The main distinctions are given in terms of possibility (3a) and necessity (3b) in reference to the speaker's knowledge of the world. For Coates (1983, pp. 18–20), auxiliary verbs with an epistemic value in English can relate to an assumption (*must*, *should*, and *ought*) or to an evaluation of possibilities (*will*, *may*, *might*, and *could*). The first group constitutes the inferential type and the second group the non-inferential type. These two classes are arranged on a scale whose extremes are confidence (*must*; *will*) and doubt (*should, ought; may, might, could*). Palmer (2001, pp. 24–31), on the other hand, distinguishes three types of epistemic modality: speculative, deductive, and assumptive. As on other occasions, the author covers with these distinctions the uses of English modal auxiliaries, in this case *may, must*, and *will*, respectively. Interestingly, Palmer (2001, p. 25) indicates that "there seem to be few languages that have a system with all three markers, but English is an exception," which I think can be taken as a good example of the role played by the English language in the inception of modal categories.

As these proposals show, in dealing with epistemic modality the notion of inference or deduction usually plays a role and is assumed to be conveyed through the auxiliary *must* and its equivalents in other languages, such as *deber (de)* in Galician. The relationship between inferential forms and epistemic modality is problematic, and will be discussed in depth later (§ 4.1.4).

2.1.2 Other proposals for the organization of modality

The modal taxonomy sketched above was the one that had the most success and diffusion in linguistic works, but is not, by any means, the only one. Even though the modal status of the three main classes is rarely discussed, the exact nature of the elements that should be included within dynamic and deontic modality is controversial. In addition, there is quite a diversity of proposals regarding the relative status of the three traditional categories.

2.1.2.1 *Dynamic and deontic modality beyond the traditional view*

The participant-internal and participant-external subtypes of dynamic modality enjoy wide acceptance. Along with these Nuyts (2005, 2016) has proposed a third subtype, which he calls *situational dynamic modality* and, he recognizes, has a controversial status. This subclass includes "possibilities/potentials and necessities/inevitabilities ... but then not related to any participant in the state of affairs in particular, but inherent in the state of affairs described in the clause as a whole" (Nuyts, 2016, p. 35). A key difference between situational and participant-external dynamic modality – *participant-imposed*, in Nuyts's (2016) terms – is precisely the role played by the first argument: the necessity or possibility is relative to this participant, albeit not internal to them, only in the case of the participant-external subtype.[2] The author illustrates the notion with examples such as the following:

---

2. It is worth noting that van der Auwera and Plungian (1998, p. 80) seem to leave the door open to include the values of Nuyts's situational modality under their participant-external modality, as the latter "refers to circumstances that are external to the participant, *if any*, engaged in the state of affairs" [emphasis added].

(5) a. All ships can sink.
 b. Little Stevie cannot have broken the vase since he was not around.
 c. John has to be the murderer, there was nobody else in the house.
 d. It is possible to open the door now, I've cleaned up the rubbish behind it.
(Nuyts, 2005, p. 8; Nuyts, 2016, p. 35)

These cases are reminiscent of alethic modality, to the extent that the type of modality they express is occupied with the logical conditions that lead to the possibility or necessity of the SoA. I am nonetheless not aware of any proposal that explicitly relates alethic modality to (situational) dynamic modality, apart from von Wright's (1951) aforementioned note.

The internal constitution of deontic modality has also been the subject of revisions. Nuyts et al. (2010) argue for an alternative definition, considering deontic modality a scalar category integrated, strictly, by degrees of moral acceptability and necessity. This excludes directives as understood by Palmer (2001). Nuyts et al. (2010) understand directives as instructions that inform about what is possible or necessary for the first argument to do, that is, as indications of obligation and permission. These authors, therefore, would include both examples in (2) in the class of directives, and exclude them from deontic modality.[3] They would, however, include under this type of modality uses of auxiliary verbs such as (6) and cases that are generally excluded in the treatment of deontic modality such as those in (7), where moral acceptability is expressed through the understudied auxiliary verb *cómpre* and through lexical resources.

(6) a. O salario dos políticos non *pode* depender do parlamento.
 'The wages of politicians cannot depend on the parliament.'
 b. O debate sobre a eutanasia *debe* abrirse este ano.
 'The debate on euthanasia must be open this year.'

(7) a. *Cómpre* non deixarse levar pola desesperación nos momentos difíciles.
 'It is necessary not to be misled by desperation in difficult moments.'
 b. O seu comportamento na escola é totalmente *deplorable*.
 'His/her behavior at school is utterly deplorable.'
 c. *Aplaudimos* que a directiva tomase esa decisión.
 'We applaud that the board of directors made that decision.'

---

3. Note that directives thus understood do not correspond only to speech acts that express orders, but also include their description (on the issue of performativity, see §3.1.3). One of the conclusions reached by Nuyts et al. (2010) is that there is a division of labor between the modal auxiliaries and the imperative mood in which, typically, the former are responsible for describing directive meaning and the latter for performing it. From this perspective, (2a) is a performative directive, because the speech act it expresses is an order, while (2b) is a descriptive directive, since it describes an order, but does not constitute a speech act of that type.

In their work on English deontic adjectives Van linden and Verstraete (2011) assume a gradual characterization like that of Nuyts et al. (2010), and also separate directive from deontic meaning, but they restrict the latter through the notion of factuality (see §2.2.2). In this way they exclude what they consider cases of non-modal evaluation, such as the last two of (7), where the SoA is factual.

2.1.2.2 *Alternative divisions of modal space*

A very common division of modal space opposes epistemic modality to the rest of the modal classes, which are then labeled as *root* or *non-epistemic* modality. It is common to include under these labels both dynamic and deontic meanings, often without making an explicit distinction between them (e.g., Coates, 1983; Declerck, 2011; Sweetser, 1990; Talmy, 2000). In this vein, Palmer (2001) distinguishes two modal systems: propositional modality and event modality. The former includes epistemic and evidential modality, both concerned with the attitude of the speaker towards the truth or the factual status of the proposition (Palmer, 2001, p. 24), whereas the second system includes dynamic and deontic modality, which refer to non-actualized or potential events (Palmer, 2001, p. 70).

Bybee et al. (1994) divide modality into four categories. The first one is agent-oriented modality, which "reports the existence of internal and external conditions on an agent with respect to the completion of the action expressed in the main predicate" (Bybee et al., 1994, p. 177). This includes specific semantic notions such as obligation, necessity, ability, desire, willingness, and root possibility, the last one resulting from the generalization of the notion of ability. This agent-oriented modality corresponds to a good extent to dynamic modality as Palmer (2001) understands it, including what have traditionally been considered deontic modal values. These values related to obligation and permission, when they constitute directive speech acts, make up speaker-oriented modality, which is the second modal category of Bybee et al. (1994). This modal category is divided into six classes: imperative, prohibitive, optative, hortative, admonitive, and permissive. The third category is the relatively uncontroversial epistemic modality, which indicates the degree of the speaker's commitment to the truth of the proposition, and has possibility, probability, and inferred certainty as the most commonly expressed subtypes. Finally, subordinating moods refer to the use of epistemic and speaker-oriented modal devices in contexts of subordination such as complement, concessive, and purpose clauses.

Van der Auwera and Plungian (1998) apply the term *modality* to those semantic domains that can be defined based on the possibility/necessity opposition. This results in four categories, two of which have already been illustrated in Examples (1) and (4), corresponding to participant-internal and participant-external modality. The third category in van der Auwera and Plungian's (1998) modal map is deontic modality, which they consider a special case of participant-external modality. Their use of the term is fairly standard, as it includes both directive and non-directive meanings. The fourth category is epistemic modality, which serves the speaker to qualify the proposition either as uncertain (possible) or probable (necessary). This dimension includes inferential evidentiality. Finally, the authors indicate that the only coherent grouping of the four classes results from combining participant-internal and participant-external (including deontic) modality, which would make up non-epistemic modality, and oppose them to epistemic modality, as this reflects obvious differences in scope: participant-related modalities affect internal aspects of the SoA expressed in the proposition, while epistemic modality has scope over the proposition as a whole.

In addition to the previous proposals, there exist other classifications of modality, which I briefly summarize below.

Within the framework of Functional Grammar, the works of Goossens (1985) and Hengeveld (2004) stand out. The former assumes the traditional tripartite division, with the peculiarity that he labels dynamic modality as facultative, which is identified with Palmer's version (meanings of ability and volition). Hengeveld's work constitutes the most elaborate proposal for the treatment of modality in Functional Grammar, and will be examined in detail later (§ 3.1.1). Regarding the types of modality, Hengeveld (2004) differentiates facultative, deontic, volitive, epistemic, and evidential. His use of deontic, epistemic, and evidential is standard. His facultative modality comprises meanings of ability and capacity, whereas his volitive modality corresponds to the modal uses of the auxiliaries *will* and *would* in English (cf. Palmer, 2001, pp. 76–80).

Narrog (2005a, 2012) elaborates a model for the diachronic study of modality that is based on two distinctions: one in terms of volitivity and another in terms of orientation towards the speech act. Volitive types of modality include deontic, boulomaic (relative to someone's desires; see below), and what Narrog calls preferential (relative to someone's preferences) and teleological (relative to someone's goals). Non-volitive types encompass epistemic, evidential, participant-internal, circumstantial, and the so-called existential (quantificational). It should be noted that the volitive/non-volitive distinction is gradual, so that some subtypes may be considered more or less volitive than others. The second distinction used by Narrog has to do with the scope of modal expressions, and is formulated as an opposition between event orientation and speech act orientation. This opposition is complementary to the one in terms of volitivity, and does not comprise modal classes as a whole, but particular uses of modal expressions. This dimension corresponds to some extent to what in historical linguistics is the notion of (inter)subjectivity (see § 4.3).

Finally, Depraetere and Reed (2011) carry out a meticulous classification of root possibility, distinguishing five subtypes (ability, opportunity, permission, general circumstantial possibility, and circumstantial permissibility) based on three criteria: the scope of modality (broad or narrow), the source of modality (internal or external to the subject), and the presence or absence of a potential barrier (the ability of the external source to impose obstacles in the realization of the SoA).

A main conclusion can be drawn from this review: the controversies in the division of modal space focus on the characterization and delimitation of dynamic and deontic modality, while epistemic modality enjoys in practically all proposals an independent status and a fairly clear definition (its problematic relationship with evidentiality notwithstanding, see §4.1.4). Taking the traditional taxonomy as a reference, the examined proposals organize modal classes mainly in two ways. On the one hand, many authors group the non-epistemic types of modality into a root (Coates, 1983) or event (Palmer, 2001) modality, sometimes distinguishing various subtypes within this class. On the other hand, a distinction between participant-internal and participant-external modality is also widely known (e.g., van der Auwera & Plungian, 1998), and constitutes an alternative to the dynamic/deontic opposition by grouping deontic meanings with a subset of dynamic ones.

2.1.2.3 *Boulomaic modality: A neglected modal class*

There is a modal category that has only been mentioned in passing: boulomaic (or bouletic) modality. It is understood as an expression of desires (Gavins, 2005; Kiefer, 1987; Portner, 2009), wishing or hoping (Hengeveld, 1988, 1989), volition or intentions (Narrog, 2009, 2012), or liking or disliking of the SoA (Nuyts, 2005). Kiefer (1987) associates this modality with the English modals *can* and *must*, and offers the following examples:

(8) a. Bill can be our leader.
    b. Bill must be our leader. (Kiefer, 1987, p. 70)

However, most authors do not recognize boulomaic values for *can* and *must*, and relate boulomaic modality with the English semi-auxiliaries *shall*, *want to*, and *will* (e.g., Narrog, 2012, p. 10), or with "modal lexical verbs" such as *hope*, *wish*, and *want* (e.g., Gavins, 2005, p. 86). Some examples follow:

(9) a. I *want* you to forgive me. (Narrog, 2009, p. 13)
    b. [W]e *shall* fight on the beaches, we *shall* fight on the landing grounds, we *shall* fight in the fields and in the streets, we *shall* fight in the hills; we *shall* never surrender. (Winston Churchill) (Narrog, 2012, p. 10)

      c. I *hope* that you will be happy.
      d. I *wish* you'd get lost. (Gavins, 2005, p. 86)

Narrog (2012, p. 10) argues that boulomaic modality has been neglected in the literature because it is hardly present in the system of modal auxiliaries and is hard to accommodate to the traditional modal distinction between necessity and possibility. However, this does not lead Narrog (2009, 2012) to include any expression of desire under boulomaic modality, since he restricts the concept of (boulomaic) modality by means of the notion of factuality (see §2.2.2). Nevertheless, others do include any expression of desire, hoping, or (dis)liking under the label, regardless of whether the SoA is factual or not:

(10) a. It's *good* that you're pregnant. (Gavins, 2005, p. 86)
     b. (It is) *Great* that you are coming to my party tonight.
     c. *Unfortunately*, I cannot come to your party tonight.
     d. I *hate* it that I cannot come to your party tonight. (Nuyts, 2005, p. 24)

These same opposing views regarding the role of factuality arose when discussing alternative understandings of deontic modality above (§2.1.2.1). This is not a trivial matter, as it is directly connected with how modality at a general level is characterized. Although boulomaic modality has been absent from most work on modality, I will argue for its inclusion in the catalog of modal categories later in this book (§5.2), where I will also address the role factuality is supposed to play in the characterization of modality.

2.1.3 Galician approaches to modality and the modals

As pointed out earlier (§1.4), there has been little theorizing around the notion of modality in Galician linguistics, but modal auxiliaries have had a constant presence in Galician grammars since Saco Arce (1868, pp. 180–181), who mentions the combination of the infinitive with *haber (de)* 'have to' and *ter que* 'have to' under "tiempos compuestos" 'compound tenses'.[4] Carballo Calero (1966, pp. 135–153) includes *ter, haber,* and *ser* 'be' as auxiliaries, but does not offer much information about their semantics: *ter* is associated with the formation of compound tenses

---

4. Whereas the examples of *ter que* provided by Saco Arce (1868) clearly convey deontic necessity, it is harder to interpret precisely his examples of *haber (de)*. This periphrasis carries not only modal meaning, but also temporal and aspectual values. The temporal value of futurity requires the auxiliary to be conjugated in the present, whereas the aspectual value corresponds to a relatively rare case of grammaticalization of the avertive category (Kuteva, 1998) and requires the auxiliary to occur in the past tense. The modal value does not require a particular tense form.

or the perfective or resultative periphrasis; *haber* expresses obligation or futurity; and *ser* is used as the passive auxiliary. He focuses the discussion on morphological issues.

More thorough accounts of the Galician modals appear in the 1970s and 1980s. Rojo (1974) carries out the first in-depth study of Galician verbal periphrases, devoting a chapter to modal verbs. He classifies modal values into "obligative action" and "hypothetical action". Obligative action is conveyed by *haber, haber de / que, ter de / que,* and *deber (de),* all of which combine with the infinitive. *Haber (de)* offers a challenging analysis, insofar as it is difficult to separate the meaning of obligation from the meaning of futurity, being the latter always present in the uses of this modal. *Haber que* can be considered a variant of the previous construction, but presents the particular feature of being used only in the third person, thus expressing an obligation with an impersonal overtone. The modal *ter que* conveys a stronger obligation than the above and possesses a variant *ter de* which is almost exclusive to the literary language. The last modal of obligation is *deber (de)*. According to Rojo (1974, pp. 161–162), the variability in the use of the preposition *de* with this modal already existed in the medieval language and continued into Present-Day Galician. As for periphrases of hypothetical action, Rojo (1974) mentions *deber (de), poder,* and *haber,* all of them conveying a meaning of doubt when followed by the indicative. He notes that *deber (de)* may appear with and without the preposition, as when expressing obligation, that *poder* conveys the same value as *quizais* 'maybe', and that the hypothetical reading of *haber* is not the most common one – additionally, he did not find cases of *haber de* with a hypothetical meaning in his corpus.

Álvarez et al. (1986) offer a similar approach, since they analyze *haber (de), hai que, ter que, ter de, deber (de),* and *poder* as modal periphrases that combine with the infinitive and express an obligation or a hypothesis. They see the expression of futurity and obligation in *haber (de)* as tightly linked, and recognize a hypothetical value for the modal, as Rojo (1974) does. Some of the examples they offer are the following:

(11) a. Obligation/futurity
Non sei por onde *hei* comezar a amece-las partes …
'I do not know where I must/will start to join the parts from …'
b. Obligation
É doado falarlles aos grandes, pero para os nenos todo *ha* ter relación, porque se non comezan a teimar nese fío que lles deixamos solto.
'It is easy to speak to the grown-ups, but for the kids everything must be linked, because otherwise they start to dwell on that thread that we left loose.'

c. Hypothesis
Ese rapaz *ha* andar polos quince anos.
'That boy must be around 15 years old.'

(Álvarez et al., 1986, p. 406)

The periphrasis *hai que* also features the verb *haber*, but only in the third person singular, since it expresses obligation in a general, impersonal manner, with no possible confusion with the future:

(12) Mais *había que* irse, pois tiñamos aínda unha hora de camiño.
'But it was necessary to leave, since we still had an hour to go.'

(Álvarez et al., 1986, p. 407)

According to Álvarez et al. (1986, p. 407), *ter que* conveys obligation in a stronger manner than the above expressions, whereas *ter de* is used above all in literary registers and is different from *ter que* in that it conveys a pending obligation.

(13) a. *Teño que* irme, xa non lembraba que hai cinco minutos que debera estar alá.
'I have to go, I didn't remember that I was to be there five minutes ago.'
b. Tencionaba voltar á aldea, non sabía cando, pero *tería de* ser.
'(S)he intended to go back to the village, (s)he didn't know when, but it had to be done.'

(Álvarez et al., 1986, p. 407)

This view on the contrast between *ter que* and *ter de* is quite unique to the work of Álvarez (Álvarez & Xove, 2002; Álvarez et al., 1986), with other grammarians seeing both periphrases as equivalent in semantic terms (Costa Casas et al., 1988, p. 226) and finding it hard to perceive the pending obligation overtone (Freixeiro Mato, 2000/2006a, p. 466). Freixeiro Mato (2000/2006a, p. 467) considers that *ter que* has come to replace *ter de* as a result of contact with Spanish and that *ter de* should be favored as the more authentic form. By contrast, Álvarez and Xove (2002, p. 349) argue that the uses of *ter de* in written language as equivalent to *ter que* are mistakes, and, according to them, *ter de* survives in popular spoken language, especially in the first person singular with the value 'action that the speaker commits to fulfill', thus being very similar to *haber (de)* in (11a).

Next, Álvarez et al. (1986, p. 408) deal with *deber (de)* and *poder*. They identify values of obligation and hypothesis for *deber (de)*, while only mentioning the hypothetical meaning for *poder*. Relevant examples are (2b) and (3), above.

Costa Casas et al. (1988, pp. 223, 226–227) and Freixeiro Mato (2000/2006a, pp. 464–473) do not deviate significantly from the ideas of Rojo (1974) and Álvarez et al. (1986). All these works distinguish two types of modal periphrases: those relating to obligation and those concerned with hypotheses. Costa Casas et al. (1988) include *haber (de)*, *haber que*, *ter de*, *ter que*, and *deber* in obligation, while only considering *deber de* under hypothesis. Freixeiro Mato (2000/2006a) follows the same classification, but adding *haber* and *poder* in the hypothetical class. Both Costa Casas et al. (1988) and Freixeiro Mato (2000/2006a) argue for a distinction between *deber* (obligation) and *deber de* (hypothesis), with Freixeiro Mato (2000/2006a) proposing a similar contrast between *haber (de)* (obligation) and *haber* (hypothesis). Nevertheless, Freixeiro Mato (2000/2006a, p. 470) concedes that these distinctions are theoretical and that real texts do not appear to follow them in a systematic way.

The works reviewed until now do not mention the non-epistemic values of *poder* when discussing the modal periphrases. Freixeiro Mato (2000/2006a, p. 470) argues that this modal is frequently used in what he terms "non-periphrastic constructions", where it retains its "basic" meanings of 'be able to' and 'have the possibility of', thus denying the grammatical status of what have traditionally been seen as dynamic modal values (§ 2.1.1). In this connection, Montero Küpper (1999) and Álvarez and Xove (2002, pp. 343–353) constitute a shift in perspective, as they discuss dynamic values in their analyses of the modals.

Montero Küpper (1999) is one of the few contributions that applies the terms *deontic* and *epistemic* to the Galician modal verbs. She lists the following deontic values:

- Obligation: *ter de/que, deber (de), haber de/que.*
- Permission: *poder.*
- Possibility (situation and availability): *poder.*
- Prohibition: *non poder, non deber (de).*
- Intentionality: *haber de.*   (Montero Küpper, 1999, p. 731)

Epistemic auxiliaries are arranged in decreasing degrees of certainty, as follows: *ter que > deber (de) > haber (de) > poder*. Montero Küpper (1999) considers that these epistemic modals are expressions of conjecture, and provides the following paraphrases: *ter que* = 'necessarily probable', *deber (de)* = 'very probable', *haber (de)* = 'quite/very probable', *poder* = 'possible or contingent'. Montero Küpper's (1999) proposal for deontic modality goes beyond the traditional classification in terms of permission and obligation, including dynamic possibility and intentionality, whereas her description of the epistemic modals combines epistemic and inferential values – namely and respectively, probability and conjecture.

According to Álvarez and Xove (2002, pp. 343–353), Galician modal periphrases are *ter que, haber que, poder, deber (de),* and *haber (de)*. They point out that the general value of modality is obligation, in two senses: as *necesidade* 'necessity' or as *deber* 'duty'. Necessity is expressed through *ter que*, whereas *deber (de)* expresses duty. They further distinguish values of possibility and impossibility, corresponding to *poder* and its negation. The difficulty to separate modal values from temporal ones in *haber (de)* forces the authors to discuss this periphrasis later, when dealing with temporal auxiliaries.

Álvarez and Xove (2002, p. 346) distinguish the modalization of the assertion (Type I) from the modalization of the event (Type II). Type I is to do with the degree of commitment of the speaker regarding the veracity of what they say, being the highest with *ter que* and *non poder*, lower with *deber (de)*, and the lowest with *poder*. Type II is further divided into Type II-1, which involves the interlocutor, and Type II-2, which does not. This distinction, rather than corresponding to the deontic/dynamic opposition within root modality (§ 2.1.2.2), seems to separate performative directive meaning (i.e., directive speech acts, such as commands) from any other expression of root necessity or possibility, as the following examples suggest (for comparable proposals see § 2.1.2.1).

(14) Type II-1
   a. De aquí en diante *tes que* poñer ti a mesa.
      'From now on you have to set the table yourself.'
   b. Esta noite *podes* quedar a durmir na súa casa.
      'Tonight you can sleep over at his/her home.'
   c. *Debes* ser máis paciente con el.
      'You must be more patient with him.' (Álvarez & Xove, 2002, p. 347)

(15) Type II-2
   a. *Ten que* termar dela para que non caia.
      '(S)he has to hold her/it so she/it doesn't fall.'
   b. Pedro *pode* marchar cando queira.
      'Pedro may leave whenever he wants.'
   c. Non respectan nada as distancias que *deberían* gardar e por iso hai accidentes.
      'They don't keep the distances they should keep at all, and that's why there are so many accidents.'
   d. Non lle gustaba nada que *houbese que* quedar alí un día máis.
      '(S)he didn't like it at all that it was necessary to stay there one more day.'
      (Álvarez & Xove, 2002, p. 347)

From these examples we see that Type II-1 expresses command, permission, and advice, while Type II-2 describes necessities or possibilities relative to the participants or the situation itself.

According to Álvarez and Xove (2002, pp. 348–349), *ter que* and *haber que* convey necessity and are partially complementary: *haber que* is restricted to the expression of Type II-2 modality with non-impersonal verbs, whereas *ter que* is used in any other context and rarely functions as a Type II-2 expression, an exception being the combination with impersonal verbs.

(Non) poder expresses (im)possibility in four different flavors: (a) the assertion is modalized as (im)possible (Type I); (b) the event is modalized in terms of ability (Type II);[5] (c) the modal expresses a(n) (im)possibility involving the interlocutor, often conveying permission, prohibition, advice, or suggestion (Type II-1); (d) the modal expresses a(n) (im)possibility that does not involve the interlocutor (Type II-2).

(16) a. Type I
O neno *podía* ter daquela tres ou catro anos.
'The boy may have been three or four years old back then.'
b. Type II: ability
Só *podo* erguer 50 quilos.
'I can only lift 50 kilos.'
c. Type II-1
Podes almorzar agora.
'You may have breakfast now.'
d. Type II-2
Oxalá *poidan* vir á voda.
'I hope they can come to the wedding.' (Álvarez & Xove, 2002, pp. 350–351)

It is difficult to match Álvarez and Xove's (2002) modal categories with more traditional ones, especially considering the following examples of Type II-2 possibility:

(17) Type II-2
a. Só *podo* saír ata as once.
'I can only go out until 11.'
b. ¿Xa *podes* move-la man?
'Can you move your hand already?' (Álvarez & Xove, 2002, p. 351)

As said, Type II-1 includes performative directive meaning expressed through auxiliary verbs, whereas any other expression of root modality is classified under Type II-2. This diverges from the traditional approach in §2.1.1, since Álvarez and Xove (2002) group dynamic meanings with a subset of deontic meanings in a quite particular way: participant-internal (17b) and participant-external (16d) dynamic modality, non-directive deontic modality (15c), and non-performative directive meaning (17a) are considered Type II-2. Moreover, Álvarez and Xove (2002) consider (16b) a borderline example of Type II modality, but it corresponds to a prototypical expression of participant-internal dynamic modality in

---

5. As in the case of Freixeiro Mato (2000/2006a), the authors think it is doubtful that the verb functions as an actual periphrasis, meaning that it lacks a grammatical status, since it is not opposed to a modal meaning of necessity.

the traditional view, just like (17b), which has no controversial modal status in Álvarez and Xove's (2002) framework.

As for *deber (de)*, Álvarez and Xove (2002) argue that the (non-)occurrence of the preposition does not affect the meaning of the modal, which expresses duty in different ways: (a) as a Type I modal it scopes over the assertion and conveys a meaning of probability; (b) as a Type II modal it scopes over the event and conveys various meanings, such as advice, convenience, moral, social, or natural obligation, etc., regardless of whether it involves the interlocutor (Type II-1) or not (Type II-2). These are some examples:

(18) a. Type I
Debe ter frío.
'(S)he must be cold.'
      b. Type II-1
Debes deitarte e tomar algún analxésico.
'You must lie down and take some painkiller.'
      c. Type II-2
Para mañá *debo* traducir un conto ao inglés.
'By tomorrow I must translate a short story into English.'
(Álvarez & Xove, 2002, pp. 352–353)

Finally, Álvarez and Xove (2002) consider *haber (de)* both a modal periphrasis and a temporal periphrasis of posteriority. When it functions as a temporal device, it conveys at the same time a modal value of 'internal obligation'. As a modal device, though, *haber (de)* does not necessarily convey posteriority. It shares characteristics with other modal periphrases, such as the ability to convey Type I and Type II modal meanings, and, according to the authors, the behavior of its preposition is comparable to that of *deber (de)*, that is, the use of the preposition is optional and does not affect the meaning of the auxiliary. When used as a Type I modal expression, *haber (de)* is equivalent to the modal uses of the morphological future (see § 4.1.1), that is, it conveys probability, as in (11c) above. Type II uses express a commitment by someone, and may involve the speaker, or they may not. Thus, the following example triggers three alternative interpretations:

(19) Mañá *ha* de vir por aquí.
'Tomorrow (s)he will come here.'

In the first interpretation *haber (de)* functions as a Type I expression ('(s)he will probably come'); in a second interpretation it functions as a Type II expression that involves the speaker ('I assure that that is the case, even actively engaging in its fulfillment'); in a third interpretation the modal functions as a Type II expression without involving the speaker ('(s)he said that, (s)he assured that (s)he would come, I am only reporting').

In sum, Álvarez and Xove (2002) distinguish two types of modality: Type I scopes over the assertion and is roughly equivalent to what has traditionally been understood as epistemic modality (§ 2.1.1); Type II encompasses what are elsewhere known as root or non-epistemic modal meanings (§ 2.1.2.2), with the alleged exclusion of dynamic meanings of ability, and is further subdivided into Type II-1, which isolates performative deontic meanings, and Type II-2, where the rest of root modal meanings are found. The isolation of (performative) directive meaning is reminiscent to some extent to the proposals of Nuyts et al. (2010) and Van linden and Verstraete (2011) introduced in § 2.1.2.1.

Lastly, Loureiro-Porto (2014) deals with Galician *cómpre*, and compares it to English *need* and *behoove*, in the first (corpus) study of this Galician device. *Cómpre* is the third person singular present indicative form of the verb *cumprir* lit. 'to comply', which can also be inflected for the third person plural in all possible verbal tenses. The verb is often seen as corresponding to two different lexemes, one meaning 'comply' (*cumprir o seu deber* 'to do his/her duty') or 'become, turn' (*cumpriu 15 anos* '(s)he turned 15') and another being a defective verb of necessity. The latter is a good candidate for a modal periphrasis, as it often combines with the infinitive and carries modal meaning.

Loureiro-Porto (2014) follows the cognitive approach to modality proposed by Sweetser (1990) and Talmy (2000) (see § 2.2.3). Thus, she distinguishes between internal necessity (*I need to eat*), external necessity (*I must pay taxes*), and general necessity, which has "an ambiguous general origin" (Loureiro-Porto, 2014, p. 178) (*I need to use the flash for this picture*). The next examples illustrate these categories with Galician *cómpre*.

(20) a. Internal necessity
ós qu'andamos polo mundo, todo nos *cómpre* saber.
'Those of us who wander in the world need to know everything.'
b. External necessity
… que é a hora das ánimas e que *cómpre* rezar as correspondentes oracións.
'… that it is the souls' time and it is necessary to (we must) pray the corresponding prayers.'
c. General necessity
… non tiven case relación con xente. Adoito falar só do que *cómpre* facé-lo e procuro non saírme do profesional.
'… I didn't socialize with people. I usually talk only about what is necessary to talk about and I try not to transcend professional matters.'
(Loureiro-Porto, 2014, pp. 184–185, her translation)

Loureiro-Porto's (2014) results show that there is a shift from internal and external necessity towards general necessity in *cómpre* and that this change is related to the decay of constructions with the experiencer (explicit in (20a)), a process which favors the general modal meaning. When compared with the English expressions, *cómpre* is similar to *need* when it occurs with an experiencer, because this fact favors internal and external necessity meanings, and is closer to *behoove* when it occurs without an experiencer, as this favors the general necessity meaning. From a syntactic point of view, Loureiro-Porto (2014) found that *cómpre* rarely occurs with a *that*-clause, showing a strong preference for bare infinitives, and that it often combines with verbs of saying in formulaic expressions, which aligns with previous findings regarding the grammaticalization of English auxiliary *can*. Thus, "it is possible to affirm that the Galician verb *cómpre* shows enough features to be considered a candidate for inclusion in the group of modal periphrases in Galician grammars" (Loureiro-Porto, 2014, p. 197).

Attention to modality and the modals in Galician linguistics has been intermittent, but interesting results have been obtained. There are several points upheld by most approaches to the matter. In the first place, there is a general agreement as to what verbs should be included in the catalog of modal periphrases: *deber (de)*, *haber (de)*, *haber que*, *poder*, and *ter que* make the cut in almost every proposal. Galician grammars have systematically excluded *cómpre* from this list, which in view of the data offered by Loureiro-Porto (2014) is probably mistaken. Secondly, there is a preference for dividing modal meaning into two categories, corresponding to what in the traditional view are deontic and epistemic meanings. Dynamic meanings are rarely discussed, but a distinction is made between dynamic necessity and possibility. The former is usually included under a broad concept of obligation, which encompasses not only deontic but also dynamic necessity, whereas the latter, when actually dealt with, is often excluded from modality – such stance on (some) dynamic modal values is not rare in other linguistic traditions (see § 5.1). Finally, there is no controversy around the modal meaning of *deber (de)*, whose equivalents in other languages, such as Italian *dovere* and English *must*, have been the object of discussion as to their epistemic vs. inferential character (see § 4.1.4): in Galician the mainstream view is that *deber (de)* conveys epistemic modality. Conflicting views exist in the Galician literature on modality, but, in my opinion, they are minor as far as modality is concerned – take, for instance, the differences regarding the interpretation of the verbs with(out) the prepositions (e.g., *ter de* vs. *ter que*, *deber* vs. *deber de*).

2.2 Theories of modality

Finding a basic, coherent, and comprehensive definition that fits all the phenomena that are usually studied under the term *modality* is far from easy. In fact, "[t]here is hardly any grammatical category which has been given more diverging definitions, and under the label of which a wider range of phenomena has been studied" (Narrog, 2005b, p. 165). According to Narrog (2005b), there are two main definitions of modality in linguistics: (a) modality as an expression of the speaker's attitudes, thus associated with the notion of subjectivity and the expression of opinions and emotions; (b) modality as an expression of factuality distinctions.

For Narrog (2005b), definition (a) constitutes a very vague characterization that does not single out modal elements against other semantic domains. As Narrog (2005b, pp. 169–176) shows, the speaker's attitudes are present in all the elements of the utterance, from the choice of vocabulary to the perspective from which a situation is conceptualized, which includes aspect, voice, tense, and modality in the traditional sense. Therefore, a definition of modality simply as the expression of speaker's attitudes is not accurate. However, the concept of attitude plays a key role in relevant proposals for the study of modality, such as the ones by Givón (2001), Kärkkäinen (2003), Nuyts (2005), Palmer (1986, 1990), and Pietrandrea (2005), and in approaches to modality concerned with discourse interaction and organization (see § 3.3).

In definition (b) modality is associated with the factual status of a proposition or an SoA. From this perspective, a modal situation is one that is located in a world different from the real one, and is therefore marked as non-factual. This proposed characterization of modality has been very successful in linguistics in general, in both formalist (e.g., Kearns, 2011; Papafragou, 2000; Portner, 2009) and functionalist (e.g., Declerck, 2011; Narrog, 2012) approaches. This conception stems from the application of possible worlds semantics to modal logic (§ 2.2.1), a model that permeates, more or less directly, a large number of works in contemporary linguistics, where possible worlds have been reworked in terms of a scale of (non-)factuality (§ 2.2.2).

Some authors combine elements of definitions (a) and (b) in their proposals. As an example, Palmer (2001, p. 8) identifies propositional modality with the speaker's attitudes in relation to the truth or factual status of the proposition, and event modality with non-factual situations. Van linden and Verstraete (2011), in turn, characterize deontic modality in terms of an attitudinal source and the factual status of the proposition.

Independently from the previous proposals, cognitive linguistics has developed its own model for understanding modality, which in this framework is conceptualized from a prior understanding of physical forces known as force dynamics (§ 2.2.3).

2.2.1 Possible worlds semantics

The development of the semantics of possible worlds was brought about in philosophy in order to fill a void in modal logic: just as the logical connectors and negation were defined in classical logic in relation to truth values, it was necessary to find a model that allowed a rigorous characterization of the modal operators of necessity and possibility (cf. Menzel, 2016).

In semantics, possible worlds refer to the various alternative forms that reality could take. The real world is one of these options, and is therefore part of the set of possible worlds. A possible world different from the real world constitutes a complete alternate universe that diverges at least in one point from reality. The set of possible worlds is infinite, because the points at which reality could diverge are infinite. In essence, this system creates a domain where the notion of truth can be applied to non-factual situations. Thus, a proposition is necessarily true if it applies to the entirety of the relevant set of possible worlds, and it is possibly true if it applies to at least one of those possible worlds. The relevant set of possible worlds is determined by the type of modality at play (cf. Kearns, 2011, pp. 82–85). For instance, in the case of deontic modality, the relevant set of worlds is that in which the valid code of norms is completely observed, that is, the worlds of absolute obedience.

(21) Os residentes deben depositar o lixo nos colectores despois das 21:00 horas.
'The residents must leave their waste in the bins after 21:00 hours.'

In (21), the utterance is modalized by the deontic auxiliary *deber (de)*. Since this device expresses deontic necessity, it entails that the proposition is mandatory according to a set of rules determined by the context, in this case, municipal regulations. In the possible worlds model the use of *deber (de)* in (21) entails that "the residents must leave their waste in the bins after 21:00 hours" is true only if "the residents leave their waste in the bins after 21:00 hours" is true in all worlds of absolute obedience. That is, a modal proposition is true or not in relation to a set of possible hypothetical situations.

Mutatis mutandis, the same analysis is applied to modal possibility and other types of modality, such as epistemic. For the latter the set of relevant worlds is the one that is epistemically possible, that is, the one in which everything that is known about the real world applies.

(22) É posible que a miña amiga estea en Lugo.
 'It is possible that my friend is in Lugo.'

In (22) the use of the modal adjective *posible* 'possible' entails that the proposition "my friend is in Lugo" is true in at least one epistemically possible world, which is the same as saying that the knowledge of reality of the speaker producing (22) is consistent with the fact that their friend is in Lugo, regardless of whether it later turned out that this was not the case.

On the one hand, the possible worlds model provides an analysis capable of handling propositions that describe hypothetical situations, and, on the other hand, it derives the concepts of necessity and possibility from logical operators such as the universal ("all worlds") and the existential ("at least one world") quantifier and negation. Thus, its focus of interest seems to lay closer to philosophical theorizing than to the analysis of linguistic expressions.

Kratzer (1977, 1981/2002) produces a more linguistic version of this model, which Portner (2009, p. 49) considers the standard theory of modality in formal semantics. Without going into the details of formalization, there are two central ideas in the work of Kratzer (1977, 1981/2002). First, the *relativity* of modality assumes that modal expressions are not ambiguous (between, for example, a deontic and an epistemic meaning), but that their meanings are relative to one or more conversational backgrounds. Therefore, it is the context that determines the set of possible worlds a particular modal expression refers to.

(23) a. De acordo coas normas do concello, é posible que os residentes tiren o lixo a partir das 21:00 horas.
 'According to municipal norms, it is possible that the residents leave their waste in the bins after 21:00 hours.'
 b. De acordo co que sei, é posible que a miña amiga estea en Lugo.
 'According to what I know, it is possible that my friend is in Lugo.'

Cases like those in (23) exemplify how context, in this case linguistic context, determines what reading should be made of a modal expression: in (23a) *posible* has a deontic interpretation due to the reference to the regulatory code that is made in the adjunct of the form 'according to X'; in (23b) the reading is epistemic because of that same adjunct, which now refers to the knowledge of the subject. According to Kratzer (1977), these types of elements constitute conversational backgrounds that provide the modal basis, that is to say, they are functions that relate the context to the relevant set of possible worlds and these to the modal expression.

The second central idea of Kratzer's theory is *ordering*. In the classical formulation possible worlds constitute a set without an internal structure, thus excluding the possibility that, in an example like (23b), several possible scenarios are considered beyond the one that is uttered. Kratzer (1981/2002) captures this possibility by giving priority to some possible worlds over others, and does so through a second conversational background, which constitutes the *ordering source*. While the modal base in (23b) provides the set of facts that are known to the speaker beyond doubt (my friend is not at home), the ordering source represents the speaker's expectations resulting from experience (my friend usually goes to Lugo once a month), second-hand information (I was told that she left from work earlier today), etc. Kratzer's model tells us that, with this modal base and this ordering source, what (23b) conveys is that among the worlds in which the previous events hold the speaker prioritizes those in which their friend is in Lugo.

Based on the above, Kratzer (1981/2002) argues that the abilities possessed by a person who masters the modal system of a language are two:

i. The ability of categorizing conversational backgrounds according to the requirements imposed by the vocabulary.
ii. The ability of drawing inferences of various strength involving two conversational backgrounds: a modal base and an ordering source.

(Kratzer, 1981/2002, p. 321)

Close to Kratzer's is the approach to modality provided by Relevance Theory. As suggested by its name, the key notion in the theory is relevance, which has its origin in Grice's (1975) Maxim of Relevance. In this framework, communication is an act of information processing that involves a speaker trying to express facts or assumptions and a hearer trying to compute information from linguistic and contextual material (Sperber & Wilson, 1995). When the processed meaning satisfies the hearer's expectations of relevance, the hearer stops processing information. Despite the fact that it apparently awards an important place to the speaker, Relevance Theory is, in practice, a theory of processing and not of production, with a clear cognitive and psychological inclination.

Relevance Theory proposes a unitary or monosemous approach to modality (e.g., Berbeira Gardón, 1998; Papafragou, 2000). In contrast with interpretations that favor polysemy and defend a rich semantics of modal expressions from which speakers make choices, the monosemous analysis based on relevance postulates a minimal semantic structure accompanied by a powerful cognitive capacity to determine meanings from context. The operation of modal expressions in Relevance Theory is essentially the same as in modal logic and in Kratzer (1977, 1981/2002): their semantics is composed of a logical relation (necessity or possibility) and a domain of propositions, that is, a set of possible worlds with which the modal unit relates the proposition over which it scopes (Papafragou, 2000, p. 40). From this perspective, expressions compatible with both deontic and epistemic meanings, such as *posible* in (23), do not specify their domain, so that the specification of this semantic value depends on the relevance-oriented pragmatic process of understanding. In this connection, the distinction between descriptive and interpretive uses of propositions is central (see Sperber & Wilson, 1995, pp. 224–231): the proposition affected by a deontic modal has a descriptive use, while the one affected by an epistemic modal has an interpretive use (Papafragou, 2000, pp. 68–71). This means that the proposition expressed as the complement of the main predicate constitutes a verifiable description of an SoA (i.e., a real-world entity) in (23a), while in (23b) it is a representation of an abstract hypothesis compatible with the speaker's beliefs (i.e., a mental object).

As Traugott (2003a, p. 663) points out, Relevance Theory "has replaced one (minimally) dyadic relationship, the deontic/epistemic 'polysemy', with another (minimally) dyadic one involving levels of representations (descriptive and interpretive)." One of the main tenets of this proposal, the monosemous approach to modal expressions, is challenged by the need for lexemes to specify, at a semantic level, whether they can operate at the descriptive level, the interpretive level, or both.

The proposals by Kratzer and Relevance Theory focus their theoretical efforts on granting a privileged role to pragmatics in the use of modal expressions. Nevertheless, the way in which this component acts is barely hinted at. There is a clear inclination towards the development of formal language and an understanding of communication as an eminently psychological task far removed from social reality.

2.2.2 The factuality approach

The core ideas of the logical approach to modality and its descendants penetrated perspectives more closely connected to communicative views of language. Functional and cognitive approaches equate modality with non-factuality and rework the discrete notions of necessity and possibility in terms of a continuum or scale.[6] This approach is found in many of the main works on modality outside formal linguistics (e.g., Frawley, 1992, pp. 385–436; Narrog, 2012; Traugott & Dasher, 2002; Van linden, 2012).

For Narrog (2005b), the definition of modality in terms of non-factuality has advantages over the one based on the attitudes of the speaker: unlike the latter, it provides a characterization at the semantic level (i.e., at the same level as categories such as tense, aspect, or negation) and allows the set of modal markers

---

[6]. Recently, this path has also been explored in formal linguistics (Lassiter, 2017), although the bases for it are already present in Kratzer (1981/2002).

to be delimited with respect to the expression of other categories. His definition follows:

> Modality is a linguistic category referring to the factual status of a state of affairs. The expression of a state of affairs is modalized if it is marked for being undetermined with respect to its factual status, i.e. is neither positively nor negatively factual. (Narrog, 2005b, p. 184)

This approach is useful for determining which units are modal and which are not. For illustration purposes, let us examine uses of the progressive such as the following:

(24) a. You're telling me you don't love me anymore. (Wright, 1995, p. 156)
    b. Estasme molestando.
       'You are bothering me.'

According to Wright (1995, p. 156), this "experiential" use of the progressive form is not aspectual, and "focusses not on an event in time, but on the (speaking) subject's consciousness of being inside an event, state, activity, looking out." It is a sign of subjectivity in language used to express the attitudes of the speaker with respect to a situation or, more specifically, "the speaker's epistemic stance and perspective of a given state of affairs" (Wright, 1995, p. 157). Cases like (24) are not considered examples of modal expressions, although they do express the attitude of the speaker. From the perspective of factuality, a definition of modality in terms of attitude/subjectivity is inadequate because it is unable to discriminate examples such as these. Conversely, a definition based on the notion of factuality, such as the one proposed by Narrog (2005b), rightly discards this type of elements, whose factuality could not be greater.

In the functional and cognitive tradition of linguistics one of the most elaborate proposals for the treatment of modality as a scalar domain based on the notion of factuality is that of Declerck (2011). In practice, it constitutes an adaptation of the possible worlds model to the framework of cognitive linguistics, and, consequently, the author devotes part of his contribution to clarifying how his version of the model should be understood.

Declerck's (2011) proposal is as follows: a possible world is always a *t-world*, that is, a world anchored to a particular time *t*. Therefore, a proposition can be true in one particular *t-world*, and false in another. The actualization of a situation is *factual* if the finite form of the sentence expressing it has a past or present temporal value. All non-factual worlds are created through linguistic mechanisms. Since non-factual worlds are equivalent to modal worlds, these mechanisms are called *modalizers*. The referent of a modalizer is a *modal state*, that is, the qualification of a situation as necessary, possible, probable, permitted, desired, etc. A modal state refers to the fact of a situation being actualized in a particular world, usually the factual one, although not necessarily, as it happens with counterfactuals. The world in which a modal state is actualized constitutes its *ground*; this phenomenon is different from *anchoring*, which refers to the temporal relationship between two worlds. In this framework, modality is defined as the phenomenon of a situation being located in a non-factual world. The author points out that "by '*nonfactual world*' we do not mean a world that is necessarily different from the factual world but rather a possible world that is not represented and/or interpreted as being the factual world" (Declerck, 2011, p. 27). This is crucial in the characterization of modality, as modalizers create worlds with various relationships with the factual world, being that of non-identity exclusive to counterfactuals.

Epistemic modality occurs when the degree of compatibility or overlap between the modal and factual worlds is taken into consideration. Therefore, epistemic modalizers express the speaker's assessment of the relationship between the modal world in which the situation described takes place and the factual world. In most cases, epistemic modality is specific, which means that a particular factuality value of the epistemic scale is applied to the relationship between the modal and the factual world. The values of this scale constitute a continuum that goes from factual to counterfactual. The continuum can be divided into as many categories as desired, but in order to account for the meanings of English modal auxiliaries Declerck (2011) distinguishes the following values:

(25) factuality > strong necessity > weak necessity > probability > possibility > improbability > impossibility > not-yet-factuality[7] > counterfactuality

The values included between the extremes of factuality and counterfactuality are relative factuality values because they all imply some degree of uncertainty on the part of the speaker, in the sense that the modal world they create is represented both as not matching and as not incompatible with the factual world. These relative values, along with counterfactuality, are modal values. Factuality is an epistemic value, but it does not have a modal character, given that it represents the factual world.

---

7. According to Declerck (2009), "not-yet-factual at t" is a modal value neglected in the literature that manifests itself in any expression that has posteriority as part of its meaning. It characterizes possible worlds foreseen by the speaker but non-factual at the time in which they are anchored. This factuality value is, according to the author, the result of the combination of counterfactual and hypothetical values – the latter covers the space that separates factuality from counterfactuality.

Non-epistemic modality, on the other hand, refers to factors that determine the actualization of the SoA (e.g., obligation and permission, ability, desire), but is not treated by Declerck (2011) in as much detail as epistemic modality.

Along similar lines is the treatment of modality in some of the main functionalist models of grammar (see Chapter 3). In Functional Grammar, the two types of objective modality (epistemic and deontic) are conceived as scales integrated by various distinctions (Dik, 1997, p. 242; Hengeveld, 1987, p. 57):

(26) a. Epistemic objective modality
certain – probable – possible – improbable – impossible
b. Deontic objective modality
obligatory – acceptable – permissible – unacceptable – forbidden

Likewise, status (≈ epistemic modality) in Role and Reference Grammar is arranged in a continuum that ranges from real to unreal:

(27) Status
real ← necessary – probable – possible → unreal
(Foley & Van Valin, 1984, p. 213)

In his monograph on epistemic modality, Nuyts (2001a) also considers a possible world where the modalized situation is located, an evaluation of probabilities, and a continuum with two poles between which modal values lie. However, Nuyts (2001a, pp. 21–22) includes certainty as both epistemic and modal, and takes negative raising into consideration, thus treating negative epistemic expressions as conveying positive probabilities of a negative SoA, rather than negative probabilities of a positive SoA (see §5.2), points where it diverges from the previous proposals.

The view of modality as a scale composed of (non-)factuality values has had a lot of diffusion in the functional and cognitive perspectives of linguistics. Such a view is a reaction to the tendency, typical of formal approaches, to treat modality in terms of discrete categories, namely possibility and necessity. It is clear, however, that in the case of deontic and epistemic modality languages distinguish more than two values, which are encoded by terms such as the ones in (26) and (27).

2.2.3 Modality as force dynamics

If Kratzer's is the standard model for modality in formal semantics, the work of Talmy (1988, 2000, pp. 409–470) on force dynamics holds an equivalent status in cognitive linguistics (see Boogaart & Fortuin, 2016; Janda, 2015; Mortelmans, 2007). In this framework, abstract conceptual domains are explained on the basis of simpler domains, from which they are often derived through processes such as metaphor and metonymy. The central idea of Talmy's model is that the linguistic dimension of deontic modality refers to social forces that we understand based on our understanding of physical forces.

Force dynamics is a semantic category that refers to the interaction of entities in relation to force (Talmy, 2000, p. 409). It has a significant presence in linguistic structure, mainly in relation to the notion of causality, and is represented grammatically in subsets of prepositions and conjunctions and, above all, in the modal categories. Modal expressions in general and auxiliaries in particular constitute the (main) grammatical category corresponding to the semantic category of force dynamics or, in other words, the grammaticalized expression of the various ways in which entities interact with respect to forces and barriers.

Force dynamics involves four main parameters: a *force opposition* between an agonist and an antagonist; an *intrinsic force tendency* (towards action or towards rest); the *relative strengths* of the opposing entities (through which the stronger entity will be able to impose its tendency); and the *resultant* of the interaction of forces (from the agonist's point of view). Take the following examples:

(28) a. John cannot leave the house.
      b. The cake can stay in the box.   (Talmy, 2000, pp. 441–442)

In (28a) the syntactic subject (the agonist) shows a tendency towards action, expressed by the auxiliary verb *can*, but an opposing force (the antagonist) blocks the realization of the SoA. The presence of negation indicates that the opposing force is greater than that of the agonist, and, consequently, the interaction results in rest. In the same context *may* would show the same configuration but limited to an interpersonal reading where the forces would be, respectively, the individual desire to carry out the action and the denial of permission by an authority. Talmy's model thus accounts for the meanings of the modals and the contrasts between dynamic and deontic interpretations. On the other hand, (28b) illustrates a case of demotion of the agonist: the subject in this case is not the agonist of the situation but the element controlled by the actual agonist, which is not expressed.

Sweetser (1990, pp. 56–68) applies Talmy's model to epistemic modality, converting through metaphor the physical and social forces of the real world into epistemic forces relative to the mental world. In the epistemic realm, barriers are always bodies of premises, so that a statement like *John may be there* is interpreted as "I am not barred by my premises from the conclusion that he is there" (Sweetser, 1990, p. 61). In this case, there is an epistemic force, exerted by a set of knowledge (the antagonist) and expressed through *may*, which allows the speaker (the agonist) to reach the conclusion expressed by the propositional content.

Sweetser's vision is not without complications. Mortelmans (2007) points out the inability of her proposal to explain why some metaphorical correspondences are better than others: while *may* or *must* allow metaphorical extensions, *can* only supports epistemic readings in the negative form, in the past, and in interrogative contexts, *need* accepts them in negative and interrogative contexts, and *shall* does not allow any type of epistemic interpretation. From a diachronic point of view, Sweetser's proposal also entails difficulties, since the discrete nature of metaphor conflicts with what is known about the evolution of modal categories. Works within the framework of grammaticalization (e.g., Nuyts & Byloo, 2015; Traugott & Dasher, 2002) have shown how epistemic values develop gradually, and have explained the shift towards these values by means of metonymy, rather than metaphor.

Talmy's model has inspired much of the work on modality in cognitive linguistics, including the influential framework of Cognitive Grammar (Langacker, 1987, 1991b, 2008). Nevertheless, the usefulness of force dynamics to separate modality from other semantic domains is disputed, as it plays a role in characterizing other conceptual dimensions as well (see §2.4).

2.3 The typological perspective on modality

Linguistic typology studies language based on the structural properties of the world's languages. Modality has an obvious typological interest, as it is a functional domain with a varied expression, and, as far as epistemic modality is concerned, likely present in all human languages (see Boye, 2012, pp. 114–124; Nuyts, 2005, pp. 18–19). Typological studies on modality focus on analyzing its expressive possibilities in the languages of the world. Given the complex nature of modality, linguistic typology has paid special attention to the compartmentalization of modal space and its semantic aspects.

The first typological approaches to modality are those by Chung and Timberlake (1985), Givón (1982, 1984), and Palmer (1986). Both Chung and Timberlake (1985) and Givón (1982) deal with modality in conjunction with mood in the context of TAM categories (tense, aspect, modality/mood) and do so in a relatively small space. Palmer's (1986) monograph develops a lengthy account of how the modal systems of different languages are organized, and has been a work of reference since its publication. In the next decades very relevant contributions to modality from a typological perspective were made, be they books (Boye, 2012; Bybee et al., 1994; Hogeweg et al., 2009; Nauze, 2008) or chapters in monographs (e.g., de Haan, 2006) and handbooks (e.g., the third part of Nuyts & van der Auwera, 2016). However, it is difficult to do justice to this comprehensive literature within the limits of this book, so I will focus the discussion on the data offered by *The world atlas of language structures online* (WALS) (Dryer & Haspelmath, 2013), one of the most ambitious projects within typological studies.

The WALS chapters we are interested in are three. They deal, respectively, with situational possibility (van der Auwera & Ammann, 2013c), epistemic possibility (van der Auwera & Ammann, 2013a), and the overlap between the two previous types of modal marking (van der Auwera & Ammann, 2013b). Van der Auwera and Ammann's (2013c) situational possibility includes deontic possibility in the traditional sense, situational possibility in the sense of Nuyts (2016), and possibility meanings related to ability. In practice, it is equivalent to non-epistemic or root possibility. The concept of modality in the WALS chapters is made up of both possibility and necessity, even though the latter is only discussed in the final chapter.[8] We thus have a view on modality very close to that of formal and logical approaches, based on the ideas that van der Auwera himself had previously proposed (van der Auwera & Plungian, 1998).

Like most WALS chapters, the three we are dealing with illustrate the distribution of a particular linguistic parameter among the languages of the world based on a sample of them. In this case, the number of languages in the sample ranges from 200 to 240, depending on the chapter. All chapters distinguish between three types of languages. In the two chapters concerned with situational and epistemic possibility (van der Auwera & Ammann, 2013a, 2013c), the three classes of languages are distinguished according to the formal strategy used to express the corresponding modal domain in affirmative declarative sentences. In the case of situational possibility (sample of 234 languages), there are languages that express it through verbal affixes (63 languages), languages that do not have affixes for this purpose, but rely on verbal constructions, that is, modal verbs (158 languages), and languages that lack markers of the previous types, but use particles, adverbs, or adjectives (13 languages). The latter are rare, and found in isolated parts of the planet. Languages that use affixes are very common in New Guinea and North America, and include numerous polysynthetic languages. The most common type, the one using verb constructions, is abundant in Europe, Africa, and South and Southeast Asia, and is rare in New Guinea and Australia.

For epistemic possibility (sample of 240 languages), a distinction is made between languages that express this modal value through verbal constructions (65 languages), languages that do not have verbal constructions but affixes (84 lan-

---

8. Van der Auwera and Ammann's (2013a, 2013b, 2013c) interest in possibility over necessity appears to have precedents in the typological literature: Chung and Timberlake (1985, p. 242) point out that "particular languages tend to be less concerned with distinguishing necessity from possibility than with distinguishing different types of possibility."

guages), and languages that only have other types of markers (91 languages). The data show that the use of modal verbs to express epistemic possibility is an eminently European phenomenon, attested in most languages of the Indo-European and Uralic families. It is also common in South India and West Africa. In the rest of the world, its presence is scarce, and in the Americas it is not found at all. Languages that use affixes and those that use other resources are distributed across most of the planet, with some areas of predominance of one type over the other (e.g., affixes in New Guinea, other resources in Central Africa).

In the third chapter, van der Auwera and Ammann (2013b) examine the extent to which the world's languages deploy common strategies for the expression of the two types of modality. They also now distinguish three classes of languages: those with modal markers that cover the entire area of modality (possibility and necessity, both situational and epistemic), those with markers that cover either situational and epistemic possibility or situational and epistemic necessity, and those with markers that in no case simultaneously encode situational and epistemic modality. These classes correspond, respectively, to languages with a high degree of overlap (36 languages), languages with some degree of overlap (66 languages), and languages with no overlap (105 languages). The former are characteristic of Europe and very rare outside this continent. The geographically prevalent pattern is the non-existence of overlap in the expression of the different types of modality, although languages with some degree of overlap are common in most of the world.

Van Olmen and van der Auwera (2016, pp.365–373) analyze modality from the perspective of Standard Average European, a linguistic area or *Sprachbund* that has the West Germanic and Gallo-Romance languages at its center, but covers most of the European continent. Based on the WALS data, they conclude that *double modal multifunctionality* – equivalent to the high degree of overlap of van der Auwera and Ammann (2013b) – and the *verbiness* of epistemic modality (i.e., the expression of this type of modality through auxiliary verbs) are prominent European traits, that is, features present in most European languages, absent in Eastern Indo-European languages, and rare in geographically adjacent languages and in most of the rest of the world's languages.

In sum, the WALS data show that (i) modal verbs are, at the typological level, the most frequent mechanism to express non-epistemic modality; (ii) in the case of epistemic modality, the use of modal verbs is an eminently European trait, although it is also frequent in other parts of the planet, such as southern India and West Africa; (iii) total modal polysemy or double modal multifunctionality is very rare outside Europe; (iv) the existence of modally polysemous verbal auxiliaries responds to the particular characteristics of European languages, and is not representative of linguistic diversity. Given the privileged place that European languages occupy in linguistic theorizing, it is not unreasonable to conclude that their particularities (viz. their multifunctional modal verbs) are largely responsible for the problematic concept of modality that is currently dominant.

2.4 Critical summary

The traditional classes of modality in linguistics are dynamic, deontic, and epistemic. Their use is widespread but far from satisfactory for everyone, considering the number of alternative arrangements of modal classes that have been proposed. This is a consequence of the difficulty to define modality and delimit its types.

Some theoretical approaches have provided explicit definitions of modality and modal classes, but they face shortcomings. The categories included under the umbrella of modality are diverse, and in order to unify them a semantic criterion is often used. The possible worlds model turns to the notions of necessity and possibility, understood as discrete categories that make up a binary distinction, especially in formal frameworks (see § 2.2.1), but not exclusively (e.g., van der Auwera & Plungian, 1998). A problem with this approach is that deontic and epistemic modality involve more values than those reflected in this binary opposition, that is, they form a scale, as seen in § 2.2.2.

Functionalist reformulations of the possible worlds approach recognize the scalar character of modal categories, identifying their values with different levels of non-factuality. This approach overcomes the difficulties of the binary perspective, but carries the same underlying problem: the lack of a common semantic substance, a coherent definition of modality as a conceptual space. In this connection, the use of non-factuality as a unifying principle seems arbitrary, to the extent that it separates values that clearly belong to the same semantic area: this is the case of certainty, clearly an epistemic value (an evaluation of probabilities) and a factual value (an evaluation as 100% probable) but, because of the latter and in accordance with the possible worlds model, a non-modal value (since modality equals non-factuality). It is worth noting that some functionalist are aware of this, and consider certainty as an epistemic modal value, but, rather than trying to amend the factuality perspective, they either give up defining modality in a coherent way (Hengeveld, 1987, p. 56; Dik, 1997, p. 241), or forsake modality altogether as an analytical category (Nuyts, 2005).

The cognitive model of force dynamics faces similar limitations. Force dynamics provides a conceptual framework for several cognitive systems, including language. In this case, force dynamics acts with a structuring function through several linguistic levels, providing conceptual coherence to unrelated domains. Thus, this model can be used to characterize a wide range of linguistic categories, not being useful for separating traditional modal classes from other semantic domains. In fact, modality is associated with various mental schemes of force dynamics, but lacks a concept that is common to all its manifestations. In addition, if we consider specific modal categories, such as epistemic modality, it is difficult to understand what would motivate the reduction of their values to another conceptual category, such as force dynamics, since probability judgments in particular and evaluations of SoAs in general are basic tools in our interaction with the world (Nuyts, 2009), and all languages encode epistemic meaning in one way or another (Boye, 2012, pp. 114–124). Lampert and Lampert (2000) carry out an extensive critical review of modality from a cognitive perspective, paying special attention to the force dynamics model, and conclude that "it seems in principle impossible to provide a holist characterization of Modality that would be based on a common conceptual substance ... as a cognitively valid category Modality is simply gratuitous" (Lampert & Lampert, 2000, p. 296).

If we admit that modality as has been traditionally conceived of lacks justification as a conceptual category, it is worth asking what led to its success as a category for linguistic analysis. A powerful reason is the existence of a strong tendency among the most studied (i.e., European) languages to have a grammatical category, namely modal auxiliary verbs, that expresses all the meanings of the traditional classes of modality, as seen in §2.3. This connection between the three traditional modal values is not only verified in the polysemy of auxiliaries, but also in the semantic development of these linguistic devices from dynamic, through deontic, to epistemic meanings, both in the diachronic (Traugott, 2006) and the ontogenetic (Hickmann & Bassano, 2016) dimensions. Non-grammatical expressions of modal meaning (e.g., lexical verbs, adverbs, adjectives) usually lack the polysemy of auxiliaries, do not show the same evolution, and raise an interest hardly comparable to that of modal verbs. Additionally, the consideration of the auxiliary system as the epitome of modality explains why evidentiality and other domains are often excluded from the list of modal categories. The pivotal role bestowed on modal auxiliaries, as a consequence of their relevance in the most examined languages, played an important part in the conception of a scarcely coherent concept of modality. Lampert and Lampert (2000, p. 296) go as far as to say that

> [t]he only incentive why Modality as a category should still be retained would ultimately have to refer to – and, as last resort, ground in – a "linguistic imperative" (unmistakably ideologically-motivated by a Eurocentric point of view) to provide a semantic correlative for the formal category of Modal Verbs.

The extreme difficulty to provide a simple and coherent definition of modality is recognized by many authors in the functionalist literature:

> The different notions generally subsumed under the heading "modality" do not seem to represent a single and coherent semantic category.
>
> (Hengeveld, 1987, p. 56)

> Mood and modality are not so easily defined as tense and aspect … In fact, it may be impossible to come up with a succinct characterization of the notional domain of modality and the part of it that is expressed grammatically.
>
> (Bybee et al., 1994, p. 176)

> [T]he phenomena which are discussed in the literature under the labels of "mood" and "modality" do not constitute a unified semantic domain which could be given a single cover-definition. (Dik, 1997, p. 241)

> Modality and its types can be defined and named in various ways. There is no one correct way. (van der Auwera & Plungian, 1998, p. 80)

However, few challenge the convenience of continuing to use modality as a category for linguistic analysis, probably because such course of action would require the deconstruction of a field of study that has been established for decades, even centuries. In my opinion, Nuyts (2005, 2017) provides a very insightful and coherent revisionist proposal, which starts from the idea that the different types of modality are, in fact, quite divergent semantic notions each deserving attention of their own. In Chapter 5 I elaborate my own proposal for the characterization of modality in Galician based on Nuyts's ideas, but first we must understand how modality is conceived of in functional approaches (Chapter 3) and what the relation of modality is with respect to neighboring categories (Chapter 4).

CHAPTER 3

Functionalist approaches to modality

Functionalist approaches have devoted much attention to modality in the context of qualifications of SoAs. Thus, tense, aspect, and modality form a triad known as TAM, and are often treated together (e.g., Ayoun et al., 2018; de Saussure et al., 2007; Hogeweg et al., 2009; Hollebrandse et al., 2005). This phenomenon of predicate evaluation, localization, and modification is central to major functionalist grammatical models, including Functional Grammar (FG) (Dik, 1997) and Role and Reference Grammar (RRG) (Van Valin, 2005; Van Valin & LaPolla, 1997), which propose a treatment in terms of layered operators. Functional Procedural Grammar (FPG) (Nuyts, 1992, 2001a) follows this path, and pays a great deal of attention to qualifying dimensions. These approaches are reviewed in §3.1, since their ideas will be instrumental in providing an overview of the Galician modal system in Chapter 5.

Functionalist approaches that clearly diverge from the previous ones are those of modality and mood in Systemic Functional Grammar (SFG) (§3.2) and in discourse-functional and interactional approaches (§3.3), which highlight the role of modality in the everyday use of language and the importance of the social and interactive context in the study of this linguistic dimension. Insights from these linguistic schools will prove crucial in the corpus study developed in Part III of the book, especially in Chapter 8.

3.1   Functional grammar models

The functional grammar models considered here assume that cross-linguistic variation of qualificational categories harbors universal patterns referring to the way in which these categories relate to each other and to SoAs and their parts, a property known as *scope*. Thus, in these models the qualifications of SoAs are ordered in hierarchical listings that reflect their relative scope. The proposals of FG, RRG, and FPG constitute different examples of how this layered ordering can be carried out.

3.1.1 Functional Grammar

One of the first treatments of modality within FG was Bolkestein's (1980) study of expressions of necessity and obligation in Latin. This, in turn, inspired Goossens's (1985) proposal for English modal auxiliaries within the same framework. Goossens (1985) considers three possible analyses to integrate modal auxiliaries in the formation of predications: (a) to treat them as full predicates (with their own argument structure and entry in the lexicon), (b) to consider them non-independent predicates subject to predicate formation rules, through which they would combine with other predicates, and give rise to derived predicates, and (c) to treat them as operators that combine with a predication, with a status equivalent to that of tense and aspect markers. These three possibilities are the reflection of three different stages in the grammaticalization process. The markers that express deontic and facultative modality (see §2.1.2.2) correspond to full predicates, those that express epistemic modality to predicate formation rules, and future and conditional forms to operators. The core ideas of Goossens (1985) will be found in future treatments of modality in FG.

Hengeveld's (1987, 1988, 1989) account became the standard model of modality in FG, which Dik (1997) closely followed. To understand how modality is integrated into FG, the building blocks of this model (see Dik, 1997) must be laid out. There are several semantic and formal levels in the organization of the clause in FG. The most basic level is the nuclear predication, which expresses an SoA, and results from the union of a predicate (designating relations or properties) with its arguments (the terms selected by the predicate and affected by its semantics). Starting from the nuclear predication, the structure of the clause is constructed by specifying in each layer the relevant grammatical operators (π) and lexical satellites (σ). This way, the nuclear predication is qualified by operators and satellites of the predicate (level 1), giving rise to the core predication, which expresses a qualified SoA. The core predication is modified by operators and satellites of the predication (level 2), which results in the extended predication, describing a qualified and localized SoA. Propositional operators and satellites (level 3) qualify the extended predication, giving rise to the proposition, which presents a possible fact through the speaker's eyes. Finally, the proposition is modified by illocutionary operators and satellites (level 4), and leads to the clause. Figure 3.1 sums up these ideas.

The operators and satellites corresponding to each level specify different properties. At level 1 additional SoA properties are added, such as qualitative aspect (π_1), manner, additional participants, and spatial orientation (σ_1). At the second level, the SoA is enriched by specifying, among other elements, tense, quantitative aspect, objective modality, polarity (π_2), and spatial and temporal location (σ_2). The qualifications of the third level (π_3 and σ_3) concern the validity of the propositional content, and specify dimensions such as subjective modalities and evidentiality. Finally, through level 4 qualifications (π_4 and σ_4) the proposition is modified with elements related to the speaker's communicative strategy, such as mitigation and strengthening of illocutionary force (see § 4.2).

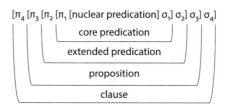

Figure 3.1 Layers and operators in FG

Regarding modality, both Hengeveld and Dik refuse to define how they understand the notion (see § 2.4), rather focusing on the study of its types and its integration into the layered model of FG. The main types of modal meaning considered in FG are three, and have different scopes (Dik, 1997, pp. 241–243; Hengeveld, 1987, 1988):

i. Inherent modality (level 1): linguistic devices that characterize the relation between a participant in an SoA and the realization of that SoA. This type of modality includes ability, volition, obligation, and permission, is internal to the SoA, and is not expressed through grammatical means.[1]

ii. Objective modality (level 2): linguistic devices through which the speaker evaluates the SoA in terms of their knowledge. They have scope over the core predication, and are expressed through predication operators (π_2), when they are realized grammatically, or compound predicates, when they are realized lexically (σ_2). Two types of objective modality exist, corresponding to two types of knowledge:
   a. Epistemic objective modality: an evaluation of the SoA in terms of the speaker's knowledge of SoAs in general.
   b. Deontic objective modality: an evaluation of the SoA relative to a set of moral, legal, or social regulations.

iii. Epistemological modalities (level 3): linguistic devices through which the speaker expresses their commitment to the truth of the proposition. This

---

1. Note that the ideas of Dik (1997, pp. 241–242) on this matter explicitly reject the grammatical status of the dynamic uses of *can*, *must*, *may*, and *have to*. This will be relevant when discussing the modal status of dynamic modality in Chapter 5.

includes subjective (epistemic and volitive) modality and evidential (inferential, quotative, reportative, and experiential) modality. When they are realized grammatically, these expressions constitute propositional operators (π_3), and when they are realized by lexical means, they form compound predicates (σ_3).

The main criterion for the classification of modality in FG is scope. The traditional modal distinctions (see §2.1.1) are overshadowed by this criterion, although the correspondences between modal classes and semantic scope are not difficult to make out. Thus, level 1 corresponds to dynamic modality, level 2 groups traditional deontic meaning with epistemic objective meaning, and level 3 includes epistemic subjective meaning, evidentiality, and what is known as boulomaic modality (see §2.1.2.3).

Hengeveld (2004) systematizes and reworks his previous proposal based on two dimensions: the target of evaluation and the domain of evaluation. The former corresponds to the semantic scope of an expression, and differentiates three types of modality: participant-oriented, event-oriented, and proposition-oriented. The domain of evaluation corresponds to what Kratzer calls the modal base (§2.2.1) or what are commonly known as the types or classes of modality (§2.1). Hengeveld (2004) defines the domain of evaluation as the perspective from which the modal judgment is carried out. This makes it possible to distinguish between facultative, deontic, volitive, epistemic, and evidential modality. Table 3.1 illustrates the combination of the three targets of evaluation (horizontal axis) with the five domains of evaluation (vertical axis), which gives rise to 15 possible combinations, five of which are logically excluded.

Table 3.1 Modal categories in FG (Hengeveld, 2004, p. 1193)

	Participant	Event	Proposition
Facultative	+	+	−
Deontic	+	+	−
Volitive	+	+	+
Epistemic	−	+	+
Evidential	−	−	+

Regarding epistemic modality, the ideas developed within FG contradict one of the few matters in the literature on which there is reasonable agreement: its propositional scope. In fact, what FG does is support the objective/subjective distinction in terms of semantic scope. This opposition dates back to Lyons (1977) and has been the object of considerable attention in the literature on modality (see §4.3). According to Hengeveld (2004, p. 1194), "event-oriented modalities describe the existence of possibilities, general obligations, and the like, without the speaker taking responsibility for these judgements", whereas "proposition-oriented modalities specify the subjective attitude of the speaker towards the proposition" (Hengeveld, 2004, p. 1196). He cites the following example:

(29)   Certainly he may have forgotten.   (Lyons, 1977, p. 808)

According to Hengeveld (2004), (29) contains an epistemic modal adverb (*certainly*) that has the rest of the utterance as its target, used by the speaker to commit themselves to the truth of the proposition "he may have forgotten". This, in turn, contains an epistemic modal verb (*may*) that targets the event and expresses the possibility that the event described by *he has forgotten* has taken place. The fact that the two epistemic judgments are non-harmonic (certainty vs. possibility) does not result in a contradiction, because they operate on different levels, so that "the speaker expresses his certainty about the existence of an objective possibility" (Hengeveld, 2004, p. 1195). This is why in FG proposition-oriented epistemic modality is subjective, and event-oriented epistemic modality is objective. We will return to the issue of objectivity and subjectivity in the next chapter (§ 4.3), and Galician corpus examples analogous to (29) will be dealt with in Chapter 8.

3.1.2   Role and Reference Grammar

Within RRG little attention has been devoted to the semantic nature of modality and of TAM categories in general. On the contrary, the traditional modal classes were refashioned in this framework, focusing on their behavior with respect to the projection of clause operators.

Like FG, RRG proposes a sentence structure divided into layers that orbit around the verbal core and its projections. A major point of divergence between the two theoretical frameworks is the number and location of layers and the terminology used to name them. In RRG the predicate is called *nucleus*, the predicate with its arguments is the core (≈ the predication(s) in FG), the core plus the adjuncts constitute the clause (≈ the proposition in FG), and the clause plus "detached position elements" make up the sentence. Similarly to FG, in RRG qualifications are applied to the various levels of the clause, and a distinction is made between grammatical expressions (operators) and lexical expressions (adverbs) of the qualifications.

Modal values are distributed in RRG between the categories of modality and status (Van Valin & LaPolla, 1997, p. 41; see also Nolan, 2008). RRG's modality encompasses root modality values expressed by auxiliary verbs, such as obligation, ability, and permission. Thus, modality acts on the core level, and refers to the relationship between the referent of the subject noun phrase and the SoA.

Status includes epistemic modality, external negation, and the realis/irrealis distinction typically associated with verbal mood (see § 4.1.3). Status, therefore, constitutes a semantic supercategory, characterized by the correlative oppositions necessity/possibility and realis/irrealis.

(30) Values of the supercategory *status*
necessity ←→ possibility
realis ←→ irrealis

This approach to status diverges from a previous formulation of the model, where the values of necessity and possibility were integrated into the real-unreal scale, represented above in Example (27):

> Status is often viewed as a binary distinction between realis-irrealis, and some languages use just such binary distinction. However, within the irrealis dimension many languages recognize further distinctions, whether the action is necessary, or likely, or merely possible. So within the irrealis poles we may have a continuum such as:
> Real ← necessary – probable – possible → unreal (Foley & Van Valin, 1984, p. 213)

Thus, the most recent accounts of modality in RRG abandon the scalar approach that characterizes its earlier versions and most of the functionalist literature on modality, embracing the binary distinction in terms of necessity and possibility, but keeping the layered approach typical of functional grammars.

3.1.3   Functional Procedural Grammar and the paradigmatic approach

In line with the above frameworks Nuyts (2001a, 2005, 2009, 2017) situates the different modal categories in a system of qualifications of SoAs, which are considered cognitively basic and universal and have an internal structure that is manifested linguistically through their relative semantic scope.[2]

(31) É moi probable que mañá chova.
'It is very likely that it will rain tomorrow.'

In Example (31) the speaker's judgment about the probabilities of the SoA is not constrained by the time marker *mañá* 'tomorrow', but located at speech time. The time marker has scope over the SoA, locating it in time, but not over the epistemic

---

2. Nuyts's proposal for (epistemic) modality goes beyond what is described here. It is worth noting his efforts to treat the phenomenon from a cognitive-functional perspective, relating epistemic modality as a linguistic category to the human conceptualization system (see Nuyts, 2001a, pp. 1–45). However, we will here focus on his characterization of modality and his paradigmatic approach to epistemic modality.

modal qualification. The same can be said, mutatis mutandis, of deontic modality and time in Example (6b). These observations, applied to the rest of categories, are summarized in a hierarchy of qualifications of SoAs represented in (32) (see Nuyts, 2001a, 2005, 2009, 2017):

(32) > inferential evidentiality
       > epistemic modality
       > deontic modality
       > time
         > quantitative aspect [frequency]
         > phasal aspect
         > (parts of the) STATE OF AFFAIRS

In this hierarchy, inferential evidentiality and epistemic and deontic modality are separated from each other and on a par with time and the two types of aspect.[3] Showing the hierarchical order of modal vis-à-vis locating categories is unproblematic, but demonstrating the separation between evidentiality, epistemic modality, and deontic modality is rather complex. According to Nuyts, these categories can hardly be combined in a single clause due to conceptual reasons related to their specific status. Nuyts (2009) proposes a "one-commitment-per-clause" principle, according to which each modal or attitudinal category refers to the speaker's commitment to the SoA in a different way, and speakers generally do not need to show their commitment in multiple ways. Inferential evidentiality and epistemic and deontic modality are three different types of qualifications that deal with the speaker's commitment to the SoA. Making a modal judgment in this sense requires taking into consideration facts external to the SoA and drawing conclusions from them: for inferential evidentiality, making deductions from evidence and assigning a degree of reliability to the inferential process; for epistemic modality, using one's knowledge of the world to assess the factual status of an event and assigning a degree of probability to that event; and, for deontic modality, determining the acceptability of a situation from the point of view of the speaker's moral system and assigning it a degree of acceptability.

The three higher qualificational categories are cognitively much more complex than the lower ones because they involve processing elements external to the SoA and making decisions about its meta-status, resulting in the assignation of a value on a scale. According to Nuyts, this is another reason why it is difficult to combine several attitudinal qualifications in the same clause: modal judgments

---

3. One must bear in mind that the hierarchy is not exhaustive. Nuyts (2009, p. 158) points out that space should be included in the hierarchy as a type of location of SoAs. The same should be applied to other locating categories, such as cause or purpose (see Dik, 1997, pp. 243–245).

intensively exploit human attentional resources, which are limited. In other words, "the restrictions on combining performative deontic, epistemic and evidential expressions may be no more than a very direct reflection of the limits of the processing capabilities of the central conceptual system" (Nuyts, 2009, p. 160). Moreover, the vast typological variability of the information used in the rational process that underlies any modal evaluation adds to this intensive exploitation of cognitive resources.[4] This idea of "one commitment per clause" is not without problems (see, e.g., Cornillie, 2009), and I will try to contribute to its empirical testing in a later chapter (§ 8.3).

Most of FPG key ideas on modality have been applied to and derived from a case study of epistemic modality (Nuyts, 2001a). In this framework epistemic modality is a basic conceptual category concerned with estimations of probability. It has characteristics in common with other types of qualifications of SoAs, but its cognitive processing and linguistic expression are particular and highly complex, which makes it worthy of being studied in its own right. Nuyts (2001a) focuses on the functional factors that motivate the existing diversity of formal devices used to express epistemic modality, and compares four types of modal expressions in German, English, and Dutch (adjectives, adverbs, auxiliaries, and mental-state predicates), accounting for their distribution in terms of four functional factors:

1. *(Inter)subjectivity*[5] refers to the individual or shared character of the epistemic judgment: subjectivity implies that the judgment is the sole responsibility of the speaker, while a judgment marked as intersubjective is presented as shared by a wider group of people.
2. *Performativity* has to do with the fact that some resources only express the modal evaluation made by the speaker at speech time (performative use), while others can also be used to describe an epistemic evaluation which is not ascribed to the speaker at speech time (descriptive use).

---

4. Despite its purported syntagmatic incompatibility, Nuyts (2009) thinks it possible to logically construe the hierarchical relationships between the higher qualificational categories: evidence about an SoA is necessary to begin to think about evaluating its probabilities, but the opposite does not make sense, so evidentiality precedes epistemic modality; considerations about the possible existence or non-existence of an SoA are necessary to begin to think about its moral desirability, so epistemic modality precedes deontic modality. Therefore, evidentiality > epistemic modality > deontic modality.
5. In earlier works Nuyts (2001a, 2001b) considered (inter)subjectivity an evidential dimension, but he later rejected its evidential status (Nuyts, 2012, 2017).

3. *Information structure*, understood as differences in the status of the informative parts of a clause in the discourse context, contrasts the epistemic qualification to the SoA under its scope. According to this factor, the types of epistemic modal expressions can be focal or non-focal.
4. *Discourse strategy* captures the observation that epistemic expressions are frequently used to achieve particular special effects in interaction, such as mitigating or managing the interaction.

In Nuyts's (2001a) proposal these factors explain why speakers choose a certain type of expression over others in a given context. The way the factors interact is complex, as can be seen in Table 3.2. The "+" sign indicates that the factor is often responsible for the use of a certain type of expression, "++" indicates that the factor is the most decisive in the use of the expressive type, "–" indicates that the factor does not play a role in the use of that formal device, and the parentheses around the signs mitigate their value.

Table 3.2 Determining factors in the use of epistemic expressions (Nuyts, 2001a, p. 227)

	epistemic qualification			
	↙	↓	↓	↘
(inter)subjectivity	–	+	++	(–)
descriptive use	–	(+)	+	(–)
focal use	–	++	(+)	–
mitigation	–	–	+	–
argumentation management	+	–	–	+
	↓	↓	↓	↓
	adverb	adjective	mental-state predicate	auxiliary

Some expressive devices are clearly determined: adjectives are used mainly for the focal expression of epistemic modality (33) and, to a lesser extent, for the expression of intersubjective judgments (33) and (36a); while mental-state predicates are used mainly for the subjective expression of epistemic modality (34), to mitigate elements of the discourse (35), and on rare occasions to express a focal qualification. In addition, both devices can be used to describe epistemic qualifications (36).

(33) Non só non é seguro, senón moi pouco *probable* que contraten un substituto.
'It is not only not certain, but barely probable that they will hire a substitute.'

(34) Eu *creo* que ela nunca confiou en ninguén como en seu avó.
'I think that she never trusted anyone the way she trusted her grandfather.'

(35) [Son as 11:55 e a reunión comeza ás 12:00. Neste contexto, A dille a B:]
Creo que debemos ir indo.
[It is 11:55, and the meeting starts at 12:00. In that context, A tells B:]
'I think we must get going.'

(36) a. Daquela non parecía *probable* que Trump fose chegar á Casa Branca.
'Back then it did not look likely that Trump would make it to the White House.'
b. O veciño *cre* que mañá vai chover.
'The neighbor thinks that it will rain tomorrow.'

Other types of formal devices seem to be neutral in terms of most of the factors: these are adverbs and auxiliary verbs, which, according to Nuyts (2001a), do not convey (inter)subjectivity, nor are they used to describe qualifications, nor as focus. Nuyts (2001a) does grant them a role in interaction management, one slightly different from the mitigating function characteristic of mental-state predicates (see §4.2.2). These two types of expressions roughly occupy the same functional area, being different in semantic terms: adverbs possess a highly specific epistemic value, compared to a greater semantic vagueness of auxiliaries. Although this difference may be relevant in the choice of one device over the other, for Nuyts the existence of these two functionally quasi-equivalent expression types is justified mainly by a fact of a syntactic nature: the possibility of using both devices in the same clause, so that the speaker can express several semantic dimensions with a proportional distribution of the load across different expression types.

The previous ideas lead Nuyts (2001a) to conclude that the different types of epistemic expressions constitute a paradigm, that is, a set of formal alternatives for the expression of the same functional category whose choice is determined by factors different from said category. Thus, Nuyts (2001a) considers that epistemic modality is inherent in the lexical semantics of the different types of expressions, and that the functional factors in Table 3.2 (almost) always act through the syntax of these formal devices.

There are important differences in specificity of the epistemic value (higher in adjectives and adverbs, lower in auxiliaries and mental-state predicates): adjectives can be more specific than adverbs (cf. Galician *moi/bastante/pouco/moi pouco probable* lit.'very/quite/little/very probable' vs. *moi/*bastante/*pouco/*moi pouco probablemente* lit.'very/*quite/*little/*very probably'), and these in turn are more specific than auxiliary verbs. These differences are explained in terms of factors external to the functional category of epistemic modality, namely information structure. A high specificity of the epistemic semantics suggests a prominent informational status of the epistemic qualification. In other words, adjectives are frequently used when the epistemic judgment is the focus of the clause because they are able to carry the greater information load that a focal expression requires.

Finally, Nuyts (2001a, p. 262) notes that epistemic expressions are organized around two syntactic patterns, illustrated in Table 3.3. If adjectives and adverbs are considered, on the syntactic level, variants of the same expression type, each of these displays two alternative syntactic patterns. In the complementating structure the epistemic qualification appears in the main clause and the SoA in a subordinate clause. In the flat structure the qualification "infiltrates" the SoA, with different degrees of integration, from very strong in auxiliaries to very weak in parentheticals. In addition, each expression type shows tendencies regarding these syntactic options, according to the results of Nuyts's (2001a) study: the two options are frequent with adjectives and adverbs, mental-state predicates have a preference for the parenthetical expression, and auxiliaries favor complementation.

Table 3.3 Syntactic patterns of epistemic expression types (Nuyts, 2001a, p. 262)

	Complementing structure		Flat structure
adjectives/adverbs	it is probable	that SoA	S probably oA
mental-state predicates	I think	(that) SoA	S, I think, oA
auxiliaries	it may be	that SoA	S may oA

These are the guidelines of the paradigmatic approach laid out by Nuyts (2001a). It constitutes a very sophisticated explanation of the variation in the linguistic expression of epistemic modality. A recent replication of the approach in Galician (Míguez, 2023) supports Nuyts's (2001a) core ideas regarding the functional factors that determine the choice between expression types (Table 3.2), and found that the syntactic behavior of Galician epistemic markers is parallel to that of West Germanic expressions (Table 3.3). From a functional point of view, Galician adjectives and mental-state predicates have very specific profiles, whereas adverbs and auxiliaries are neutral in terms of most of the factors in Table 3.2, and can be considered variants of the same expression type at a functional level. From a syntactic perspective, Galician adjectives and adverbs clearly complement each other – the former appear in the complementing pattern, the latter in the flat structure – but auxiliaries and mental-state predicates have a very strong preference for the flat structure and the complementing pattern, respectively – in Nuyts's (2001a) results is the other way around – and they can hardly be considered ambivalent in syntactic terms.

3.2 Systemic Functional Grammar

Systemic Functional Grammar is an influential functional model in today's linguistics. Its greatest exponent was the British linguist M. A. K. Halliday, whose work draws from J. R. Firth's, who in turn took inspiration from anthropologists such as Bronisław Malinowski. As a result, among functionalist models of grammar, SFG places special emphasis on the social and cultural functions of language and communication (see Butler, 2003, pp. 43–48; Robins, 2000, pp. 301–307). Linguistic communication involves, in this framework, three metafunctions (Halliday, 1970b, pp. 141–144; Halliday, 2014, pp. 82–86): *ideational* or *experiential*, that is, language as the expression of meaning from the perspective of the speaker; *interpersonal*, the use of language to create and maintain social relationships; and *textual*, which allows linguistic elements to be combined with elements of the context or other linguistic elements in order to build texts.

Modality in SFG (see Halliday, 2004, 2014) is a product of the interpersonal metafunction, and is closely linked to the system of MOOD, which determines linguistic choices related to the exchange of information in the clause and the management of speaker and hearer roles. More specifically, MOOD has to do with the choice between the imperative and the indicative and, in the case of the latter, between declarative and interrogative. When the indicative mood is chosen, *modality* appears as an option. Modality is divided into *modalization* and *modulation*, which are respectively related to *probability* and *usuality*, on the one hand, and to *inclination* and *obligation*, on the other hand. SFG thus avoids using traditional terms such as epistemic modality and deontic modality.

Modality as explained by Halliday (2004, 2014) enables the study of a large number of formal devices and their distinctive characteristics based on the role they play in interaction. Martin and White (2005) develop Halliday's model of modality under the label of *appraisal*, which includes three types of evaluation: *attitude* is related to the speaker's emotions; *engagement* is concerned with the reference to the source of the speaker's attitudes and the interplay of different voices in discourse; and *graduation*, as its name suggests, graduates (i.e., either raises or lowers) elements of discourse. The category closest to modality in the traditional sense is engagement, which constitutes a system of options that indicate the degree of commitment to the evaluation. Resources usually linked to evidentiality, modality, and mitigation are associated with this category. This theoretical approach is dialogic, meaning that it accounts for modal elements in real contexts of use. An application of these ideas is found in the work of Simon-Vandenbergen and Aijmer (2007), which will be reviewed briefly at the end of the next section. In this way, SFG is intimately connected with approaches that deal with modality in discourse and interaction.

3.3 Discourse-functional and interactional approaches[6]

This section deals with different approaches, not necessarily linked to a particular theoretical model, which study modality from the point of view of the construction and organization of interaction and discourse. More specifically, these approaches are characterized by an interest in analyzing modality using authentic linguistic data extracted from corpora and explaining the functions of modal expressions in terms of discourse structure, communicative situation, text type, and medium.

A widely used term in these approaches is *stance* (e.g., Biber & Finegan, 1988; Du Bois, 2007; Kärkkäinen, 2003; Ochs, 1996), which refers to the functions of modal elements not only in linguistic studies, but also in disciplines such as sociolinguistics, discourse analysis, and anthropology. Close and sometimes equivalent terms are *commitment* (Stubbs, 1986), *engagement* (Martin & White, 2005; White, 2003), *evidentiality* (Chafe, 1986; Downing, 2001), and *modality* itself (Schoonjans, 2019). A very influential model for understanding stance is Du Bois's (2007) stance triangle, which breaks down stance into three triangularly related actions: *evaluation*, *positioning*, and *alignment*. In this framework stance is understood as a triple act by which a social actor evaluates an object, positions a subject (usually the self), and aligns it with other subjects. These ideas are summed up in the following definition: "Stance is a public act by a social actor, achieved dialogically through overt communicative means, of simultaneously evaluating objects, positioning subjects (self and others), and aligning with other subjects, with respect to any salient dimension of the sociocultural field" (Du Bois, 2007, p. 163).

In discourse-functional and interactional approaches *modality* is often used to designate the linguistic expression of stance. In the same way that stance is a broad concept, its linguistic expression goes well beyond modal auxiliary verbs, and includes all those devices that express attachment or detachment in a specific communicative situation. In this connection, a key role is awarded to frequency of use in establishing a limited number of devices as modal markers. Kärkkäinen's (2003) study of epistemic stance in American English illustrates this perspective. In her data, the most frequent marker is the "epistemic phrase" *I think*, which performs several functions in initial position. One of them is the "recipient-oriented design of utterances", illustrated in (37).

---

6. I borrowed this label from Aijmer (2016).

(37) DORIS: Isn't that what you gave the neighbor one time?
      SAM: I...
      DORIS: You gave him some kind of herb.
      SAM: I gave him a red pepper.
      DORIS: *I think* ... *I think* you gave him ... some ... herb of some kind.
      SAM: I may have given ... given him some basil.
                              (adapted from Kärkkäinen, 2003, p. 147)

In this example, one of the participants, Doris, shows disagreement with what was expressed in the previous turn, and uses *I think* to introduce her assertion. In this case, the speaker does not use the epistemic marker to make an estimation of probabilities, but she is resuming a previous statement introduced without a modal qualification. The function of *I think* in this context is to introduce a counterargument to the immediately preceding utterance, which, moreover, has already been rejected by the interlocutor. In other words, what the speaker is doing is resorting to a device that encodes doubt in order to mitigate the illocutionary force of an assertion that, in this context, constitutes a threat to the interlocutor's face. Therefore, Kärkkäinen (2003) concludes, *I think*, and epistemic markers in general, play a key role in the (re)design of interventions in interactive contexts.[7]

This kind of approach has been applied to a wide number of epistemic markers in different languages. For instance, Downing (2001) considers English *surely* a "fighting word"; Cornillie (2015, pp. 136–137), on Spanish *a lo mejor*, points out that it is not only used to introduce hypotheses, but also to invite the interlocutor to confirm or reject the SoA, thus playing a role in turn-taking procedures; and González-Vázquez (2021, p. 91) argues that Galician *seica* "is used not only to attenuate the rights of the speaker's claims but [also] to highlight the hearer's epistemic rights."

In understanding the connection of modal markers with the discourse and social context the notions of *indexicality* and *reflexivity* are crucial (cf. Simon-Vandenbergen & Aijmer, 2007, pp. 44–50). The former is developed in the work of anthropologists such as Gumperz (1982) and Ochs (1996), who argue that contexts are vital in the interpretation of utterances and that there is a relatively conventionalized relationship between both elements. Ochs (1996) pays special attention to this idea, arguing that linguistic markers that convey epistemic stance

---

7. It should be noted that the same device can have different functions depending on context: Simon-Vandenbergen (2000) contrasts the uses of *I think* in political discourse and in informal conversation, and shows how social context determines the function of the device. Thus, the *I think* that appears in political discussions is not used to weaken illocutionary force but to fight for power in the interaction.

point indirectly towards actions, identities, and social relations. The second key concept in discourse approaches to modality is reflexivity, which refers to the ability of language to reflect on itself and to the metalinguistic processing that enables speakers to monitor their own linguistic activity and structure the evolving discourse.

Simon-Vandenbergen and Aijmer (2007) apply these notions to the semantic field of modal certainty in a corpus study of English adverbs. On the one hand, the adverbs have an indexical character to the extent that they encode information implicit in the context, linked, for example, to social identity, solidarity, or politeness. On the other hand, the adverbs have a reflexive character that results in a central role in discourse structuring and conveys the speaker's awareness of how their interventions are related to the preceding or following discourse. A further ingredient in Simon-Vandenbergen and Aijmer's (2007) recipe for the study of adverbs of certainty is dialogicity. They take inspiration from the concept of heteroglossia (see Bakhtin, 1981), assuming that discourse is fundamentally argumentative and that, as a consequence, it is necessary to distinguish between the epistemic meaning of adverbs and their rhetorical function. For this, they take White's (2003) model, which explains the dialogic potential of linguistic devices on the basis of different types of strategies. In the particular case of adverbs of certainty, Simon-Vandenbergen and Aijmer (2007) identify categories such as challenging, concession, concurrence, countering, and endorsement. *Of course* offers an illustration:

(38) And *of course* during the nineteenth century we can't hide the fact Egypt became very much of a hunting ground for agents on behalf of museums in Europe.   (Simon-Vandenbergen & Aijmer, 2007, p. 205)

According to the authors, *of course* in (38) restores the balance of power between the speaker, as the provider of information, and the hearer, as the recipient of it. In this type of contexts, the adverb means 'as you already know', but it doesn't matter if the interlocutor really knows: it is a mechanism for saving face, in two ways. On the one hand, by implying that the hearer knows as much as the speaker, *of course* is a mark of solidarity and equality that protects the interlocutor's face. On the other hand, the speaker saves their own face by flagging the information as common knowledge, and avoids sounding naive by implying that the information they provide is new to the hearer. Thus, *of course* also encodes superiority, so that it is precisely in this "ambivalent expression of power relations" that its rhetorical potential lies. In conclusion, in this model "adverbs of certainty can be analysed as social markers and as contextualization cues signalling or guiding the organization of the message in the evolving discourse" (Simon-Vandenbergen & Aijmer, 2007, p. 50).

CHAPTER 4

Modality and neighboring categories

A conclusion can be drawn from Chapters 2 and 3: modality is a broad category whose definition and delimitation is far from being firmly established. The main approaches involve understanding modality as a logical opposition between necessity and possibility (§ 2.2.1), as a gradual dimension that accommodates several non-factual values (§ 2.2.2), as a cognitive category described in terms of force dynamics (§ 2.2.3), or as a pragmatic notion based on the attitudes of the speaker (§ 3.3).

Firstly, the result of this great diversity of approaches is a wide range of views on the relationships between modality and the categories of tense, aspect, mood, and evidentiality, together known as TAME. These relationships, reviewed in § 4.1, range from the functional interaction between clearly independent categories (the case of modality and aspect) to the overlap between adjacent functional domains (this is the well-known case of epistemic modality and evidentiality, but to some extent also that of modality and tense), and sometimes involve problematic associations, such as the view of verbal mood as the grammatical expression of modality. As Squartini (2016, p. 51) points out, the controversies affect the grammatical expression of these domains (verbal tenses, periphrases, and moods), but not lexical markers (e.g., the temporal adverb *tomorrow* or the evidential adverb *supposedly*).

Secondly, the difficulty of defining modality, on the one hand, and the relevant role that modal markers play in interaction, on the other, often lead to subsuming modality to discourse strategies such as mitigation and strengthening. However, this view risks blurring the borders between semantics and pragmatics, as will be shown in § 4.2.

Finally, subjectivity and intersubjectivity do not overlap with modality, but deeply influence how modality and modal categories are understood. For this reason § 4.3 is devoted to shedding some light on the relationship between modality and the different notions of (inter)subjectivity.

4.1 Modality and TAME

Tense, aspect, and mood have traditionally been considered grammatical categories of the verbal domain, namely, morphemes and periphrases of the verb that express closed classes of semantic values. However, it is not always obvious which values are included within each category. In this connection, Dik (1997, Chapter 9) argues for a distinction between the set of semantic values related to the category (*temporality, aspectuality, modality*) and the subset of these that is expressed by grammatical means (*tense, aspect, mood*[1]). In this double triad, it is the modality/mood distinction that entails the greatest difficulties (Bybee et al., 1994, p. 176; Chung & Timberlake, 1985, p. 241), since mood as an inflectional category of the verb is too restrictive to be considered as the main (grammatical) expression of modality (Narrog, 2012, p. 1). Because of this, *modality* often takes the place of *mood* in the acronym TAM (e.g., Ayoun et al., 2018; Hogeweg et al., 2009). In the following pages I will review how modality relates to each of the TAME categories, focusing on discussing the Galician data.

4.1.1 Tense

A few decades before the recent discussion on the (non-)modal status of evidentiality, the boundaries between modality and tense were debated in similar terms in the linguistic literature. For example, Lyons (1977, p. 820) goes so far as to state that "tense is a kind of modality." In fact, relations between temporal reference and modality still enjoy the attention of cognitive approaches to language (e.g., De Wit, 2017; Patard & Brisard, 2011).

In an already classic characterization (Comrie, 1985) tense, conceived as the grammatical(ized) codification of the cognitive category of temporality, locates an SoA on the temporal axis, specifically in three alternative positions: present, past, or future. In this view tense is clearly different from modality, as it involves an objective location on the temporal axis compared to the subjective qualification of the SoA entailed by modality. Nevertheless, when discussing the future tense, non-factuality and, by extension, modality come along.

The relationship between futurity and non-factuality is philosophical in nature, and, in general, linguists prefer not to address it. Attention is paid, however, to the reasons for speaking about the future, which, according to Dahl (2000), are three: to make predictions, to communicate intentions, and to express future plans (scheduling). The last category is the one involving greater factuality and the only one that is not encoded through future but present tense markers in the European languages studied by Dahl (2000). In these languages the future tense is mainly used to refer to posterior events whose factuality is doubtful (i.e., predictions and intentions).

---

1. Note that these terms are also frequently used to designate the formal correlates of the semantic categories, namely, certain sets of verbal morphemes and auxiliaries.

Futurity in Galician is expressed not only by the future tense (*futuro*), but also by the *pospretérito*, also known as the conditional. Whereas the *futuro* typically expresses future SoAs (predictions and intentions), as in (39a), the *pospretérito* conveys posteriority with respect to a previous event (i.e., future-in-the-past), as in (39b).

(39) a. Mañá *choverá* todo o día.
         'Tomorrow it will rain all day.'
     b. Ela pensaba que ao día seguinte *chovería* todo o día.
         'She thought that the next day it would rain all day.'

However, these tense markers are used in an additional manner that breaks away from their canonical time reference. In an example such as (40a) the future tense does not convey a prediction or intention (a future SoA), but a conjecture about a present SoA. Similarly, the *pospretérito* in (40b) does not refer to the future-in-the-past, but rather to a conjecture about a past SoA. I will refer to these as *modal uses*.[2]

(40) a. (Agora) haberá 30 persoas aí fóra.
         '(Now) there must be 30 people out there.'
     b. (Onte) habería 30 persoas aí fóra.
         '(Yesterday) there must have been 30 people out there.'

The two examples in (40) describe the same SoA, but with different temporal references: (40a) is a conjecture about the number of people present outside at speech time, whereas (40b) is a conjecture about the number of people present outside the day before speech time. These modal uses are well known in Romance languages. However, the controversy arises when discussing their epistemic or inferential nature.

According to Pietrandrea (2005), the Italian future only encodes epistemic modality, whereas according to Hennemann (2014) the Spanish future only encodes inferential evidentiality. Other authors assign both epistemic and inferential values to future forms (see Oliveira, 2015, for Portuguese; Rodríguez Rosique, 2017, for Spanish). Similarly, Squartini (2001) considers modal uses of Romance future oriented forms inferential, without excluding the possibility of finding epistemic values in particular cases.

---

2. I am not including cases of prediction, as Giannakidou and Mari (2018) do, nor intention under modality. Also excluded are those uses of the *pospretérito* that convey a counterfactual SoA, typically found in, but not restricted to, conditional clauses (e.g., *Se tivese tempo, faríao* 'If I had the time, I would do it'). This I will call the *conditional* use. According to Thieroff (2010, p. 13), the overlap between the temporal future-in-the-past use and the conditional use is common in European languages.

In Galician grammars modal uses of the *futuro* and the *pospretérito* are accounted for in terms of probability, an epistemic dimension (Álvarez & Xove, 2002, pp. 280–281; Freixeiro Mato, 2000/2006a, pp. 349–354). According to Álvarez and Xove (2002), tense makes up a scale that consists of three positions, represented in (41) and illustrated in (42).

(41)   non-probable > probable > unreal

(42) a. Non-probable (*presente*)
A estas horas aínda *está* no traballo.
'At this time (s)he is still at work.'
b. Probable (*futuro*)
A estas horas aínda *estará* no traballo.
'At this time (s)he must still be at work.'
c. Unreal (*pospretérito*)
Segundo el, aquí *teriamos* un caso claro de prevaricación.
'According to him, here we would have an obvious case of perversion of justice.' (Álvarez & Xove, 2002, p. 281)

We must point out that Álvarez and Xove (2002, p. 280) use *non-probable* in (41) in the sense of *certain*, that is, to describe a factual SoA and, by extension, the absence of a modal judgment. The present tense illustrates this category in (42a). The notion of *probable* is illustrated by the *futuro* in (42b), and also by the examples in (40). As for the unreal category, it is illustrated by a conditional use of the *pospretérito* in (42c). Thus, the "non-canonical" uses of tense are explained in terms of the factual status of the SoA, that is, in terms of modal distinctions. In fact, Álvarez and Xove (2002) see the system of tense in Galician intimately related to that of mood, where factuality/reality status plays a key role. Therefore, we will return to the scale in (41) and delve deeper into modality and tense when discussing mood later on (§ 4.1.3).

It is obvious that modality and tense are intertwined in complex ways that have not gone unnoticed for Galician grammars. Yet, despite recognizing the contribution of tense to modal distinctions, both Álvarez and Xove (2002) and Freixeiro Mato (2000/2006a) do not stray from the consensus view that modality and tense are different categories, the modal uses of future-oriented tenses being a "deviation" from their canonical, temporal use.[3] Both agree as well in viewing the modal uses of tense as expressions of probability, an epistemic value. However,

---

3. A major exception to this conception comes from Cognitive Grammar (De Wit, 2017; Langacker, 1991b), where the modal component of tense is considered basic, whereas its temporal component is seen as specific.

the issue of the epistemic vs. inferential nature of modal uses of tense markers is a thorny one, and will be reexamined in § 4.1.4.

4.1.2 Aspect

The connections between aspect and modality are not as far-reaching as those between the latter and tense. The traditional definition of aspect leaves no room for confusion with any modal category: aspect is the grammatical(ized) expression of the internal temporal constitution of an SoA (Comrie, 1976). The appearance of an SoA may correspond, in the most basic version, to ongoing situations that are still unfinished (imperfective aspect) or to culminated events (perfective aspect). From this perspective, aspect has little to do with necessity and possibility, with non-factuality, or with the attitudes of the speaker.

Nevertheless, some interactions between aspect and modality exist. In fact, the two notions have been the object of joint attention on several occasions (e.g., Ameka & Kropp Dakubu, 2008; Böhm, 2016; Hatav, 1997). Different aspectual choices are used to present the same SoA in different ways, which can be more or less compatible with particular modal interpretations. As Leiss (2008) indicates, there is an affinity between perfective aspect and deontic modality, on the one hand, and imperfective aspect and epistemic modality, on the other, as far as modal verbs are concerned. (43) and (44) illustrate the interaction.

(43) a. Debe *marchar* xa.
        '(S)he must leave now.'
     b. Debe *estar marchando* xa.
        '(S)he must be leaving now.'

(44) a. Débelles *dar* o diñeiro.
        '(S)he must give the money to them.'
     b. Débelles *estar dando* o diñeiro.
        '(S)he must be giving the money to them.'
                                    (adapted from Leiss, 2008, p. 17)

In series (a) the modal verb *deber (de)* yields a deontic/directive interpretation – '(s)he has the obligation to leave/to give them the money' – while in series (b) the same modal introduces the same non-finite verb in the progressive, and yields an epistemic reading – 'it is likely that (s)he is leaving/giving them the money'. Similar results would be obtained with an imperfective past form and a perfective past form: *debía marchar xa* (imperfective aspect) yields a deontic interpretation, whereas *debeu marchar xa* (perfective aspect) leads to an epistemic reading.

Some authors argue that the link between aspect and modality may be due to an interaction between modality and tense determined by futurity (Narrog,

2008) or to a general connection between imperfective aspect and subjectivity (Boogaart, 2011). However, these links are not very strong, as deontic/directive readings are also favored in some progressive contexts (e.g., *debe estar durmindo antes de que volvamos* '(s)he must be sleeping before we are back'). At any rate, it is obvious that aspect and modality are different categories.

4.1.3 Mood

Mood has attracted the attention of philosophers and grammarians since Antiquity (§1.3), and is still the subject of much linguistic research. According to Malchukov and Xrakovskij (2016), two alternative views exist regarding the relationship between modality and mood. One view does not distinguish between the two poles from a conceptual perspective: mood is the formal reflection of the semantic dimension of modality. This is the traditional approach, which conceives of mood as the grammatical(ized) counterpart of modality (e.g. Bybee et al., 1994, p. 181; Palmer, 2001, p. 4), or as a category intimately related to modal meaning (e.g., Portner, 2018). In the alternative view, mood and modality are conceptually different. This approach is found in *The Oxford handbook of modality and mood* (Nuyts & van der Auwera, 2016), where *modality* refers to the semantic domains traditionally included under this label (dynamic, deontic, epistemic), whereas *mood* has to do with, on the one hand, sentence types, such as declarative and interrogative, and the illocutionary forces expressed by them (i.e., sentence or illocutionary moods), and, on the other hand, with the distinctions between the indicative and the subjunctive, and between realis and irrealis (i.e., grammatical or verbal moods). In this section we will focus on the domain of verbal mood, and delve into its relationship with modality.

Verbal mood is one of the great enigmas of linguistics, even today. It is a very widespread category among the languages of the world, and its analysis is extremely complicated. The main proposal to account for mood as a formal category is the functional domain of reality status, that is, the location of an SoA in either the real world (realis) or some unreal world (irrealis) (see Elliot, 2000). Typologically oriented works such as Foley and Van Valin (1984), Givón (1994, 2001), Palmer (2001), and Van Valin and LaPolla (1997) rely on reality status to explain the contrasts between the indicative and the subjunctive, so that, in very general terms, the indicative would cover the area of realis and the subjunctive the area of irrealis. However, some criticism has been raised regarding the typological validity of reality status as an autonomous grammatical category.

According to Nikolaeva (2016, pp. 80–84), the criticism is related to two facts. On the one hand, the formal distinctions of verbal mood are not necessarily related to reality status distinctions. Thus, in some languages, the irrealis marker expresses potentiality, and this, in turn, can imply non-factuality/counterfactuality in particular contexts; in other languages, the irrealis marker weakens epistemic certainty, with different semantic effects depending on the syntactic context. On the other hand, the types of sentences marked as realis or irrealis vary greatly across languages, obscuring the role that reality status may play. In fact, there are well-known examples, such as the Galician ones in (45), where the indicative is selected in a context of non-factuality (irrealis) and the subjunctive is chosen in a context in which the SoA is factual (realis), contrary to theoretical expectations.

(45) a. Creo que *está* na casa. [non-factual: IND]
'I think (s)he is at home.'
b. Alégrome de que *estea* na casa. [factual: SBJV]
'I am happy (s)he is at home.'

It would seem that in cases like these the syntactic context determines mood selection and that mood does not make a semantic contribution to the sentence. This idea of mood as a semantically vacuous category is one of the numerous proposals that have been put forward to explain the phenomenon. Other accounts understand the subjunctive as a mark of dependency or intentionality, as a stance marker, as a clue on how the utterance should be interpreted in its context, as a device to evaluate the information value of clauses, etc. (see Lunn, 1995; Mauri & Sansò, 2016, pp. 171–178; Nikolaeva, 2016, pp. 80–84). None of these explanations is entirely satisfactory.

When discussing mood, it is common to propose language-specific explanations. In the case of Galician, Freixeiro Mato (2000/2006a, p. 337) points out that mood is a "property" of the verb that expresses the attitudes of the speaker in relation to their message, which includes certainty, doubt, assumption, command, etc. Thus, the indicative is the mood of reality, and presents the SoA as known or real; the subjunctive is the mood of non-reality, and presents the SoA as not known or not real; and the imperative expresses command, advice, exhortation, supplication, or invitation. As regards the indicative/subjunctive opposition, this account is based on the realis/irrealis distinction, and is faced with clear counterexamples, such as those in (45).

A more sophisticated proposal is found in Álvarez and Xove (2002), who distinguish, in the first place, between the area of illocutionary moods and the domain of "verbal moods of probability and unreality." They characterize illocutionary moods as functional domains concerned with "implicacións que o locutor establece co alocutario ou respecto de si mesmo" (Álvarez & Xove, 2002, p. 175) 'implications that the speaker establishes with the addressee or with respect to himself'. Thus, mood and tense verbal morphemes partially contribute to identifying the illocutionary mood of a main clause: the indicative characterizes declarative and interrogative illocutionary moods, the subjunctive is used with desiderative and imperative illocutionary moods, and the imperative verbal morpheme is exclusive to the imperative illocutionary mood.

Álvarez and Xove (2002) understand verbal moods in a very similar way: "relacións de implicación en distintos sentidos que se establecen entre os interlocutores e o dito na oración" (Álvarez & Xove, 2002, p. 264) 'relationships of implication in different respects that are established between the interlocutors and what is said in the sentence'. They claim that there is no biunivocal relationship between morphological mood categories (indicative, subjunctive, imperative) and the notional distinctions of verbal mood (unreal/non-unreal, probable/non-probable) (Álvarez & Xove, 2002, p. 266). In fact, the relationship between the formal and the conceptual dimension is quite complex, as illustrated in Table 4.1, which summarizes Álvarez and Xove's (2002) model for verbal mood.

In Table 4.1 morphological mood labels are in small caps, notional mood categories are in italics, and tense categories are in regular font. Regarding the moods of unreality, the INDICATIVE is always *non-unreal*, whereas the INDICATIVE and the SUBJUNCTIVE can be either *unreal* or *non-unreal*. The latter is the unmarked and most frequent element of the opposition vis-à-vis the *unreal*, which is concerned with "'distanciamento' en varios sentidos, sobre todo para referirse a situacións inexistentes, contrarias ó que existe ou pode existir, e para expresar peticións, preguntas e declaracións moi atenuadas, corteses" (Álvarez & Xove, 2002, p. 279) ''distancing' in several senses, above all to refer to situations that are non-existent, contrary to what exists or can exist, and to express requests, questions, and statements in a very mitigated and polite way'. The following are examples of the unreal mood.

Table 4.1 Verbal mood in Galician (Álvarez & Xove, 2002, p. 267)

	INDICATIVE		SUBJUNCTIVE	IMPERATIVE
	non-probable	probable		
non-unreal	presente, pretérito, futuro, copretérito, antepretérito, pospretérito	futuro pospretérito	presente pretérito	imperativo
unreal	pospretérito, copretérito, antepretérito		pretérito	

(46) a. Unreal declarative: IND
   Faríacho, pero non podo.
   'I would do it for you, but I can't.'
   b. Unreal interrogative: IND
   ¿*Faríasmo* de seren outras as circunstancias?
   'Would you do it for me under different circumstances?'

c. Unreal desiderative: SBJV
      ¡Ogallá *estivese* agora alí con ela!
      'I wish I were there now with her!' (Álvarez & Xove, 2002, p. 279)

Then there are the moods of probability, which are only relevant for the *non-unreal* INDICATIVE and oppose *probable* to *non-probable* SoAs. *Non-probable* mood is the unmarked term and conveyed by all INDICATIVE tenses, whereas the *probable* mood is restricted to modal uses of the *futuro* and the *pospretérito*, like the ones in (40). The *probable* mood is seen by Álvarez and Xove (2002, p. 280) as equivalent to the mitigation of the utterance, which leads them to understand the scale in (41) as a politeness continuum. The interpretation of (epistemic) modality distinctions in terms of politeness is not unprecedented, but a recurrent pattern in the literature (see § 4.2).

Álvarez and Xove's (2002) account illustrates the interplay of tense and mood categories in the construction of verbal meaning. In their account of verbal mood in Galician there is no single functional factor that explains the distribution of morphological categories, but rather a complex interaction of reality status (non-unreal/unreal), epistemic modality (non-probable/probable), discourse strategy (mitigation), and illocutionary mood (declarative, interrogative, desiderative, imperative). Mood can only be considered as an expression of modality distinctions if modality is conceived of in a very broad and vague way. In a more narrow conception of modality (i.e., as traditionally characterized, see § 2.1.1) mood plays only a very marginal role, limited to the opposition between non-probable and probable SoAs, which is not directly expressed through morphological mood markers, as it is only relevant in the indicative. In sum, modality and morphological mood have a very weak link, since the latter does not directly encode any modal value in the traditional sense (dynamic, deontic, epistemic).

4.1.4 Evidentiality

Evidentiality occupies a prominent place in current linguistics, especially in the functional and typological traditions, but this was not always the case. The languages that laid the foundations of the European linguistic tradition, namely Greek and Latin, do not possess a grammatical category that clearly corresponds to the concept of evidentiality. This emerged when the languages of the world, particularly those of North America, began to be studied seriously, which happened early in the 20th century: Waldemar Jochelson is credited with the first use of *evidential* as a term for linguistic description in 1905 (Izquierdo Alegría et al., 2016, p. 11), whereas Franz Boas mentions *information source* as a notion of mandatory expression through grammatical means in some Amerindian languages in 1911 (Aikhenvald, 2004, pp. 12–13). During the 1980s studies on evidentiality were consolidated, and during the 1990s the notion began to be applied to European languages. This resulted in the bibliographic explosion on evidentiality that we have witnessed in the last two decades and that continues to this day.

Currently, evidentiality is used as equivalent to source of information, rather than evidence (e.g., Aikhenvald, 2004, p. 3). Izquierdo Alegría (2019) shows how *source* is applied to very different notions and, in general, used very vaguely in the literature on evidentiality. He argues for a triple distinction that aims to break down the concepts that underlie the use of *source*, namely: the mode of access to information (direct, reportative, inferential), the bases of information (sensory, enunciative, cognitive), and the source of information (the "agent" that creates the information). While the bases and the source are relevant to understanding the functioning of evidential expressions at the epistemological level, it is the modes of access that receive linguistic codification. This is consistent with Willett's (1988) seminal work, where the main division is between direct and indirect access to information. With direct evidentials the speaker conveys that they know the SoA through one of their senses, usually sight or hearing; with indirect evidentials the speaker conveys that they either inferred the event from witnessed or known facts (inferential evidentiality), or learned about it through communication with other people (reportative evidentiality).

In many languages evidentiality is expressed through verbal morphology, and thus reference to the mode of access to information is mandatory when using a verb. Languages lacking a grammatical expression of evidentiality can convey evidential meanings using adverbs and particles or more complex constructions. A major debate in the delimitation of evidentiality stems from these formal differences: in linguistic typology, with Aikhenvald (2004) as a prominent figure, the term is only applied to grammatical expressions of the mode of access to information, while in the linguistics of many European languages evidentiality is understood as a functional dimension that may be expressed through either grammatical or lexical means. The latter view will be held here.

Evidentiality has been associated with semantic dimensions such as *mirativity*, that is, the marking of information as unexpected or surprising (e.g., Aikhenvald, 2012; DeLancey, 2001; Lazard, 1999), and *(inter)subjectivity*, understood as the status of a judgment as individual or shared with others (Nuyts, 2001a, 2001b). However, the boundaries between epistemic modality and evidentiality have attracted the most attention.

Links of different sorts have been proposed between evidentiality and epistemic modality. Some authors consider evidentiality a part of epistemic modality or so closely related to it as to regard both as the same subtype of modality (e.g., Chafe, 1986; Palmer, 1986). Others treat them as different categories within an epistemological or propositional modality (e.g., Boye, 2012; Palmer, 2001). Among those who separate evidentiality from epistemic modality, some include evidentiality within modal categories (e.g., Chung & Timberlake, 1985; Hengeveld, 2004), whereas others do not (e.g., Aikhenvald, 2004; Bybee et al., 1994; de Haan, 2006; González Vázquez, 2006). Yet, another group of linguists include inferential evidentiality within (epistemic) modality, and reject the modal status of other evidential categories (Narrog, 2009, pp. 10–11; Nuyts, 2017; van der Auwera & Plungian, 1998).

The conceptual confusion between the two categories has to do with the subjective and deictic nature of evidentiality, which connects with the definitions of modality in terms of attitude and non-factuality (see §2.2). From this perspective, it is not surprising that correspondences are sought between evidential and epistemic modal values. For example, Bybee et al. (1994, p. 180) argue that "an indirect evidential, which indicates that the speaker has only indirect knowledge concerning the proposition being asserted, implies that the speaker is not totally committed to the truth of that proposition and thus implies an epistemic value." However, a number of counterexamples to this approach have been raised (Aikhenvald, 2004; Cornillie, 2009; González Vázquez, 2006, pp. 101–134). Givón (1982, pp. 34–35) illustrates the mismatch between the degree of certainty and particular evidential values with a lama's account of the *Life of the Buddha* in Sherpa: there is no truer story for a Buddhist, yet the monk tells it using the hearsay/indirect-evidence mode, which, according to Bybee et al.'s (1994) approach, is associated with a lack of commitment to the truth of the proposition.

It is difficult to find stable links between evidential and epistemic values. Nevertheless, telling apart inferential evidentiality from epistemic modality with regard to some particular linguistic devices has proved to be quite challenging. In Galician, such devices include the modal verbs *deber (de)* 'must' (3b), repeated here as (47), and *haber (de)* (48), and the modal future, that is, the uses of the *futuro* and the *pospretérito* discussed above (40), repeated here as (49).

(47) A acusada *debe de estar* ocultándolles información.
'The accused must be withholding information from them.'

(48) *Ha de haber* 30 persoas aí fóra.
'There must be 30 people out there.'

(49) a. (Agora) *haberá* 30 persoas aí fóra.
'(Now) there must be 30 people out there.'
b. (Onte) *habería* 30 persoas aí fóra.
'(Yesterday) there must have been 30 people out there.'

In the Galician grammatical literature, Álvarez and Xove (2002, pp. 280–281, 343–356) and Freixeiro Mato (2000/2006a, pp. 349–354, 470–473) use terms such as *probability* and *doubt* to describe the devices under consideration, whereas Montero Küpper (1999) deals with the *epistemic values* of the periphrases (see §2.1.3). This apparently symbolizes a consensus on the epistemic character of these devices, but one must bear in mind that these works do not consider evidentiality nor inferentiality as separate semantic dimensions. It is quite telling in this regard that Montero Küpper (1999) characterizes the epistemic periphrases as expressions of conjecture, which has traditionally been considered an inferential value.

There is a rich literature on equivalent devices in other Romance and Germanic languages, where they are the object of diverging considerations: from a purely evidential status, to a purely epistemic one, through an intermediary position that considers them hybrid epistemic and inferential expressions. For Portuguese, the language closest to Galician, Oliveira (2015) shows that the modal future has inferential and reportative values, and argues that the inferential uses are also epistemic, since the future can be replaced by the modal *dever* 'must'. She offers the following examples of the inferential uses:

(50) a. A esta hora o João *estará/deve estar* em casa.
'By this time John must be already home.'
b. Quando a conheci, ela *teria/devia ter* uns 15 anos.
'When I first met her, she must have been 15 years old.'

(Oliveira, 2015, p. 102, her translation)

According to Oliveira (2015), in Portuguese the modal future is both inferential and epistemic, whereas the modal *dever* is epistemic. However, the use of replacement as a method has undesired consequences: if the future must be considered epistemic on account of its replaceability by the modal, the modal must be considered inferential on account of its replaceability by the future. As will be seen below, this is a methodological quagmire faced by other contributions to the literature.

Squartini (2001, 2004, 2008) offers a framework for studying these devices in Romance. He introduces an "inferential gradient" (Squartini, 2008, pp. 921–927), which has at one end the most subjective type of reasoning, conjectures, and at the other end the most objective type of reasoning, based on external evidence and dubbed circumstantial inferences; in an intermediary position are generic inferences, based on knowledge of the world.[4] According to Squartini (2008), the

---

4. This gradient can be seen as deriving from a distinction between different types of information bases within the inferential mode of access: a sensory base for circumstantial inferences, a cognitive base for generic inferences, and no information base for conjectures.

Italian future conveys generic inferences (51a) and conjectures (51b), but not circumstantial inferences (51c).

(51) a. [Suonano alla porta] *Sarà* il postino.
'[The bell rings] It must be the postman.'
b. [Suonano alla porta] Non aspettavo nessuno; *sarà* Gianni.
'[The bell rings] I was not expecting anybody. It might be G.'
c. ??[Indicando un ragno] Attento, *sarà* ancora vivo, perché ho visto che si muove.
'[Pointing to a spider] Be careful! It must be still alive, for I saw it moving.'
(Squartini, 2008, pp. 923–924, his translation)

Conjectures expressed by the Italian future match different epistemic values, as shown by the combination with epistemic adverbs such as *sicuramente* 'certainly' (52a) and *forse* 'perhaps' (52b).

(52) a. [Suonano alla porta] *Sarà* sicuramente il postino.
'[The bell rings] It is certainly the postman.'
b. [Suonano alla porta] Forse *sarà* il postino.
'[The bell rings] Perhaps it is the postman.'
(Squartini, 2008, p. 926, his translation)

The above examples are supposed to show that the modal future is inferential and that inferentiality is different from epistemic modality, because, according to Squartini (2008), the future encodes various types of inferential evidentiality, which match different epistemic values. Nonetheless, Pietrandrea (2005, pp. 70–72, 93–98) argues against the evidential character of the Italian future, considering it a purely epistemic expression unmarked in terms of the degree of certainty. Similarly, Hennemann (2014) considers that the Spanish future only encodes inferential evidentiality, whereas González Vázquez (2006, p. 160) rejects this idea, and argues in favor of the epistemic nature of the future.

Turning now to *deber (de)* and its equivalents, we are confronted with a similar scenario. Some authors argue against any association with evidential values (Aikhenvald, 2004; de Haan, 2006), yet many others acknowledge the evidential (either inferential or reportative) character of Romance *deber (de)*, *devoir*, and *dovere*, and Germanic *moeten* and *must* (e.g., Cornillie, 2009; Pietrandrea, 2005; Squartini, 2004, 2008). Squartini (2008) examines Italian *dovere* along with the modal future. The auxiliary verb is different from the future in that it conveys generic (53a) and circumstantial (53c) inferences, but not conjectures (53b). Additionally, *dovere* combines with *sicuramente* (54a), but not with *forse* (54b).

(53) a. [Suonano alla porta] *Deve essere* il postino.
'[The doorbell rings] It must be the postman.'

b. ??[Suonano alla porta] Non aspettavo nessuno; *deve essere* Gianni.
'[The bell rings] I was not expecting anybody. It must be G.'
c. [Indicando un ragno] Attento, *deve essere* ancora vivo, perché ho visto che si muove.
'[Pointing to a spider] Be careful! It must still be alive, for I saw it moving.'
(Squartini, 2008, pp. 922–924, his translation)

(54) a. [Suonano alla porta] *Deve essere* sicuramente il postino.
'[The bell rings] It must certainly be the postman.'
b. ??[Suonano alla porta] Forse *deve essere* il postino.
'[The bell rings] Perhaps it must be the postman.'
(Squartini, 2008, p. 927, his translation)

Let us now reflect on how the Galician devices fit in this type of contexts. At first glance, the Galician modal future and *deber (de)* show the same distribution as the Italian examples:

(55) a. [Chaman á porta] *Será/debe ser* o carteiro.
'[The bell rings] It must be the postman.'
b. [Chaman á porta] Non esperaba a ninguén; *será/??debe ser* Xan.
'[The bell rings] I was not expecting anybody. It must be the postman.'
c. [Sinalando unha araña] Coidado, aínda ??*estará/debe estar* viva, vina moverse.
'[Pointing to a spider] Be careful! It must be still alive, for I saw it moving.'

Regarding the combinability with epistemic adverbs more differences arise: whereas both devices combine with probability adverbs (56a) and only the future is acceptable with possibility adverbs (56b), neither combines easily with certainty adverbs (56c).

(56) a. [Chaman á porta] Probablemente *será/debe ser* o carteiro.
'[The bell rings] It must probably be the postman.'
b. [Chaman á porta] Quizais *será/??debe ser* o carteiro.
'[The bell rings] Perhaps it must be the postman.'
c. [Chaman á porta] Certamente ??*será/??debe ser* o carteiro.
'[The bell rings] It must certainly be the postman.'

Regardless of minor differences between close languages like Galician and Italian, it is not clear whether the contexts used by Squartini (2008) actually isolate inferential meanings. If we place prototypical epistemic adverbs, such as Galician *probablemente* 'probably' and *quizais* 'maybe' in the same contexts, we get similar patterns.

(57) a. [Chaman á porta] *Probablemente/quizais* é o carteiro.
 '[The bell rings] It is probably/maybe the postman.'
 b. [Chaman á porta] Non esperaba a ninguén; ??*probablemente/quizais* é Xan.
 '[The bell rings] I was not expecting anybody. It is probably/maybe Xan.'
 c. [Sinalando unha araña] Coidado, *probablemente*/??*quizais* aínda está viva, vina moverse.
 '[Pointing to a spider] Be careful! It is probably/maybe still alive, for I saw it moving.'

The adverb *probablemente* has the same distribution as the auxiliary *deber (de)*: it occurs in contexts of generic and circumstantial inference, but not with conjectures. *Quizais*, in turn, has the same distribution as the modal future: it is compatible with generic inferences and conjectures, but not with circumstantial inferences. De Haan (2001, p. 8) uses contexts of this kind to argue that both strong (*must*) and weak (*may*) epistemic markers might be associated with processing evidence. De Haan (2001) also claims that both types of epistemic markers are diachronic sources of evidentials, thereby rejecting the inherent relationship between strong epistemic modality and inferentiality.

Epistemic modality and inferentiality are clearly separated areas in the conceptual domain (Cornillie, 2009, pp. 57–59; Nuyts, 2017, pp. 72–73). Both are connected from a logical point of view, because they involve a process of reasoning based on evidence aimed at assessing the factual status of the SoA.[5] However, the two categories are different insofar as they refer to different parts of the same cognitive process. Epistemic modality encodes the outcome of that process, in terms of degrees of probability, and says nothing about the process itself. It does imply, sometimes very strongly, that there is evidence to carry out the assessment, but it does not point to this evidence directly. Inferentiality refers to the reasoning process itself, and assigns it a degree of reliability, but does not encode the probability that the SoA will occur. Certainly, when a speaker expresses, for example, high reliability of the inference of an SoA, the hearer might surmise that they also see its realization as highly probable. However, one must not lose sight of the fact that inferentiality and epistemic modality are two separate conceptual categories that denote different aspects of the same reasoning process.

---

5. Epistemic possibility constitutes an exception, as far as it does not entail, on a purely semantic level, the existence of such a process, but simply that the speaker lacks any reason to deny the existence of the SoA. Nevertheless, epistemic possibility judgments usually have some kind of justificatory support, and are rarely true professions of ignorance (see Przyjemski, 2017, pp. 187–190).

The question, then, is what part of the reasoning process the modal future and the auxiliaries *deber (de)* and *haber (de)* point towards. Since it is hard to find contexts that accept inferential markers and exclude epistemic ones, or vice versa, it would appear that the only alternative is to pay attention to their interpretation in the same context. Nonetheless, ad hoc contexts favor the inclinations of their author, as shown by the variety of opinions on the interpretation of these devices, and corpus evidence should be preferred. Later in this book (§ 8.3) I will use corpus data to argue that the modal future and the auxiliaries *deber (de)* and *haber (de)* convey inferential values.

4.2 Modality and discourse strategy

The term *discourse strategy* covers phenomena of linguistic production such as mitigation, strengthening, concession, and challenging. Mitigation and strengthening are our focus here, as they have an intricate relationship with epistemic modality. Concession will also be paid some attention, since it is often discussed along with mitigation and strengthening. Mitigation and strengthening are discourse strategies that modify the illocutionary force of the speech act, downplaying the utterance or reinforcing it, respectively (Holmes, 1984). While epistemic modality acts on the semantics of the clause, mitigation and strengthening operate on the speech act level. In formal terms, epistemic modality is known to constitute a complex paradigm, consisting of modal auxiliaries, cognitive verbs, adjectives, and adverbs (Nuyts, 2001a), whereas mitigation arises as an implicature when using preexisting linguistic forms (Albelda Marco & Estellés Arguedas, 2021b, p. 81). It is not clear, however, which category strengthening fits into. According to Albelda Marco and Estellés Arguedas (2021a, pp. 22–23), strengthening mirrors mitigation in that it is a context-dependent meaning. Yet, in the realm of discourse markers catalogs of strengthening operators are found (e.g., Freixeiro Mato, 2005, pp. 105–106), which suggests that strengthening, rather than being derived contextually in all cases, might be encoded by some expressions.

On paper, epistemic modality and discourse strategies are clearly different linguistic phenomena. However, we often see epistemic values readily translated into strategic ones. Thus, the expression of an epistemic value of uncertainty tends to be considered an instance of mitigation, and something similar applies to strengthening, with the expression of certainty being automatically labeled as a case of reinforcement of the utterance. The next example offers an illustration of this approach:

(58) probabilmente è una conseguenza di un problema intestinale che è cominciato con l'influenza eh?
'it is probably a consequence of an intestinal problem that began with the flu eh?'

(adapted from Caffi, 2007, p. 103, her translation)

(58) is an Italian example extracted from an interaction between a doctor and a patient. In the example, the doctor makes his diagnosis, using *probabilmente* 'probably' to introduce it. According to Caffi (2007, p. 103), this constitutes a case of mitigation, since the adverb "weakens the speaker's degree of certainty about the whole proposition: the overall effect on the utterance is that the diagnosis is downgraded to a hypothesis." This way, mitigation is directly associated with the "degree of certainty" of the proposition, that is, epistemic modality. Similarly, Hummel (2018, p. 111) uses "epistemic mitigation" to refer to the fact that Romance equivalents of English *surely* "downgrade the truth value of the proposition," and Álvarez and Xove (2002, p. 280) understand the probable mood as "a 'mitigación' con que se formulan as predicacións" 'the "mitigation" with which predications are formulated' (see § 4.1.3). From this perspective, literal uses of epistemic expressions of possibility and probability are by definition cases of mitigation: what defines these linguistic devices semantically – their epistemic value – is the downgrading of the truth value of the utterance, which is in turn equated with mitigation. A parallel example concerning strengthening can be found in Labov (1984, p. 44), who defines intensity as "the commitment of the self to the proposition," and analyzes English *really* as establishing a *surreal mood* that designates "a state of reality greater than normal," thus equating a discourse strategy of intensity to epistemic and reality status values.

In this context, the boundaries between the semantic content of epistemic expressions and their pragmatic use is distorted by equating the semantics of uncertainty with a mitigating pragmatic strategy, and the semantics of certainty with a strengthening pragmatic strategy. When dealing with the pragmatics of epistemic modal devices, it is necessary to take into consideration whether the use of a marker of doubt or certainty conveys the mental state of the speaker or if (besides that) it has the goal of achieving some type of special effect in discourse, such as downplaying or boosting the force of the assertion. The guiding assumption of this book will be that the categories of discourse strategy should only be applied in the second scenario.

4.2.1 Mitigation

Although drawing the line between the semantics of linguistic expressions and their pragmatic effects is not always easy, previous work shows that the distinction can be operationalized. In her analysis of Spanish adverbial expressions of evidentiality, Albelda Marco (2016) considered the involvement of public face as a fundamental criterion for recognizing mitigating uses of evidential markers. Her results show that there is no perfect match between evidentiality and mitigation thus understood: the latter is very frequent in conversations and interviews, where the interlocutors interact face to face, but is very infrequent in journalistic prose and political debates, where the purely evidential and the dissociative function respectively prevail. These results (and those of similar works, such as Albelda Marco, 2018; Carretero & Zamorano-Mansilla, 2019; Figueras Bates, 2018) show the key role played by the concept of public face in characterizing mitigation as a discourse phenomenon, and have paved the way to recent theoretical and methodological breakthroughs. In this connection, Albelda Marco and Estellés Arguedas (2021b) propose an operational definition of mitigation based on three dimensions: cognitive ("mitigation is the result of a speaker reading her hearer's mind and suspecting her image in the hearer's eyes might be endangered," p. 83); social and rhetorical ("mitigation aims to achieve goals of human communication," p. 83); and linguistic ("mitigation is realized through linguistic forms and mechanisms that minimize semantic or illocutionary intensity, increase vagueness, or defocalize the sources of enunciation," p. 84).

The recognition of the mitigating uses of epistemic markers is probably the most challenging (see Albelda Marco, 2010). Epistemic markers typically occur in declarative sentences that perform an assertive speech act, but their use as mitigators might also occur with directives and commissives expressed through declarative sentences. An example is (35), repeated below as (59).

(59) [Son as 11:55 e a reunión comeza ás 12:00. Neste contexto, A dille a B:]
Creo que debemos ir indo.
[It is 11:55, and the meeting starts at 12:00. In that context, A tells B:]
'I think we must get going.'

In an example like (59) the mental state predicate *creo* 'I think' is used by the speaker to turn a command into a hypothetical SoA, thus making their utterance less threatening to the interlocutor. The same utterance without the epistemic expression would constitute a direct order that would threaten in a more serious way the public face of the hearer. Cases like this are easy to detect, because a directive speech act expressed indirectly (i.e., not through the imperative mood) is likely to play a role in public face management.

From the point of view of mitigation, problematic cases are those where epistemic expressions of possibility and probability occur in assertive speech acts, since it is often difficult to tell whether they convey an authentic doubt in the mind of the speaker (epistemic modality), or are part of a strategy to minimize potential threats to someone's public face (mitigation). In this connection, analyzing contexts in their full complexity can shed light on the process of meaning creation. Albelda Marco (2010) offers a number of criteria for the recognition of mitigation based on corpus data, including the interaction of speech act types with sentence types and situational features that usually favor mitigation, such as an interaction of a transactional nature, inequality in the social status of the interlocutors, or a lack of mutual acquaintance between speaker and hearer. Regarding epistemically modalized assertives, she argues for a distinction between opinions and assertions of factual truths, with the former being more likely to affect the public face of another individual. Thus, epistemic markers occurring in opinions are likely to perform a mitigating function, whereas when they accompany assertions of facts they are more likely to restrict the truth of what is said. A further distinction is pertinent:

- Mitigation of assertives aimed at saving the hearer's face. Some factors favor the involvement of the addressee's face and, as a consequence, the occurrence of mitigation. These include conflicting topics that may prompt the expression of disagreement, negative responses that contradict what was introduced by others, the adjacency and interrelationship between the interlocutors' utterances, and metalinguistic mechanisms such as turn overlap, interruption, or digression.
- Mitigation of assertives aimed at saving the speaker's face. The intention to protect one's own image can be detected by paying attention to whether the epistemic marker is integrated into a larger turn or stands alone. In the latter situation, mitigation is less likely, because the modal marker does not accompany the content that is problematic for the speaker. One must also include here reformulations and corrections and the anticipation of possible negative elements, all of which point towards the presence of compromising matters for the speaker.

The use of epistemic expressions of uncertainty as mitigators is very prominent. According to Albelda Marco and Cestero Mancera (2011, pp. 19–20), they account for more than 12% of mitigating devices in their spoken language corpus.

4.2.2 Concession

Nuyts (2001a) puts forward discourse strategy as one of the functional factors influencing the use of epistemic expressions (see §3.1.3). This factor captures the observation that epistemic markers are frequently used to obtain certain special effects in interaction. Specifically, Nuyts (2001a) associates mitigation with cognitive verbs, and argument managing with modal auxiliaries and adverbs. By argument managing Nuyts (2001a, pp. 224–227) refers to examples like (60), featuring the Dutch modal *kunnen* 'can' – the focus is on the second occurrence of *kan*.

(60) Deze betekenisverandering kan volgens Jespersen verklaard worden door het feit dat kinderen de uitdrukking 'to count one's beads' onbewust anders gingen analyseren dan hun ouders, de vorige generatie. Deze factor *kan* een rol gespeeld hebben, maar het is onmogelijk om dit te bewijzen.
'According to Jespersen, this meaning change can be explained by the fact that children unconsciously started to analyze the expression "to count one's beads" differently from their parents, the previous generation. This factor can/may have played a role, but it is impossible to prove this.'
(Nuyts, 2001a, p. 225, his translation)

In this example, the author uses *kunnen* to qualify Jespersen's argument as possible in order to indicate that he cannot or does not want to reject it but does not support it either. As Nuyts (2001a, p. 225) points out, the main purpose of this strategy is to avoid threatening the face of the person who originally issued the argument, in this case Jespersen. It seems, then, that we are dealing with a case of mitigation: what the author does is convey its rejection in a softened manner for the sake of politeness. One must bear in mind that what is carried out in a polite manner in (60) is rejection and that this is not achieved (solely) by means of the modal expression.

Both (60) and the example provided by Nuyts (2001a, p. 226) as an argumentative use of an epistemic adverb have in common the fact that the clause qualified by the modal element is followed by another clause introduced by an adversative conjunction. It is the second clause that conveys rejection and the first clause that achieves the mitigating effect, but the coordination of the two is necessary for the politeness strategy to work. These are cases of mitigation through concessive constructions: the author recognizes that they cannot fully or partially deny the opposing argument, and, in this way, counteracts the potential discrepancies and face threats (see Albelda Marco & Cestero Mancera, 2011, pp. 29–31; Briz Gómez, 1998, p. 149; Couper-Kuhlen & Thompson, 2000; Haverkate, 1994, pp. 118–120). The same effect is obtained if an expression with a different epistemic value is used, as in the following example featuring the Galician adverb *certamente* 'certainly'.

(61) *Certamente*, existen obras que se presentan e comercializan en formato dixital, pero non son maioría nin moito menos a data de hoxe.
'There certainly exist works that are presented and commercialized in a digital format, but they are not the majority by any means at the present time.'
(CORGA)

The adverb *certamente* in (61) reinforces the content of the first clause in the coordinated structure, thus creating a context of concession in which the introduction of disagreement becomes less threatening. This is the same strategy followed in (60). There is, however, one aspect worth mentioning: *certamente* reinforces the content of the first clause, while the modal qualifies it as a possibility. That is, there can be a difference in the strength given to the concession – "how much" the speaker decides to concede – but the mitigation mechanism is independent of such a difference, which relies directly on contextual factors such as the topic of conversation or the relationships between the interlocutors. In fact, in a case like (61), the presence of the strengthening adverb is not a requirement for there to be mitigation: (61) without *certamente* produces a similar mitigating effect.

We must conclude that the strategy of mitigation through concession is independent of epistemic expressions and, as a consequence, that there is no argument managing use of epistemic auxiliaries and adverbs – if anything, there is an argument managing use of concession. It is interesting to point out that, in a later work with other researchers (Byloo et al., 2007, p. 48), Nuyts and colleagues do not grant an independent status to the concessive uses of English *certainly* and Dutch *zeker*, and explain the emergence of the concessive meaning as "entirely due to interaction with the context."

4.2.3 Strengthening

Strengthening, also known as *emphasis, intensity*, or *reinforcement*, has been paid far less attention than mitigation (Schneider, 2017, p. 24). Nevertheless, there also exist previous research that shows the appropriateness of distinguishing strengthening from the semantics of devices that typically express it, such as certainty adverbs (Byloo et al., 2007; Simon-Vandenbergen & Aijmer, 2007) or general knowledge evidentials (Kotwica, 2020). Byloo et al. (2007) study English *certainly* and Dutch *zeker*, distinguishing several uses, among which are epistemic modality and strengthening. Their results reveal a predominance of strengthening and a marginal character of epistemic modality: strengthening is the most frequent meaning for *certainly*, and is quite relevant for *zeker*, whereas epistemic modality is the least frequent meaning for both adverbs.

We can easily find examples of the Galician equivalent of *certaintly* and *zeker* where it has a strengthening reading and an epistemic interpretation ('it is 100% likely') cannot be obtained. Such an example is (62), where *certamente* occurs in the context of the verb *constatar* 'confirm, validate'.

(62) No seu ir e vir a domicilio coa súa ilustrada mercadoría, Suso constatou que *certamente* os xeranios son xenerosos regalando primores florais, pero piden coidados.
'In his coming and going from home to home with his illustrated merchandise, Suso confirmed that geraniums certainly are generous in gifting floral delicacies, but require attention.' (CORGA)

In (62) *certamente* does not convey a judgment in terms of likelihood, but reinforces the subordinate clause. According to Byloo et al. (2007), expressions of certainty such as *certamente* and *certainly* are rarely used as epistemic markers. They conclude that "talking about certainty has a quite different conversational role from talking about uncertainty" and that maybe "terms specifically dedicated to expressing epistemic certainty are relatively less often 'needed'" (Byloo et al., 2007, p. 56). The reason for this lies in what can be dubbed the "certainty paradox": "the fact that we only say we are certain when we are not" (Halliday, 2004, p. 625). Qualifying an SoA with the strongest epistemic value (i.e., certainty) instead of using a bare assertion often has apparently undesirable pragmatic effects, such as indicating that the speaker is not really sure of what they are saying. Sometimes authors are fully aware of these effects, as shown by the metalinguistic comment on epistemic adverbs in (63).

(63) E, obviamente, nos territorios da incerteza antes referidos, en que, máis unha vez, nos moveremos, non poderei evitar os «tal vez», os «quizais», os «segura-», os «probábel-» ou os «posibelmente», e mais os «sen dúbida», os «con certeza» ou os «evidentemente», que, de maneira directa ou paradoxal, sosteñen as precarias reconstrucións e as salutares dúbidas ...
'And, obviously, in the aforementioned territories of uncertainty, in which more than once we will be moving, I will not be able to avoid «tal vez» ['perhaps'], «quizais» ['maybe'], «seguramente» ['probably' lit. 'surely'], «probabelmente» ['probably'] or «posibelmente» ['possibly'], nor «sen dúbida» ['no doubt'], «con certeza» ['for sure' lit. 'with certainty'] or «evidentemente» ['evidently'], which directly or paradoxically support the precarious reconstructions and the salutary doubts.' (TILG)

Crucially, the author of this excerpt from a study on Galician medieval literature divides markers of uncertainty into two groups: those directly pointing to doubt, that is, possibility and probability adverbs, such as *quizais* and *probabelmente*; and those doing so paradoxically, namely, certainty adverbs, such as *sen dúbida* or *con certeza*. Expressions of certainty signal that certainty cannot be taken for granted. They draw attention to the speaker's own doubts over the SoA, and, as a consequence, lead to inferences of uncertainty. Thus, certainty is a problematic meaning to convey, whereas strengthening is free from this restriction, and is much more prominent from the point of view of discourse. This explains why a dedicated class of strengthening operators exists and why epistemic meanings of certainty are rare in texts. The forthcoming pragmatic analysis (§ 8.2) should add evidence to support these claims.

4.3 Modality and (inter)subjectivity

Subjectivity is a recently emerged notion in linguistic studies. Albeit one of the first mentions of the term was in Bréal's work on semantics in 1900 (Traugott & Dasher, 2002, p. 19), it was not until the 1990s that the first monographs on the subject appeared (Iwasaki, 1993; Stein & Wright, 1995), and the topic did not attract wide attention until the publication of work on the diachronic dimension of (inter)subjectification by Traugott and Dasher (2002) (Narrog, 2012, p. 1). In current cognitive and functional linguistics there are three influential notions of (inter)subjectivity, derived from the works of Langacker (1990, 1991a, pp. 315–342, 2000, pp. 297–316), Nuyts (2001a, 2001b, 2014, 2015), and Traugott (1989, 2010; Traugott & Dasher, 2002). Many authors have dealt with the differences and links between these three understandings of the notion, and have reached the conclusion, in most cases, that they have little to do with each other (e.g., Brisard, 2006; Krawczak, 2016; López-Couso, 2010; Narrog, 2012, pp. 13–46, 2016; Nuyts, 2012; Portner, 2009, pp. 122–129; Verstraete, 2001). The discussion is undoubtedly too extensive to do it justice here, so in the pages that follow I will deal only with those notions of immediate interest to the present book – that is, those that will be instrumental in the coming chapters. This amounts to discussing the ideas of Nuyts and Traugott.

Subjectivity has been associated with epistemic modality since at least Lyons (1977). In order to explain how the relationship between the two notions should be understood, the British linguist used this famous example:

(64) Alfred may be unmarried. (Lyons, 1977, p. 797)

According to Lyons (1977), there are two ways in which (64) can be interpreted. In the first and most common reading the speaker subjectively qualifies the utterance based on their own uncertainty. In the second and more marked reading the speaker presents the SoA as an objective possibility. For the latter interpretation Lyons (1977) suggests a scenario in which the speaker knows that Alfred belongs to a community of 90 people and that 30 of them are single, but they do not know who is single and who is not. In this situation the speaker can use (64) to indicate that there is a mathematically computable chance (1/3) that Alfred is single. In this view, the existence of an objective possibility that something is the case is opposed to a subjective feeling of uncertainty about a hypothetical event. The objectivity/subjectivity opposition, as understood by Lyons or in a very close spirit, has become popular in cognitive and functional linguistics, especially when dealing with modality (e.g., Coates, 1983; Dik, 1997; Hengeveld, 1988; Olbertz & Dall'Aglio Hattnher, 2018; Palmer, 1986; Rodríguez-Espiñeira, 2010), but it was also adopted in the formalist school of linguistics (e.g., Kratzer, 1981/2002).

Nuyts (2001b, 2012) considers the objectivity/subjectivity opposition problematic, insofar as it is very hard to operationalize and its discussion remains confined to impressions and intuitions. As an alternative, Nuyts (2001a, 2001b, 2014, 2015) argues for approaching the subjective nature of modal expressions from a purely functionalist perspective. Thus, if we pay attention to what the speakers do when they express modal qualifications of SoAs, the most appropriate interpretation of subjectivity has to do with the responsibility of modal evaluation. As a consequence, Nuyts reformulates the distinction using the labels *subjective* and *intersubjective*: a modal (epistemic, deontic…) evaluation is subjective when it is presented as the sole responsibility of the speaker, and it is intersubjective when it is presented as shared between the speaker and other individuals. According to Nuyts, modal markers do not encode (inter)subjectivity directly, but rather through their syntax. This restricts the expression of the dimension to predicative categories (lexical verbs and adjectives), so that a subject in the first person expresses subjectivity and an impersonal subject intersubjectivity. Consequently, adverbs and auxiliary verbs do not encode this dimension, because they do not have the ability to control a grammatical subject, being considered neutral forms. Nuyts illustrates these ideas with the following examples of epistemic (epi) and deontic (deo) modality:

(65) a. *I think* they left already. [subjective epi]
b. *I really regret* that they left already. [subjective deo]

(66) a. *It is quite probable* that they left already. [intersubjective epi]
b. *It is unacceptable* that they left already. [intersubjective deo]

(67) a. They *probably* left already. [neutral epi]
b. *Unfortunately* they left already. [neutral deo]

(68) a. They *may well* have left already. [neutral epi]
b. They *must* leave right away. [neutral deo]

(Nuyts, 2012, p. 59)

(Inter)subjectivity as understood by Nuyts is a semantic dimension that responds to certain communicative needs: taking responsibility for a judgment while avoiding involving others, opposing one's opinion to others', indicating that one's own stance is not strictly personal, expressing the existence of agreement between interlocutors, etc. Although the author does not clarify what the theoretical status of (inter)subjectivity is, he argues in favor of considering it a category external to the realm of qualifications of SoA, similarly to mirativity (Nuyts, 2017). In fact, the two dimensions *parasite* other – usually modal – expressions, but among modal devices there are those considered neutral that do not convey (inter)subjectivity, as seen in (68). In other words, (inter)subjectivity is encoded by speakers as a dimension of modal expressions only when it is necessary to do so, and, therefore, languages offer resources that are neutral in terms of this semantic category.

The concepts of Lyons and Nuyts were formulated in the context of modal qualifications. Although it is often applied to the modal domain, Traugott's notion of (inter)subjectivity emerged in the context of another discussion, namely her studies on diachronic change, where the process of (inter)subjectification plays a key role. (Inter)subjectification is one of the most influential hypotheses in semantic change. It claims that meanings evolve from the description of the world, to the expression of speaker's attitudes, and, finally, the speaker's stance towards the hearer, as reflected in (69).

(69) non-subjective > subjective > intersubjective

(Traugott & Dasher, 2002, p. 281)

Subjectification is the process whereby linguistic forms develop subjective meanings out of non-subjective (or objective) ones. Non-subjective meanings are concerned with the description of the objective world, whereas subjective meanings express the speaker's stance with respect to the objective world, that is, they "encode and regulate attitudes and beliefs" (Traugott, 2010, p. 35). Thus, Traugott's subjectivity is opposed to objectivity, constituting an opposition that strongly reminds one of the distinction originally formulated by Lyons, which Traugott (2010, p. 33) acknowledges taking as a starting point. Intersubjectification is an ulterior step whereby linguistic forms with subjective meaning develop addressee-oriented meaning. This must be understood in a broad sense, since Traugott's intersubjectivity not only includes meanings that regulate the interaction between the interlocutors, but also those that perform textual functions.

An important assumption in Traugott's work (e.g. Traugott, 2003b, 2007; Traugott & Dasher, 2002) is the unidirectionality of (inter)subjectification: meanings change in the direction of increased (inter)subjectivity, but not the other way around. In other words, (69) cannot be run through from right to left – there is no de(inter)subjectification. A typical illustration of this idea is found in the evolution of modal auxiliaries: Traugott and Dasher (2002, Chapter 3) focus on the subjectification of English *must* and *ought to*, whereas Nuyts and Byloo (2015) account for the diachronic trajectory of Dutch *kunnen* 'can' and *mogen* 'may' in terms of subjectification and intersubjectification. Nevertheless, some counterexamples to unidirectionality have been spotted in different domains of grammar (see López-Couso, 2010, pp. 142–143), the most prominent collection of which is found in the realm of epistemic and evidential expressions, particularly in the work of Cornillie (2008, 2016). This author shows that the development of expressions such as the Spanish evidential (semi-)auxiliaries *resultar* 'turn out' and *parecer* 'seem', the epistemic adverbs *tal vez* 'perhaps' and *quizás* 'maybe' and even some of Traugott and Dasher's (2002) own applications of the notion to modality contradict the unidirectionality principle, insofar as they instantiate cases in which modal expressions develop intersubjective readings before subjective ones. Míguez (2021) argues that this is also the case of Galician *certamente* and *seguramente*, as their intersubjective meanings developed before and led to subjective (i.e., modal) meanings.

In sum, subjectivity and intersubjectivity can be understood in two clearly different ways. Nuyts views them as dimensions floating over modal meaning (a matter of either individual or shared responsibility over a modal judgment), whereas Traugott conceives them as broad groupings of meanings of fundamental diachronic importance. Modality is the (main) playground of (inter)subjectivity from Nuyts's perspective, and one of many subjective meanings from Traugott's. Since both notions of (inter)subjectivity will be frequently used in Part III and there is an obvious potential for confusion, I will reserve the terms *subjective* and *intersubjective* exclusively for Nuyts's notion. As for Traugott's perspective, the different meanings of the adverbs under examination will be grouped under *modality*, *discourse*, or *other*, respectively corresponding to subjectivity, intersubjectivity, and objectivity/non-subjectivity.

CHAPTER 5

Modality revisited
The Galician system

In this chapter I will outline a framework for the discussion of modal categories based on Nuyts's (2005, 2017) work. Starting from the theoretical underpinnings to reassess modality provided by Nuyts (2005, 2017), I will propose the existence of four basic modal categories in Galician, and will discuss their different internal structure. This should not be taking as an exhaustive development, but rather as a point of departure for the discussion of modality and modal classes in Galician. First (§ 5.1), the chapter will lay the foundations for an understanding of modal categories that overcomes the shortcomings of traditional approaches. Subsequently (§ 5.2), it will provide empirical support for and illustrate the main modal categories with Galician examples.

5.1   A revision of modality and modal categories

In § 2.4 the main factor hindering the definition of modality was identified with the lack of a semantic substance common to the three traditional modal categories. The use of the distinction between necessity and possibility as a unifying criterion is problematic because this binary opposition does not accommodate the scalar values of deontic and epistemic modality. Non-factuality, as a non-discrete alternative, is not satisfactory either, since it arbitrarily excludes factual modal values, such as epistemic certainty, as well as deontic judgments of factual SoAs. Moreover, there are dramatic differences in scope between the traditional classes of modality, namely dynamic modality, on the one hand, and deontic and epistemic modality, on the other.

At this juncture, it seems sensible to focus on categories that are manageable and can be given a coherent definition. This means studying epistemic and deontic modality on their own, on a par with other qualificational domains such as time, space, and aspect. Let us bring back the hierarchy of qualifications represented earlier in (32), in a modified version.

(70)   > inferential evidentiality
       > epistemic modality
       > deontic modality   [attitudinal]
       _____
       > time
       > quantitative aspect / dynamic modality   [situating]
       _____
       > phasal aspect   [detailing]
       > (parts of the) STATE OF AFFAIRS

                                        (adapted from Nuyts, 2017, p. 73)

In (70) modal categories such as inferential evidentiality and epistemic and deontic modality have an independent status, just like time and the different types of aspect. Nevertheless, this should not prevent us from identifying superior levels of organization where some of the basic categories are grouped. According to Nuyts (2005, 2017), the hierarchy is first split between phasal and quantitative aspect: under this separation, qualificational categories refer to the internal properties, or details, of the SoA. The next split is found between time and deontic modality: time and quantitative aspect – and additional categories such as space, cause, purpose, or condition – constitute a supercategory concerned with the temporal, spatial, and logical location of the SoA. Finally, the remaining categories at the top of the hierarchy involve some type of commitment towards the SoA on the part of the speaker, that is, different kinds of attitudes.

The definition of modality as the expression of speaker's attitudes is widespread but problematic. As Narrog (2005b) shows (see §2.2), the attitudes of the speaker are expressed in many ways in language, not just through modal markers. However, the notion of attitude becomes manageable when restricted by the concept of qualification: modality is a supercategory that comprises different kinds of attitudinal qualifications. Attitudinal qualifications are defined by three properties (cf. Nuyts, 2017, pp. 62–66):

- Scalar structure. The semantic domain of an attitudinal qualification has three or more values corresponding to different degrees of the same property.
- Wide scope. Attitudinal qualifications operate over the SoA, but also over other non-attitudinal qualifications of SoAs.
- Performative flexibility.[1] Attitudinal qualifications perform the attitude of the speaker, meaning that they express a commitment on the part of the speaker, and identify them as responsible for the qualification, but their expressive devices also allow for uses where speaker's commitment is "suspended."

---

1. Bear in mind that this take on *performativity* is different from how it is understood in the influential speech act theory (Austin, 1962).

The scalar structure of the semantic domain of attitudinal qualifications (first property) is in line with their higher cognitive complexity: they involve the processing of information external to the SoA in order to obtain a particular degree of speaker commitment relative to a gradual dimension. As a consequence, they exploit human attentional resources intensively, and have a very different cognitive status from other qualifications of SoAs (Nuyts, 2009, 2017), which is linguistically reflected in their wider scope (second property). Thus, attitudinal qualifications are not restricted by temporal, spatial, or aspectual markers, but the opposite is true. However, their performative flexibility (third property) makes it possible for attitudinal meanings to fall under the scope of other, lower range qualifications, or, in other words, to constitute SoAs of their own. This, of course, has to do with the distinction between performative and descriptive uses (see §3.1.3), and involves some degree of formal complexity, namely the availability of devices with and without verbal support. These properties single out modal categories from other expressions of attitudes in language. I will illustrate them with Galician examples in the next section.

This revision of modal categories has two main consequences. The first one is that some traditional modal categories do not meet the above criteria, and must be excluded from modality, whereas other domains that have been traditionally excluded from modality must be included for the opposite reason. This second scenario covers categories such as inferential evidentiality and affective modality, which fit the above criteria, as I will show in the next section. In the first scenario we are dealing with dynamic modality: its values do not form a scale, but a binary opposition, it has narrow scope, being restricted by temporal or spatial markers, and lacks performative uses, as it is oriented towards the first argument participant in the SoA, rather than the speaker. In this connection, it is worth noting that Dik (1997, pp. 241–242) considers inherent (i.e., dynamic) modality (see §3.1.1) a peripheral notion with no grammatical status that is "mainly mentioned under Modality because the predicates used to express these SoA inherent features often develop into more strictly 'modal' expressions over time." Along these lines, Nuyts (2005, 2017) classifies dynamic modality as a category of quantitative aspect, whereas Gisborne (2007) accounts for the dynamic meanings of English *can* and *will* as the preservation of older lexical meanings. Excluding (some) dynamic meanings from modality has also been a common stance of Galician approaches to modal auxiliaries (§2.1.3).

The second consequence of this revision is that the internal structure of some categories must be reshaped. Evidentiality contains inferential values, which are modal in the proposed sense, and reportative and experiential values, which are not, since they are not performative and do not form a scale (Nuyts, 2017, pp. 68–72). The inclusion of inferential evidentiality within modality and the exclusion of other evidential categories are far from being unprecedented, and have been put forward in the literature several times (e.g., Narrog, 2009, pp. 10–11; van der Auwera & Plungian, 1998). Similarly to evidentiality, deontic modality must be reshaped so as to fit the above criteria. This involves defining deontic modality as an evaluation in terms of moral (in)acceptability, thus excluding directive meaning, following the steps suggested by Nuyts et al. (2010) and Van linden and Verstraete (2011). From the point of view of semantic coherence, there is no reason to exclude moral (in)acceptability when applied to factual SoAs, as Van linden and Verstraete (2011) argue, just like there is no reason to leave epistemic certainty out of epistemic modality.

5.2 The expression of modal categories in Galician

For this illustration of modality in Galician, we start from a narrow definition of conceptual categories and a broad view on their formal expression. The behavior of languages warrants this way of proceeding, since in the modal domain there often is a division of labor between grammatical and lexical means of expression (see Nuyts, 2001a, for epistemic modality; Van linden, 2012, pp. 75–76, for deontic modality). Therefore, I will offer an overview of the different expression types for each category.

There are four semantic domains that can be considered attitudinal qualifications in the above sense: deontic modality, affective modality, epistemic modality, and inferential modality. Below, I offer a characterization and examples of each of them. I will use the examples to illustrate the scalar nature of the categories, and, later, I will show that they all have a wide semantic scope. As a source of linguistic examples I will use CORGA (Centro Ramón Piñeiro para a investigación en humanidades, 2022). In the illustration of the categories the examples correspond to performative uses, although I will show afterwards that they all possess formal resources that allow speakers to describe, rather than perform, modal content.

DEONTIC MODALITY is an indication of the degree of moral desirability of the SoA. Devices that serve this function include the auxiliaries *deber (de)* 'must', *haber (de)* 'have to', *haber que* 'have to', *poder* 'can, may', and *ter que* 'have to', the (semi-)auxiliary *cómpre* 'be necessary', adjectives such as *aceptable* 'acceptable', *esencial* 'essential', and *lamentable* 'deplorable', and lexical verbs such as *aplaudir* 'applaud' and *condenar* 'condemn, deplore'. Deontic values are set on a scale ranging from moral necessity to moral unacceptability, with an intermediary position of moral acceptability. Moral necessity is expressed by the auxiliary *deber (de)* in (71a), the adjective *esencial* in (71b), and the lexical verb *aplaudir* in (71c).

(71) a. Nun divorcio *debe* primar o sentido común, e sobre todo no que atinxe aos fillos.
'During a divorce common sense must prevail, especially with regards to children.' (CORGA)
b. *É esencial* que o novo presidente executivo, Matthias Müller, actúe con transparencia nos próximos meses para aclarar este escándalo.
'It is essential that the new CEO, Matthias Müller, acts with transparency in the coming months in order to clarify this scandal.' (CORGA)
c. *Aplaudimos* que recoñeza como pendente a situación legal dos traballadores autónomos, a pesar das súas carencias con respecto ao réxime xeral da Seguridade Social …
'We applaud that he recognizes the situation of self-employed workers as pending, despite its shortcomings with respect to the general Social Security system …' (CORGA)

Moral acceptability is expressed by the auxiliary *poder* in (72a) and the adjective *aceptable* in (72b). As a bonus, (72a) includes an underlined expression of moral necessity – the auxiliary *deber (de)*.

(72) a. Se temos claro que Galiza necesita un proxecto nacionalista, centrado na defensa dos intereses do país e non supeditado a estratexias alleas, todo o demais *pode* e <u>debe</u> debaterse.
'If it is clear to us that Galiza needs a nationalist project, focused on defending the interests of the land and not subordinated to external strategies, everything else can and must be debated.' (CORGA)
b. Ben sabes que non son celosa e que atopo perfectamente *aceptable* que te deites con quen sexa …
'You know well that I am not jealous and that I find it perfectly acceptable that you sleep with anyone …' (CORGA)

Moral unacceptability is often achieved through the negation of expressions of moral acceptability, such as the auxiliary verb in (73a), or through adjectives such as *lamentable* in (73b) – external negation of the auxiliary is underlined in (73a).

(73) a. No extremo oposto atópanse dous tipos de xeados sen azucres engadidos … Con todo, <u>tampouco</u> este tipo de xeados sen azucre *pode* cualificarse como saudable.
'At the other end are two types of ice creams with no added sugars … Nevertheless, this type of ice creams with no sugar cannot be qualified as healthy either.' (CORGA)
b. É *lamentable* que te esqueceras ata do irmán enfermo, parece mentira en ti.
'It is deplorable that you forgot even about your sick brother; that's not typical of you.' (CORGA)

The three deontic values illustrated form a scale by themselves, but moral necessity and moral unacceptability are gradable domains. There exists a large number of adjectives that contrast strong and weak deontic necessity (see Van linden, 2012, for English): in Galician an adjective like *esencial* conveys strong deontic necessity, whereas *conveniente* 'convenient' expresses weak necessity and allows for a finer-grained modulation of the semantic dimension by taking grade modifiers, such as *moi* 'very' and *bastante* 'quite'. As for moral unacceptability, strong values are represented in (73), while weaker values are obtained by combining the adjective *aceptable* with negative modifiers such as *pouco* 'a little' and *moi pouco* 'very little'.

Figure 5.1 represents the semantic structure of a modal category like deontic modality. It has a central position, corresponding to a neutral stance towards the modal dimension (e.g., moral acceptability), and two subdimensions splitting from the central point, representing increasing degrees of the modal dimension in positive or negative terms (e.g., moral necessity vs. moral unacceptability). Affective modality possesses this semantic structure as well, whereas epistemic and inferential modality differ in this respect.

Figure 5.1 Semantic structure of deontic and affective modality

AFFECTIVE MODALITY is an indication of the degree of affection towards the SoA.[2] The little recognition of this dimension as a modal category is probably related to the fact that it is not expressed through grammatical means such as the auxiliary verbs. Additionally, it can hardly be understood in terms of the traditional values of possibility and necessity. Devices with an affective value include adverbial expressions such as *afortunadamente* 'fortunately', *lamentablemente* 'unfortunately', *por desgraza* 'sadly', and *por sorte* 'luckily', the complex predicate *dar igual* 'to be the same', and constructions with verbs such as *gustar* 'like', *encantar* 'love', *odiar* 'hate', and *aborrecer* 'detest'. Affective values are set on a scale ranging from affection to disaffection, with an intermediary position of indifference. Affection is conveyed by *afortunadamente* in (74a) and by *gustar* in (74b).

---

2. Although Nuyts (2005) uses *boulomaic modality* in this sense, I will avoid the term because it has been used in at least two other ways in the literature: in reference to desire (e.g., Gavins, 2005; Kiefer, 1987) and in reference to volition and intention (e.g., Narrog, 2012, p.9) (see §2.1.2.3).

(74) a. A pediatra especialista en VIH do hospital La Paz de Madrid, Isabel de José, explica a situación actual dos pequenos afectados e o seu futuro.
ENTREVISTADOR: ¿Cal é a incidencia real da sida nos nenos españois?
ENTREVISTADO: *Afortunadamente*, o número de nenos afectados en España por este virus é moi pequeno.
'A pediatrician who specializes in HIV at La Paz Hospital in Madrid, Isabel de José, explains the current situation of the affected children and their future.
INTERVIEWER: What is the real incidence of AIDS in Spanish kids?
INTERVIEWEE: Fortunately, the number of kids affected by this virus in Spain is very small.' (CORGA)
b. A min *gústame* que a xente opine, sempre que o faga argumentando.
'I like that people voice their opinions, as long as they do so with arguments.' (CORGA)

Disaffection is expressed by *lamentablemente* in (75a) and by *odiar* in (75b).

(75) a. *Lamentablemente*, os sistemas de saúde non dispoñen na actualidade dos medios necesarios para realizar un óptimo seguimento dos pacientes ...
'Unfortunately, health systems lack at present the necessary means to monitor patients optimally.' (CORGA)
b. *Odio* que alguén mire nas miñas cousas.
'I hate when somebody goes through my things.' (CORGA)

A neutral stance of indifference is achieved through the complex predicate *dar igual*.

(76) *Dános igual* que sexa neno ou nena.
'We do not care whether it is a boy or a girl.' (CORGA)

Affective values also fit the semantic structure represented in Figure 5.1. The positive subdimension (affection) is illustrated in (74), the negative one (disaffection) in (75), and the neutral point (indifference) in (76). Further modulations of the semantic subdimensions are obtained with *encantar* and *aborrecer*, denoting a greater degree of (dis)affection than *gustar* and *odiar*, respectively. The latter represent the weaker values of the positive and negative subdimension, and are susceptible of taking quantifiers such as *un pouco* 'a little', *bastante*, and *moito* 'a lot'.

The relationship between affective and deontic modality is analogous to that between epistemic modality and inferential evidentiality (see §4.1.4): moral acceptability or unacceptability can imply affection or disaffection, respectively, in the affective domain, whereas affection or disaffection can imply moral acceptability or unacceptability, respectively, in the deontic domain. However, liking, disliking, or feeling indifference towards the SoA (affective modality) is not the same as considering the SoA morally desirable, acceptable, or unacceptable (deontic modality).

EPISTEMIC MODALITY is an indication of the degree of likelihood of occurrence of the SoA. Devices that serve this function include the modal auxiliary *poder*, cognitive verbs such as *coidar* 'think', *crer* 'believe', *dubidar* 'doubt', and *pensar* 'think', adjectives such as *certo* 'certain, true', *improbable* 'unlikely', *seguro* 'sure', *probable* 'likely', and *posible* 'possible', and adverbs such as *certamente* 'certainly', *probablemente* 'probably', *posiblemente* lit. 'possibly', *quizais* 'maybe', *se cadra* 'perhaps', and *seguramente* lit. 'surely'. At first sight, epistemic values are set on a scale similar to the one represented in Figure 5.1, ranging from certainty to impossibility, with an intermediary position in terms of possibility. However, as Davidse et al. (2022, p.10) argue, "epistemic modal markers express inherently positive degrees of probability." Thus, negative epistemic expressions, such as *dubidar* and *imposible*, do not convey negative probabilities of a positive SoA, but positive probabilities of a negative SoA. In other words, negation of the SoA can be placed on the epistemic marker, which explains why the next series of examples are roughly semantically equivalent.

(77) a. *Creo* que *non* está na casa.
 'I think (s)he is not at home.'
 b. *Non creo* que estea na casa.
 'I don't think (s)he is at home.'
 c. *Dubido* que estea na casa.
 'I doubt (s)he is at home.'

(78) a. *É probable* que *non* estea na casa.
 'It is likely that (s)he is not at home.'
 b. *Non é probable* que estea na casa.
 'It is not likely that (s)he is at home.'
 c. *É improbable* que estea na casa.
 'It is unlikely that (s)he is at home.'

This phenomenon, known as negative raising (see Nuyts, 1992, Chapter 3, for a thorough account), is not exclusive of epistemic modality (pace Davidse et al., 2022, p.11),[3] but shows that epistemic modal qualifications are always positive,

---

3. Negative raising interpretations are possible with some deontic and inferential expressions. Although most expressions of deontic modality do not allow negative raising interpretations, the mid-scalar predicate *conveniente* does (e.g., *é conveniente que non prime a crispación* 'it is convenient that exasperation does not prevail' / *non é conveniente que prime a crispación* 'it is not convenient that exasperation prevails'). Similarly, the inferential (semi-)auxiliary *parecer* 'seem' triggers this reading (see below).

despite the existence of negative epistemic expressions. Deontic and affective modality have negative expressions that do not behave like the epistemic ones in (78), but rather convey a qualification in negative terms, as seen in (73) and (75).

In sum, epistemic modality lacks a negative subdimension, and is restricted to a neutral stance and a positive subdimension, as represented in Figure 5.2.

Figure 5.2 Semantic structure of epistemic modality

The neutral point corresponds to epistemic possibility, and is expressed by the auxiliary *poder* in (79a) and the adverbs *quizais* in (79b) and *se cadra* in (79c).

(79) a. Hoxe é Irlanda, onte foi Grecia, mañá *pode* ser Portugal e pasado mañá o Estado español.
'Today was Irlanda's turn, yesterday was Greece's, tomorrow may be Portugal's, and the day after the Spanish State's.' (CORGA)
b. *Quizais* a idea de usar auga fervendo para cocer alimentos se lle ocorrese a algún destes homes ou mulleres do Paleolítico cando se escaldou coa auga dalgunha burga, e isto fíxolle pensar que podía abrandar ou coce-la carne nunha poza natural chea de auga quente.
'Maybe the idea of using boiling water to cook food came to the mind to some of these men or women of the Paleolithic when (s)he scalded himself/herself with the water of a hot spring, and this made him/her think that (s)he could soften or cook the meat in a natural well filled with hot water.' (CORGA)
c. Kromer. Kromer e non Kramer. *Se cadra* o dono era xudeu, porque algo no apelido así llo facía pensar.
'Kromer. Kromer and not Kramer. Perhaps the owner was Jewish, because something in the family name made him think so.' (CORGA)

The positive subdimension involves increasing degrees of probability, and has certainty (100% probable) at its end.[4] Epistemic certainty is conveyed by the adjectives *certo* in (80a) and *seguro* in (80b) and the adverb *certamente* in (80c) – additional discussion of (80c) can be found in §8.2.1.

---

4. Although, from a purely semantic perspective, certainty corresponds to a particular probability value, there are reasons to separate certainty from probability (see §6.1).

(80) a. <u>Coido</u> que ao Tío lle importaban pouco eses rituais. Nunca tropecei con el na igrexa, agás o día do seu enterro. *É certo* que en cada cuarto había un crucifixo, que seguramente colgarían as súas esposas antes de morrer. Fóra destes detalles, ignoro se tiña crenzas ou pasaba delas.
'I think the Uncle did not care much about these rituals. I never ran into him at church, except for the day of his funeral. It is true that in every room there was a crucifix, which was probably hung by his wives before dying. Apart from these details, I ignore whether he had beliefs or he did not care about them.' (CORGA)
b. Onte á noite entrou na baía de Fisterra unha goleta inglesa por culpa dunha tormenta. Pediron xente na vila para repararen os danos do trebón e eu fun un dos que subiu a bordo como calafate. Estiven á espreita e *estou seguro* de que levan un cargamento moi importante na adega.
'Last night a British schooner entered the bay of Fisterra because of a storm. They asked for people in the town to repair the damages of the storm, and I was one of those who went on board as a caulker. I was lurking around, and I am sure that they carry a very important shipment in the hold.' (CORGA)
c. Foi esta indeterminación o que o induciu a non dicir nada á policía. Esto e os reberetes fantásticos do sucedido, que *certamente* farían pensar á policía nunha historia de drogas ou alcohol.
'It was this lack of resolution what led him not to tell anything to the police. That and the fantastic details of what had happened, which would certainly lead the police to think of a story of drugs or alcohol.' (CORGA)

In between certainty and possibility a relevant number of epistemic values are found. These amount to different degrees of probability, and are conveyed by the cognitive verb *crer* in (81a) (see also the underlined fragment in (80a)), the adverb *probable* in (81b), and by a subset of *-mente* adverbs that describe increasing degrees of probability, namely, *posiblemente* > *probablemente* > *seguramente* (see §8.2.1).

(81) a. – Foron ver a don Servando, o cura de Calabarda, en Porto do Son. E non sei moito máis. *Creo* que os detiveron alí mesmo.
'–They payed a visit to Mr. Servando, the priest of Calabarda, in Porto do Son. And I don't know much more. I think they were arrested right there.' (CORGA)
b. Actúen con prudencia. *É probable* que haxa homes armados no seu interior.
'Proceed with caution. It is likely that there is armed men inside.' (CORGA)

INFERENTIAL MODALITY is an indication of the degree of reliability of the inferential process that justifies the existence of the SoA. This dimension is expressed in Galician by auxiliary verbs such as *deber (de)*, *haber (de)*, and *ter que*, adverbs such as *aparentemente* 'apparently', *claramente* 'clearly', *evidentemente* 'evidently', and *obviamente* 'obviously', the adjectives *claro* 'clear', *evidente* 'evident', and *obvio* 'obvious', the (semi-)auxiliary verb *parecer* 'seem', the modal future, and cognitive verbs such as *imaxinar* 'imagine', *sospeitar* 'suspect', and *supoñer* 'suppose'. Inferential values are arranged along a gradual dimension of reliability. Low levels of reliability are encoded by *haber (de)* in (82a) and *supoñer* in conjunction with the modal future in (82b).

(82) a. Temos que falar con ela. A estas horas *ha de* estar no café. Vamos!
'We must speak with her. At this time she might be at the café. Let's go!'
(CORGA)

b. –Como che foi onte?
–Xa che contei, pero tal e como sobabas *supoño* que non te *lembrarás* de nada. É longo, despois de comer falamos.
'–How did you do yesterday?
–I already told you, but as you were soundly asleep I suppose you don't remember anything. It's long, we'll talk after lunch.' (CORGA)

Medium levels of reliability are conveyed by *deber (de)* in (83a) and *parecer* in (83b).

(83) a. Muras *debe* ser dos poucos Concellos de Galiza que non ten solo industrial ...
'Muras must be one of the few municipalities in Galiza that lacks industrial land ...' (CORGA)

b. Nietzsche *parece* estar influído aquí por Gobineau – encargou de feito os seus libros á universidade de Basilea–, ao atribuír á mestura de razas o auxe das ideas democráticas e socialistas.
'Nietzsche seems to have been influenced in this regard by Gobineau – in fact he ordered his books from the University of Basel – as he assigned the raise of democratic and socialist ideas to the mixing of races.' (CORGA)

High levels of reliability are expressed by *obviamente* in (84a) and *evidente* in (84b).

(84) a. Con este exemplo vedes que o can amosa o rango de tamaños e pesos máis amplo de todas as especies animais. A variedade débese, *obviamente*, á man humana, que nunha acción de enxeñaría xenética foi cruzando os seus compañeiros caninos ao longo da historia para potenciar certos trazos e tamaños.

'With this example you see that dogs show the widest range of sizes and weights of all animal species. Variety is obviously due to human action, who by resorting to genetic engineering crossbred his canine companions throughout history to develop particular features and sizes.' (CORGA)

b. *É evidente* que aínda que a nosa actual capacidade cranial é similar á do Homo sapiens primitivo, ao ser os respectivos medios vitais moi diferentes, a nosa conciencia e os nosos estados cerebrais han de diferir notablemente dos daquel.
'It is evident that, even though our current cranial capacity is similar to that of primitive Homo sapiens, the respective living environments being very different, our consciousness and our brain states must differ notably from theirs.' (CORGA)

As in the case of epistemic modality, there are no negative inferential values, and negative inferential expressions trigger a negative raising interpretation – the next examples are roughly semantically equivalent.

(85) a. *Parece* que *non* está na casa.
'It seems that (s)he is not home.'
b. *Non parece* que estea na casa.
'It does not seem that (s)he is home.'

Where inferential modality differs from any other modal class is in its lack of a neutral point. In the case of epistemic modality, the neutral point is possibility, which indicates that the SoA is compatible with the speaker's knowledge. Similarly, the formulation of a deontic judgment in terms of acceptability conveys that the speaker does not see the SoA as desirable or condemnable. Inferential modality lacks this neutral point, since it refers to the reliability of a mental process that justifies the existence of the SoA. There is no possible neutral stance in such semantic domain. Thus, the semantic structure of inferential modality corresponds to a single gradual dimension, as represented in Figure 5.3.

Figure 5.3 Semantic structure of inferential modality

Let us now turn our attention to semantic scope. Modal categories are part of a system of qualifications of SoAs with a hierarchical organization, as illustrated in (70) (see also §3.1). The most direct reflection of the internal structure of the hierarchy arises from the combination of several qualifications in the same utterance. I will illustrate the relation between modal categories, on the one hand, and situating and detailing categories, on the other. I will not deal with the relative scope of categories within each level. Consider the following examples:

(86) a. *deontic modality* > time
O goberno *debe* aumentar o gasto en defensa o ano que vén.
'The government must increase defense expenditure next year.'
b. *affective modality* > time
Afortunadamente, o paquete chegará pola tarde.
'Fortunately, the parcel will arrive in the afternoon.'
c. *epistemic modality* > space
Probablemente chove en Santiago.
'It is probably raining in Santiago.'
d. *inferential modality* > time
Parece que onte non veu.
'It seems that (s)he did not come yesterday.'
e. *epistemic modality* > time > **aspect**
Seguramente **deixou de** traballar pola mañá.
'(S)he probably stopped working in the morning.'

In (86a), *deber (de)* expresses a deontic evaluation that is not limited by the temporal expression *o ano que vén* 'next year': the moral necessity of the government increasing its defense budget in the coming year is an attitude of the speaker at the moment of speech, and does not start at a point in the future, as would be the case if the temporal marker had scope over the modal expression. Similarly, the SoA in (86b) will happen in the coming afternoon, but the speaker's liking of it is in force from the moment of speech. The epistemic evaluation expressed in (86c) by means of *probablemente* is valid in any place where the utterance is produced, which need not be Santiago de Compostela. Mutatis mutandis the same is true for the inferential qualification in (86d), by which the speaker communicates that they infer the SoA at the moment of speech, and not the day before. Finally, the cessative aspectual periphrasis *deixar de* in (86e) is constrained by the temporal marker *pola mañá* 'in the morning', inasmuch as the cessation of the SoA, signaled by the periphrasis, takes place in the frame established by the temporal expression. In addition, the two expressions, together with the rest of the predication, are under the scope of the epistemic evaluation expressed by *seguramente*. In conclusion, modal categories scope over situating categories, and these, in turn, scope over detailing categories, but not vice versa.

These examples, as well as the rest of examples in this section, illustrate performative uses of modal categories. The wider scope of the latter is determined by performativity, which links modal meaning to the speaker at the moment of speech: by definition, modal qualifications cannot fall under the scope of locating or detailing categories because they express the point of view of the speaker at the moment of speech, rather than contributing information about the SoA. Nevertheless, modal categories can be expressed in ways that suspend their performative character. Deictic mechanisms such as verbal inflection are used to ascribe the modal judgment to entities different from the speaker at speech time, as the following examples show:

(87) a. *time* > <u>deontic modality</u>
<u>Condenei</u> o seu comportamento *ata que o coñecín*.
'I condemned his behavior until I knew him.'
b. *space* > <u>affective modality</u>
En Antuerpe <u>encantábame</u> *pasear pola zona vella*.
'In Antwerp I loved to go for a walk in the old town.'
c. *aspect* > <u>epistemic modality</u>
O veciño *deixou de* <u>crer</u> que mañá vai chover.
'The neighbor stopped thinking that tomorrow it's going to rain.'
d. *time* > <u>inferential modality</u>
Daquela <u>parecíame</u> que Trump non ía chegar á Casa Branca.
'Back then it seemed to me that Trump was not going to make it to the White House.'

In these examples, the modal devices ascribe modal content not to the speaker, but to other entities, be it the speaker at some location other than the here and now, be it an entity other than the speaker. These uses of modal markers do not convey modal qualifications, but constitute SoAs by themselves. Evidence of this is that they can be detailed and localized, that is, fall under the scope of categories such as phasal aspect and temporal location, as highlighted in the examples.

The intention of this section has been to flesh out the main ideas for understanding modality in the way previously proposed (§ 5.1). It has focused on providing support for the claim that the four modal categories possess a scalar structure, wide scope, and performative flexibility. Despite this commonalities, it has shown that each category has its own distinctive features, be they a particular type of semantic structure or a specific set of linguistic devices, which highlights the idea that each modal category is a basic semantic domain. Galician linguistics offers an almost unspoiled landscape with regard to modality studies, which offers the opportunity to overcome the obstacles presented by other linguistic traditions. This was an attempt to take a first step in this direction by proposing an alternative way of approaching modal meanings and devices. In this proposal modality and its classes, as traditionally understood, are reorganized to obtain semantic categories whose definition is simple and unproblematic. Four of these categories have been identified. Being similar to each other, they are expressed through a variety of formal devices, and constitute linguistic domains deserving of individual attention. The proposal is not exhaustive, and cannot be developed further within the limits of this book, as each of the modal categories under discussion is highly complex and amenable to a monographic approach. This chapter has dealt with different modal categories, and, in doing so, has set the scene for the discussion of epistemic adverbs that will be the focus of the rest of the book.

PART III

A focus on epistemic adverbs

CHAPTER 6

Corpus and method

This third part of the book zooms in on epistemic adverbs, featuring a corpus investigation of six Galician adverbs. The reasons why adverbs were chosen as a case study among the range of epistemic expressions have to do with two main facts: (i) adverbs are in some accounts (e.g., Nuyts, 2001a) an unmarked form for the expression of epistemic meaning, and (ii) they nevertheless exhibit a remarkable internal diversity that remains unaccounted for. This chapter will address general considerations for the study of the adverbial expression of epistemic modality, and introduce the basic methodological characteristics of the corpus investigation. It begins by examining the main properties of epistemic modality relevant for the adverbial domain (§ 6.1) and describing the sample of Galician epistemic adverbs considered in the corpus study, showing their arrangement on the epistemic scale and providing a brief overview of their diachronic development (§ 6.2). It later focuses on the empirical basis for the corpus investigation (§ 6.3), and explains and illustrates the variables the data were coded for (§ 6.4). Finally, it presents the statistical methods used (§ 6.5).

6.1 Epistemic modality as expressed by adverbs

Epistemic modality was previously defined as an indication of the degree of likelihood of occurrence of the SoA (§ 5.2), which is a widespread characterization within functional linguistics (see § 2.2.2). Epistemic modality has a scalar semantic structure constituted by a neutral stance in terms of possibility and increasing degrees of probability. This scalar character may lead to conclude that epistemic modality is a gradual category. However, not all subdimensions of epistemic modality are gradable, an often neglected fact (but see Jiménez Juliá, 1989, pp. 202–204; Rodríguez-Espiñeira, 2010, pp. 196–198). Three dimensions must be distinguished: possibility, probability, and certainty (cf. Hoye, 1997, p. 240).

Although from a purely semantic perspective certainty can be seen as a particular value within the realm of probability, specifically '100% probable', several reasons advise to separate both areas. On the cognitive side, certain information occupies a prominent place in conceptualization, unlike uncertain information (Nuyts, 2001a, p. 364). On the linguistic side, expressions of certainty (e.g., Galician *certamente*, English *certainly*) differ greatly from expressions of possibility and probability as regards non-epistemic uses (Byloo et al., 2007, p. 56). Also, importantly for our case, adverbs of uncertainty license the indicative/subjunctive alternation in Iberian Romance, whereas adverbs of certainty do not.[1]

Expressions of possibility present the SoA as compatible with the speaker's knowledge, but they only entail a neutral stance towards its occurrence. Expressions of probability, in turn, present the SoA as the preferred scenario to a particular degree. From this characterization follows that probability is, but possibility is not, a gradual category. A relevant observation is that probability adverbs seem to be able to take grading expressions as modifiers (e.g., *moi probablemente* 'very probably'), whereas this is not the case of (prototypical) possibility adverbs (e.g., **moi quizais* 'very maybe'). The above definition also entails a difference as regards speaker's commitment. As (88) shows, two alternative SoAs can be qualified in terms of possibility in the same utterance, but not in terms of probability.[2]

(88) a. Possibility
    Quizais aínda está na casa ou *quizais* xa marchou.
    'Maybe (s)he is still at home or maybe (s)he already left.'
  b. Probability
    ??*Probablemente* aínda está na casa ou *probablemente* xa marchou.
    '(S)he is probably still at home or (s)he probably already left.'

This contrast in gradability must not obscure the fact that possibility and probability do form a scale: probability entails possibility, as exemplified by utterances such as *it is possible and even likely that…* (see Leech, 1970, p. 224; Matthews, 1991, p. 62). The same applies to certainty, which entails both probability and possibility.

Also in the realm of the semantics of epistemic adverbs is the issue of (inter)subjectivity, or whether the epistemic qualification is exclusively attributed to the speaker or shared between the speaker and others (see § 4.3). According to Nuyts (2001a), the (inter)subjective character of an epistemic expression depends on the syntactic structures it appears in. Thus, adverbs are considered neutral as regards (inter)subjectivity, since they do not partake in personal or impersonal syntactic constructions, unlike adjectives (cf. *I am sure that this is the case* vs. *It is probable that this is the case*). However, (inter)subjectivity can also be encoded in the semantics of an epistemic expression. The adjectives *cierto* 'certain' and

---

1. The finite verb form following an adverb of uncertainty may appear either in the indicative or in the subjunctive (e.g., *Quizais está$_{IND}$/estea$_{SBJV}$ na casa* 'Maybe (s)he is at home'), whereas adverbs of certainty only allow the indicative (e.g., *Certamente está$_{IND}$/*estea$_{SBJV}$ na casa* 'Certainly (s)he is at home').
2. Tellingly, some languages lacking a dedicated disjunctive marker use an epistemic possibility adverb before each clause to achieve disjunctive coordination (Dixon, 2009, p. 33).

seguro 'sure' in Spanish express intersubjective and subjective certainty, respectively. According to Delbecque (2009), this is not (entirely) due to diverging syntactic patterns (*estoy seguro* 'I am sure' vs. *es cierto* 'it is certain'), since the (inter)subjective differences also arise when the adjectives occur in the same kind of construction. The epistemic adverbs originating from these adjectival bases inherit not just their epistemic value, but also the (inter)subjective flavor that comes with it – and this seems to be generalizable to several Romance languages. Thus, in Italian, *certamente* acts as a "polyphonic trigger" whereas *sicuramente* triggers "a paradigm of alternative monophonic judgments" (Pietrandrea, 2008, p. 242). The Galician cognates are susceptible of comparable considerations (see § 6.2.1). Although (inter)subjectivity is not a decisive factor in determining the use of epistemic adverbs vis-à-vis other epistemic expressions – and the (inter)subjective component of epistemic adverbs is surely less marked than that of adjectives – it does play a role in the paradigmatic relations between epistemic adverbs.

The coming pages, focused on Galician epistemic adverbs, should make the above points clearer.

6.2   Galician epistemic adverbs

Epistemic adverbs have not been studied in their own right in Galician linguistics, but they have been dealt with in Galician grammars. In this connection, Álvarez and Xove (2002, pp. 607–608, 627–628) include uncertainty adverbs in their class of "modalizers," whereas Freixeiro Mato (2000/2006a, pp. 511–512) includes them in his "adverbs of doubt." In these taxonomies, prototypical epistemic adverbs such as *quizais, talvez, se cadra, ao mellor* (all of the above expressing possibility), *posiblemente, probablemente,* and *seguramente* (these three expressing probability) are lumped together with inferential and reportative expressions such as *disque, seica, polo visto,* and *ao parecer* and non-adverbial expressions such as *pode que* 'it may be that'. As for adverbs of certainty, Álvarez and Xove (2002, p. 628) grant *abofé* 'of course', *certamente* 'certainly', *realmente* 'really, actually', and *verdadeiramente* 'truly' the status of modalizers. To find comparable expressions in the work of Freixeiro Mato one must look into the domain of discourse markers, particularly into the class of strengthening operators (Freixeiro Mato, 2005, pp. 105–106, 2003/2006b, p. 171).

Álvarez and Xove (2002, pp. 607, 627–628) explicitly distinguish adverbs with a reportative value from adverbs with an epistemic value, and point out that the latter may convey increasing degrees of probability: *posiblemente > probablemente > seguramente* (see § 6.2.2 on the fact that *posiblemente* conveys probability, rather than possibility). In order to give a consistent account of the adverbial expression of epistemic modality, the present work will study forms spanning over the whole epistemic scale. Hence, I will consider not only markers of probability, but also expressions of possibility and certainty. The chosen adverbs and their mutual arrangement are captured in (89).

(89)

> *certamente*	[certainty]
> *seguramente*	
> *probablemente*	[probability]
> *posiblemente*	
> *quizais, se cadra*	[possibility]

Certamente is probably the only adverbial form in Galician encoding epistemic certainty (i.e., 100% likelihood).[3] I consider adverbs such as *abofé*, *efectivamente*,[4] and *verdadeiramente* strengtheners in their sentential uses, rather than markers of epistemic certainty (regarding meaning categories, see Chapter 8).

In terms of different epistemic values, probability is the richest dimension in (89), although the three forms considered exhaust the adverbial expression of probability in Galician, which can only be further modulated by adverb modifiers. The inclusion of *seguramente* and *posiblemente* within probability might strike the reader as odd, since their lexical bases, *seguro* 'sure' and *posible* 'possible', belong in opposite poles of the scale, namely and respectively, certainty and possibility. This apparent contradiction is the result of diachrony, that is, the fact that the two adverbs have taken the same development path in opposite directions on the epistemic scale, finally converging in nearby semantic locations.

Possibility is not a gradable dimension. Therefore, different possibility expressions encode the same epistemic value. This apparent semantic simplicity is in contrast to the wealth of adverbial forms that express possibility in Galician: *quizais, talvez, acaso, se cadra, ao mellor, igual, o mesmo*... (cf. Álvarez & Xove, 2002, p. 627; Freixeiro Mato, 2000/2006a, pp. 511–512). Albeit the motivations for such remarkable case of variation are no doubt multiple and complex, some authors have pointed out the existence of functional contrasts between adverbs of possibility. Thus, Matte Bon (1995, pp. 257–258) groups possibility adverbs in Spanish according to the newness of the hypothesis they introduce: *quizá(s)* and *tal vez* present hypotheses as already known for the speaker, *a lo mejor* (cf. Gali-

---

3. Another form one can think of is the adverbial adjective *seguro*, but its status as a fully-fledged adverb is in question: it must be followed by a complementizer in order to occur in sentence-initial position, while the complementizer is optional with *certamente* and *seguramente*.

4. Rivas and Sánchez-Ayala (2012) consider *efectivamente* in Spanish as a reactive confirmation marker, rather than an epistemic expression with a primary meaning of certainty.

cian *ao mellor*) introduces hypotheses as devised by the speaker at the moment of speech.[5] Cornillie (2010) develops a similar distinction. He studies modal (mostly epistemic) adverbs in Spanish, and shows how units such as *a lo mejor, lo mismo* (cf. Galician *o mesmo*), and *igual* convey an "open perspective" to the SoA and perform specific interactional functions in conversation, whereas *quizá(s)* and *tal vez* do not yield an "open perspective" and are not so successful in interaction.

There are also important historical differences between adverbs of possibility: those presenting the hypothesis as the result of a more careful reflection (Type A) are long-established forms that trigger the mood alternation; conversely, those possibility adverbs that present the hypothesis as a more recent development (Type B) have entered the paradigm of epistemic expressions only recently, and do not trigger the mood alternation – they only combine with the indicative. Possibility adverbs originate from temporal phrases (e.g., *talvez* 'such time'), conditional protases (e.g., *se cadra* 'if it happens to be'), the semantics of sameness (e.g., *igual* 'equal, same', *o mesmo* 'the same'), desiderative-like constructions (e.g., *ao mellor* 'to the best'), etc. This is the case of both Type A and Type B possibility adverbs. The semantic and syntactic differences between Type A and Type B adverbs do not stem from diverging historical origins, but are rather due to different stages of development: as recent members of the epistemic modal system, Type B adverbs are semantically transparent – whence their "open conceptualization" and the newness of the hypotheses they introduce – and syntactically underdeveloped – they do not trigger the mood alternation, or do so only marginally. A consistent account of epistemic possibility must consider both Type A and Type B adverbs. Thus, in (89) I have included *quizais*, arguably the oldest possibility adverb in Present-Day Galician, as a representative of Type A, as well as *se cadra*, a very recent epistemic form, first documented in the second half of the 19th century, as a representative of Type B.

Below, a brief overview of the diachronic development of each adverb under examination is offered.

6.2.1 *Certamente* and *seguramente*

Together with *quizais*, *certamente* and *seguramente* are the only forms studied here that are documented in Old Galician (approx. 1200–1500).[6] According to

---

[5]. Matte Bon (1995) applies the terms "thematic" and "rhematic" to this distinction, which I find misleading, since qualificational adverbs are known for introducing newly asserted (i.e., rhematic) information (Verhagen, 1986, pp. 82–86), regardless of the newness of the hypothesis.

[6]. I am using TMILG (Varela Barreiro, 2007) as a source for old language data.

Míguez (2021), these adverbs evolved from being very similar in Old Galician to being quite different in the present-day language.

Romance adverbs ending in -*mente* developed out of a Latin instrumental construction, so that in Old Galician both *certamente* and *seguramente* were mainly used as manner adverbs (i.e., as verbal adjuncts within the verb phrase), meaning 'truthfully' and 'safely', respectively (notice the connection with the adjectives *certo* 'certain, true' and *seguro* 'safe, secure'). Their subsequent diachronic development consisted in a shift towards modal and discourse functions. Thus, already in the old language, both adverbs had an epistemic meaning of certainty and a strengthening meaning, and these functions became dominant over the course of several centuries at the expense of the manner use.

Nowadays, *certamente* has strengthening and certainty meanings (the former being predominant), *seguramente* has become a probability expression, and manner uses are extremely rare for both adverbs. The different semantic evolution of *certamente* and *seguramente* is a consequence of the pragmatic problems faced by epistemic certainty (see Chapter 8) and their, respectively, intersubjective and subjective features. Thus, the intersubjective certainty of *certamente* favored the maintenance of the certainty/strengthening polysemy, whereas the subjective certainty of *seguramente* facilitated the shift towards weaker epistemic values (cf. Hummel, 2018).

6.2.2 *Probablemente* and *posiblemente*

These adverbs are not documented in Old Galician, and in Modern Galician (approx. 1500–1975) their first occurrences are as recent as the end of the 19th century (*probablemente*) and the 1920s (*posiblemente*).[7] Nevertheless, they are (scarcely) found in Old and Modern Spanish (Suárez Hernández, 2018, pp. 154–170).[8] The Spanish data shows that these adverbs underwent a development similar to that of *certamente* and *seguramente*: they emerged as manner adverbs intimately related to their adjectival bases, *probable* 'probable' and *posible* 'possible'.

Probable derives from the verb *probar* 'prove' and originally meant 'that can be proved, provable', a meaning that can only be retrieved in very marked contexts today (cf. Rodríguez-Espiñeira, 2010, p. 195). Therefore, in its early stages *prob-*

---

7. For modern language data I resorted to TILG (Santamarina et al., 2018).
8. The diachronic evolution of Romance -*mente* adverbs and equivalent forms in other European languages (e.g., -*ly* adverbs in English) is, in general terms, crosslinguistic rather than language specific (Hummel, 2013), so that parallel developments are expected in different (but related) languages.

ablemente functioned as a verbal complement with the meaning 'in a provable manner'. Both the adverb and its adjectival base developed an epistemic value of probability that became the main meaning of both expressions. In the case of the adverb, such development included the emergence of sentential scope.

Posible is linked to the verb *poder* 'can, may'. As a manner adverb *posiblemente* is rarely attested in Old Spanish (Suárez Hernández, 2018, pp. 155–156), and conveyed situational dynamic possibility (see § 2.1.2.1). In Present-Day Galician (1975 – today) the dynamic meaning must be extremely rare: the use of *posiblemente* in (90), an example retrieved from Android operative system's welcome screen, most probably a literal translation from English, sounds hardly acceptable.

(90) Ao continuar, aceptas que este dispositivo tamén poida descargar e instalar automaticamente actualizacións e aplicacións de Google, do teu operador e do fabricante do teu dispositivo, *posiblemente* mediante datos móbiles.
'By continuing, you accept that this device may also automatically download and install updates and applications from Google, from your network operator, and from your device's manufacturer, possibly through mobile data.'

The intended meaning of *posiblemente* in (90) is situational dynamic possibility. Such meaning can be conveyed in Galician through the adverb *potencialmente* 'potentially' or a construction with *posible* (e.g., *é posible (que)* 'it is possible (that)'). *Posiblemente* triggers an epistemic meaning of probability in (90), which is unexpected in such context – how can the computer system *know* that the user will probably be relying on mobile data?

The modal dynamic meaning in *posiblemente* is probably hard to access because of the shift of the adverb towards epistemic probability. (91) is a version of (88) that shows that *posiblemente* does not allow for conjoining two alternative epistemic qualifications, a feature that distinguishes probability from possibility expressions. Note also that *posiblemente* can be modified by grading expressions (e.g., *moi posiblemente*).

(91) ??*Posiblemente* aínda está na casa ou *posiblemente* xa marchou.
'She is probably still at home or she probably already left.'

As regards (inter)subjectivity, both adverbs convey intersubjective epistemic probability, thus opposing the subjective probability of *seguramente*.

6.2.3 *Quizais* and *se cadra*

The origins of *quizais* have been traditionally traced back to the Latin phrase QUĪ SAPIT 'who knows' (e.g., Lorenzo, 1977, s.v. *quiçá*). However, such analysis poses an important phonetic problem regarding the presence of a <ç> (representing an affricate sound) in the old language, which could not have originated from the Latin phrase. Espejo Muriel and Espinosa Elorza (2012) suggest instead that *quizais* and its cognates come from French *qui ça* (interrogative pronoun + emphatic particle), through its Occitan equivalent *qui çai*, and were reinterpreted as QUĪ SAPIT through folk etymology. This last part of Espejo Muriel and Espinosa Elorza's (2012) analysis entails that the affricate sound was already lost in Ibero-Romance when the Occitan expression was borrowed, thus reconciling the traditional interpretation as QUĪ SAPIT with the presence of <ç> in written texts. Nonetheless, despite the willingness to obtain a compositional analysis of the adverb in etymological studies, Present-Day Galician *quizais* and its variants are opaque forms whose origins are not obvious for speakers, on account of the formal distance between *quen sabe* [kɛnˈsaβɪ] (today's QUĪ SAPIT) and *quizais* [kiˈθajs].

The linguistic string *se cadra* consists of the conditional conjunction *se* 'if' and the present indicative third person singular form of *cadrar* 'to be convenient' or 'to coincide'. It is a very recent epistemic adverb in Galician, being first documented in TILG in 1854. A close equivalent of this form is the Portuguese expression *se calhar* (see Pinto de Lima, 2008). Rodríguez-Espiñeira (2019) explores the origins of *se cadra* in the context of the Galician Spanish calque *si cuadra*. She puts forward the grammaticalization path subordinate clause (conditional protasis) > reduced parenthetical clause > epistemic adverb. She argues (pace Pinto de Lima, 2008) that the sense of the verb *cadrar* that triggered the grammaticalization process was the one of 'coincidence, chance' (*se cadra* 'if the chance arises'), in line with the development of other epistemic expressions such as Latin *forte* 'by chance', Spanish *acaso* 'chance', and English *perhaps* (see López-Couso & Méndez-Naya, 2021, 2023). In Present-Day Galician the three evolutionary stages coexist, that is, *se cadra* can function either as a conditional clause, as a reduced parenthetical clause or as an epistemic adverb. Therefore, *se cadra* and *quizais* are at opposite ends of the grammaticalization spectrum.

6.3 Corpus design

The six adverbs were studied through the use of present-day language data, which were extracted from the biggest corpus for present-day Galician, CORGA. This corpus has more than 43 million words of (mostly written) language from 1975 to 2020. The raw data extracted from CORGA totaled 17,368 observations. Given material limitations and the in-depth nature of the analysis, not all observations could be considered. Therefore, the final sample was limited to 300 occurrences of each adverb, resulting in 1,800 analyzed observations, which were randomly selected from the raw data with the help of LibreOffice Calc *RAND()* function.

Observations were excluded on linguistic grounds. The main objective of this study is to delve into (the expression of) epistemic modality. Thus, observations were left out if they met any of the following criteria:

- *The adverb has non-sentential scope.* This covers the rare cases where the adverb functions as a manner adjunct within the verb phrase, as well as more usual cases in which it acts as a "post-manner" (i.e., modal or discourse-oriented) device, but scopes over just a part of the SoA (e.g., *He is at home, probably since yesterday*). This also includes the very frequent uses of *certamente* as an adjective intensifier (e.g., *certamente bo* 'really good').
- *The adverb scopes over a sentence with no finite verb.* The categories of analysis include mood and time reference of verb forms. In order to study these categories, observations with an adverb scoping over a non-finite verb form (an infinitive, a gerund, or a participle) had to be excluded.[9]
- *The verb form is ambiguous between two morphological categories.* For some verb forms ending in *-ra*, it could not be determined whether they corresponded to the *antepretérito* (pluperfect), an indicative tense, or the past subjunctive. Therefore, observations with ambiguous *-ra* forms were left out.

Further exclusions happened because of a lack of context or clarity.

6.4 Variables

The way adverbs function needs to be examined in the context in which they are used. Thus, the analysis takes, for the most part, a syntagmatic approach, focusing on co-appearing expressions and the properties of the linguistic context. The restrictions laid out above allowed for a high degree of consistency to be reached as regards linguistic context. This, in turn, facilitated the inclusion of a relatively high number of variables in the analysis. Alongside the syntagmatic variables, other categories concerning the functioning of the adverb (e.g., in terms of performativity) and the extra-linguistic context were considered. The observations in the final samples were annotated for all variables, which are illustrated in the following pages. I will provide the justification for the inclusion of the variables when hypotheses are discussed (§ 7.1; § 8.1).

---

9. Bear in mind that the analysis of epistemic adverbs in non-finite clauses has proven fruitful (e.g., Tucker, 2001), but is beyond the research goals of this monograph.

A final step in the annotation process was to ascribe one or more meaning categories to every adverb in every observation. This required a contextualization process that went beyond syntagmatic factors, and involved looking at the context of production and reception of texts in a broad sense in order to understand and obtain information on what adverbs do in the utterances they appear in. This part of the analysis will be the focus of Chapter 8.

6.4.1 The adverbial phrase

Adverbial phrases are, at least in Galician, quite simple compared to verb and noun phrases. Phrases headed by epistemic adverbs are even simpler, since they can only take one modifier, which is necessarily a quantifier. In my dataset, the only modifiers found were *moi* 'very' and *máis* 'more'. This variable provides us with information on the gradability and specificity of the semantic value encoded by the adverb.

6.4.2 The verb phrase

All observations included in the samples feature a finite verb form. I took into consideration its mood (indicative or subjunctive) and lemma (i.e., the lexical item the finite verb belongs to). I did not include tense as a variable, since it correlates with temporal reference, which is covered in the study and has a more obvious relation with epistemic modality. Nevertheless, I did code the data for morphological tense,[10] for instrumental purposes – see below the indications concerning the annotation of modal future forms.

In the immediate periphery of the finite verb we find another relevant variable, polarity. Data were coded for negative polarity if the finite verb was under the scope of an *n*-word, such as *non* 'no', *nin* 'nor', *nada* 'nothing', *ninguén* 'nobody', *nunca* 'never', or *tampouco* 'neither', and for affirmative polarity otherwise.

---

10. Excluding the potential ambiguity of *-ra* forms, annotating tense in Galician is straightforward. There are six indicative tenses – *presente* (e.g., *como* 'I eat'), *futuro* (e.g., *comerei* 'I will eat'), *pretérito* (e.g., *comín* 'I ate [perfective]'), *copretérito* (e.g., *comía* 'I ate [imperfective]'), *antepretérito* (e.g., *comera* 'I had eaten'), *pospretérito* (e.g., *comería* 'I would eat') – and two subjunctive tenses – *presente* (e.g., *coma*) and *pretérito* (e.g., *comese*). Indicative tense forms ending in *-amos*, *-emos*, or *-imos* are potentially ambiguous, as the *presente* and the *pretérito* are syncretic in the first person plural; however, context was always rich enough to settle any possible confusion. As for the future subjunctive, it has been lost in spoken Present-Day Galician, and is confined to very formal written registers (see Freixeiro Mato, 2000/2006a, pp. 359–370). In the samples used here it did not show up.

In some cases, the finite verb was a modal auxiliary. Modal auxiliaries are characterized by considerable polysemy. When a particular occurrence of a modal auxiliary could be interpreted as (near-)epistemic (i.e., epistemic or inferential) the lemma of the modal (*deber (de)*, *haber (de)*, *poder*, *ter que*) was added to the annotation. If the modal had dynamic, deontic, directive, or other value, but no (near-)epistemic interpretation, it was not reflected in the annotation.

Another way the finite verb may express (near-)epistemic values is by means of the modal future. Example (40) illustrates this category. In essence, modal uses arise in future-oriented indicative tenses (viz. the so-called *futuro* 'future' and *pospretérito* 'future preterite') when, instead of conveying a future perspective from a present or a past reference point, they locate the SoA in the present or the past, adding an inferential interpretation. Thus, annotating modal future values was a matter of matching a tense form with its time reference: when the *futuro* had present time reference and the *pospretérito* had past time reference (as opposed to their prototypical values 'future' and 'future-in-the-past', respectively), observations were coded as modal future.[11]

A variable that no doubt transcends the limits of the verb phrase, but is worth discussing in relation to verb morphology is time reference. In its most basic account, time reference comprises three categories (past, present, and future), which do not exhaust temporal distinctions, but are usually adequate for most purposes. I drew on this "simplistic" system, and further distinguished future-in-the-past and indeterminate time reference. The former is associated with modality and factuality, whereas the latter corresponds to cases in which the SoA cannot be located in the time axis – typical instances include generic statements such as *growing up is probably just a matter of getting to know oneself*. Cases of ambiguous time reference, that is, an observation that could be assigned more than one temporal value, were excluded.

Future-in-the-past and its relation with tense are worth further discussion. Romance languages have a tense form that expresses future-in-the-past time reference and counterfactual reality status, often dubbed "the conditional" and regarded as a non-indicative mood by some authors (see Thieroff, 2010, pp. 11–14). As Thieroff (2010) argues, conditional forms have modal uses, just like past and future tense forms, and should not be considered independent moods. The modal uses of conditional forms emerge as implicatures from the combination of past time reference and future potentiality: when the speaker uses a form that conveys a future perspective from a past reference point they imply that the SoA did not happen, since, in case the SoA had taken place, they would have been more infor-

---

11. Additionally, when an indeterminate time reference (see below) is expressed in the *futuro*, this was also counted as a case of modal future.

mative by using a past tense form – Verstraete (2005) offers a similar analysis of counterfactuality, showing that it arises as an implicature of past potentiality.

Thieroff (2010, p. 13) claims that "in general Futures-in-the-past occur only in one mood, either in the Indicative or in the Subjunctive" and that "[a]s for the Romance languages the Indicative is the only choice."[12] The Galician *pospretérito* is consistently classified as an indicative tense on morphological grounds (Álvarez & Xove, 2002, p. 265; Freixeiro Mato, 2000/2006a, p. 338). Yet, the *pospretérito* is not the only tense in Galician that expresses future-in-the-past. The latter can also be expressed by means of the past subjunctive, as (92) demonstrates.

(92) a. Non sabía canto tempo durmira, probablemente o día non *tardaría* moito en abrir.
'He did not know for how long he had slept, probably it would [IND] not take too long to get light.' (CORGA)
b. Qué desgusto ían levar seus pais. Á avoa Florentina íalle subir a tensión a vinte e catro. Quizais non o *resistisen*.
'His parents would get disappointed. Grandma Florentina's blood pressure would rise up to 24. Maybe they would [SBJV] not withstand it.' (CORGA)

The forms of the two subjunctive tenses in Galician have the ability to convey the same temporal values expressed by the six more temporally-specialized indicative tenses – as far as declarative clauses with an epistemic adverb are concerned. Present and future time references are expressed by the present subjunctive, whereas absolute and relative past time references, including the future-in-the-past, are conveyed by the past subjunctive. Thus, the indicative and the subjunctive in Galician can be compared across different time references, since both moods span over the whole temporal axis.

6.4.3 The clause

Clauses were classified into main, subordinate, comparative, and insubordinate.[13] Observations were also classified according to their sentence type or illocutionary

---

12. Thieroff (2010, p. 13) goes on to add that the reason for this is that "in these languages there is no Future Subjunctive." While Galician and many other Romance languages have lost their future subjunctive, Portuguese still retains a fully functional future subjunctive. Moreover, the loss of the future subjunctive in Galician did not involve a shift of the subjunctive future-in-the-past in favor of the *pospretérito*, but in favor of the past subjunctive (see Veiga, 1991, 1992, for an account of the consequences of the loss of the future subjunctive in Galician and Spanish).

13. Insubordination is defined by Evans (2007, p. 367) as "the conventionalized main clause use of what, on prima facie grounds, appear to be formally subordinate clauses." A Galician example

mood. There are three major sentence types in Galician: declarative, interrogative, and imperative.[14] Although, in principle, epistemic qualifications can only occur in declarative sentences, in my sample epistemic adverbs also showed up in interrogative sentences, which is not completely unexpected (see Nuyts, 2001a, pp. 57–59).

The syntactic position of the adverb within the clause was taken into account. Sentential adverbs in Galician enjoy a high degree of positional freedom. Given the breadth of syntactic possibilities, I have distinguished four general positions, considering the SoA and the finite verb form. In *initial position* the adverb occurs on the left of the SoA (i.e., before the verb and all its complements). This is not readily equivalent to utterance-initial, since, if an element external to the SoA (e.g., a textual marker or a coordinated sentence) precedes the epistemic adverb, this is still considered initial position (cf. Kärkkäinen, 2003, p. 55). Both examples in (92) above count as initial position – note that (92a) features two different SoAs separated by a comma and that *probablemente* is in initial position as regards the SoA it scopes over. Adverbs in *pre-verbal medial position* appear on the left of the verb and on the right of at least one of its complements (including the subject), be they arguments or adjuncts, as in (93).

(93) O bo acollemento posiblemente tivo que ver coa ausencia de literatura e filosofía durante case toda a guerra …
 'Its good reception *probably* had to do with the absence of literature and philosophy throughout almost the whole war.' (CORGA)

Determining the position of adverbs in relative clauses is a thorny issue: subordinate clauses are introduced by a marker, which in the case of relative clauses is a pronoun with some function within the predication of the relative clause – therefore a part of the SoA. Applied strictly, the above criterion would make it impossible to encounter an adverb in initial position in relative clauses. However, I decided to ignore subordinate markers when determining adverb position within a subordinate clause, since subordinate markers always fill the initial slot.

---

of an insubordinate clause is *que me deixes en paz!* 'leave me alone!', where the complementizer *que* has no subordinator and the whole clause functions as a main sentence.

14. Exclamative sentences are a minor sentence type, dependent on or overlapping with the major sentence types (see Aikhenvald, 2016; Álvarez & Xove, 2002, pp. 188–189). Álvarez and Xove (2002, pp. 175–189) consider desiderative sentences as an additional sentence type in Galician. They grant this status to desiderative sentences on account of them expressing the speaker's attitudes and featuring the subjunctive mood and the adverb *oxalá*. Following this logic, sentences with an epistemic adverb followed by the subjunctive mood, such as (92b), should be considered an additional sentence type.

Thus, we find both initial and pre-verbal medial uses of an adverb in any subordinate clause, as in the relative clauses in (94).

(94) a. Initial position (relative clause)
O outro conxunto *que* <u>probablemente</u> *deixe esta categoría será o Alfoz* ...
'The other team that will probably leave [lit. 'that probably leave'] this division is the Alfoz.' (CORGA)
b. Pre-verbal medial position (relative clause)
Naquel intre tiña algo especial *que nestes tempos,* <u>se cadra</u>, *perdeu*.
'At that moment it had something special that nowadays it has perhaps lost [lit. 'that nowadays perhaps (it) lost'].' (CORGA)

When in *post-verbal medial position* the adverb appears on the right of the verb and on the left of at least one of its complements, be they arguments or adjuncts, as in (95).

(95) Post-verbal medial position
O primeiro *tería* <u>seguramente</u> unha importancia maior ...
'The first one probably had [lit. 'would have surely'] greater importance.' (CORGA)

If the adverb occurs on the right of the SoA (i.e., after the verb and all its complements), it is in *final position*. This may amount to utterance-final, as in (96a), but not necessarily: in (96b) *certamente* is in final position relative to the SoA it scopes over, which is followed by a coordinated sentence (cf. (92a)).

(96) a. Absolute final position
Sucedeu algo máis tarde, <u>quizais</u>.
'It happened somewhat later, maybe.' (CORGA)
b. Non-absolute final position
Gañamos tempo, <u>certamente</u>, e desta maneira pasamos máis horas ó aire fresco.
'We bought some time, certainly, and this way we got to spend more hours outdoors.' (CORGA)

It might be argued that disregarding the position of the adverb in the whole utterance is misleading. However, I do not consider it a flaw: the position of the adverb relative to the SoA matches its position in terms of the intonation unit, as the above examples show, which is the unit of reference to determine the syntactic position in spoken discourse (Kärkkäinen, 2003).

The distance between the adverb and the finite verb form was measured in number of syllables and independently from the relative position of adverb and verb. The measure considered the number of syllables that would be realized in (formal) speech. The counting procedure disregarded irrelevant written conventions: for example, a clitic is written as a separate word when it appears before the verb, and is graphically attached to the verb when in post-verbal position; in either case, the clitic was not considered a part of the verb, and was therefore counted as a syllable.

Finally, some aspects of the semantics of the SoA do not depend exclusively on the verb or the verb phrase, but rather result from the combination of the verb and its complements throughout the clause. Two semantic categories were considered in this connection: control and dynamicity. Control is concerned with whether the first argument carries out the SoA voluntarily, whereas dynamicity has to do with the presence of some change or internal dynamism in the SoA – whether or not "something happens" (see Dik, 1997, pp. 107–115). There exists a number of well-known diagnostics to detect these two semantic dimensions (e.g., Dowty, 1979, pp. 55–60). (96a) above is an example of a dynamic SoA, and (95) is an example of a non-dynamic SoA. The category of control is exemplified below:

(97) a. Controlled SoA
... supuxo que aquela noite Celia non só rachou con el, senón que ademais, *probablemente tomou tamén unha decisión liberadora.*
'... he supposed that that night Celia not only broke up with him, but that, moreover, she probably also made a liberating decision.' (CORGA)
b. Non-controlled SoA
... e debía ser tan estúpida que *probablemente descoñecía que existise a morte* ...
'... and she must be so stupid that she probably ignored that death existed...' (CORGA)

6.4.4 Beyond the clause

Performative uses are the default uses of epistemic expressions (see §3.1.3). However, most epistemic devices can also be used to describe, rather than perform, an epistemic qualification. A key difference between adjectives and adverbs is that the former allow for structurally descriptive uses whereas the latter do not (see Nuyts, 2001a, pp. 72–76). Yet, epistemic adverbs are used descriptively. In this study, I have considered any means by which the speaker/writer shifts the orientation of the epistemic qualification from themselves to another entity (i.e., any other than the speaker/writer at the moment of speech). In the corpus data, there are two formal means by which this is achieved, corresponding to either indirect speech or pseudo-indirect thought:[15] complement clauses and *according to*-phrases. Crucially, the fact that these are the only possibilities documented in the corpus confirm the structural limitations of adverbs. Nevertheless, descriptive uses are found, and must be considered in a general account of epistemic adverbs. The examples below illustrate the two formal devices.

(98) a. Complement clause: indirect speech
Leo *díxome que* don Maximino tiña moitos anos e visto moito mundo, e que <u>probablemente</u> coñecese a sobriña moito mellor ca nós ...
'Leo told me that Mr. Maximino was many years old and had seen a lot of the world, and that he probably knew his niece much better than we did ...'
(CORGA)
b. Complement clause: pseudo-indirect thought
Creu que <u>quizá</u> fose produto da excitación e desbaratou a idea inicial, instintiva, de arramplar con todo.
'He thought that maybe it had been a figment of excitement, and dismissed the initial instinctive idea of sweeping everything away.' (CORGA)
c. *according to*-phrase: indirect speech
Segundo o Xornal, <u>posiblemente</u> o crego tropezou.
'According to the newspaper, the priest probably stumbled.' (CORGA)

I have not considered direct speech and direct thought as descriptive uses, because they are performative from the perspective of the represented subject and partially overlap with the category MEDIUM, to be discussed below.

6.4.5 The extra-linguistic context

As advanced earlier, CORGA is composed mainly of written language – only about 1% of its data corresponds to spoken language. Nevertheless, written texts sometimes resemble or even mimic spoken language. Thus, I have incorporated the contrast oral/non-oral as a variable. Observations coded as oral correspond to the few examples of spoken language in CORGA, but also to dialogues in fictional prose, direct quotes in press, and interviews in essay and press. The language of such observations cannot be considered, strictly speaking, as oral (the mediation of the written word is obvious), but it does possess features typical of spoken registers, which may constitute a source of variation.

---

15. As Chafe (1994, p. 220) notes, cases that "look like indirect quotations of inner language actually express beliefs, opinions, or decisions." Therefore, the term *indirect thought* would be inappropriate.

6.4.6 Summary of variables

Table 6.1 summarizes the variables and their levels. I use mnemonic names for the variables (in small caps) and their levels (in typewriter font). These codes will figure in the exposition of the statistical analyses and results in the coming chapters.

In order to meet the requirements of the statistical modeling, some variables were recoded. Thus, MODIF, CLAUSE, and PERFORM have only two levels each. In these cases at least one of the variants had a very low frequency, and the contrast between the variants given their frequency was deemed of minor importance (e.g., the contrast between *máis* and *moi* as modifiers, and between complement and *according-to* phrases as descriptive structures). In the case of CLAUSE, comparative and insubordinate clauses were pooled together with subordinate clauses, since they showed up quite infrequently (three and four times, respectively). This should not pose a problem in terms of syntactic context, since all comparative and insubordinate clauses were introduced by a complementizer typical of subordinate clauses, either *que* 'that', *porque* 'because', or *como* 'as'.

The number of different verb lemmas found in the dataset was 374. The full array of lemmas and their frequencies are available in Table A.1 (Appendix A). Given their large number, lemmas were grouped according to their frequency. Thus, the five most frequent lemmas (*estar* 'be', *haber* 'have', *poder* 'can/may', *ser* 'be', *ter* 'have') were considered independently, while the rest were grouped under the same category. As a consequence, VERB has six levels.

Finally, DISTANCE was recoded into a categorical variable, since it lacked a normal distribution and its relationship with the dependent variable was not linear.

Table 6.1 Summary of variables

Type of variable	Variable	Levels
Adverb variable	ADVERB (adverb lemma)	cert (*certamente*)
		segu (*seguramente*)
		prob (*probablemente*)
		posi (*posiblemente*)
		quiz (*quizais*)
		seca (*se cadra*)
	MODIF (adverb modification)	mod (adverb modified)
		non-mod (adverb not modified)
Verb variables	VERB (finite verb lemma)	estar (*estar*)
		haber (*haber*)
		poder (*poder*)
		ser (*ser*)
		ter (*ter*)
		other (none of the above)

Table 6.1 *(continued)*

Type of variable	Variable	Levels
	MOOD (verbal mood)	ind (indicative)
		sbjv (subjunctive)
	POLARITY	aff (affirmative)
		neg (negative)
Co-occurrence variables	AUX (presence of (near-)epistemic auxiliary verb)	deber (*deber (de)*)
		haber (*haber*)
		poder (*poder*)
		ter (*ter que*)
		non-aux (absence of (near-)epistemic auxiliary)
	MODFUT (modal use of future tense)	mod (modal use)
		non-mod (absence of modal use)
Variables related to clause syntax	SENTENCE (sentence type)	declar (declarative sentence)
		inter (interrogative sentence)
	CLAUSE (clause type)	main (main clause)
		subord (subordinate clause)
	POSITION	ini (initial)
		pre-v (pre-verbal medial)
		post-v (post-verbal medial)
		fin (final)
	DISTANCE (between adverb and verb)	adj (adjacent)
		near-adj (1–3 syllables)
		non-adj (4–12 syllables)
		distant (>12 syllables)
Variables related to clause semantics	TIME (time reference)	fut (future)
		futpast (future-in-the-past)
		indet (indeterminate)
		past (past)
		pres (present)
	CONTROL	ctrl (controlled SoA)
		non-ctrl (non-controlled SoA)
	DYNAM (dynamicity)	dyn (dynamic SoA)
		non-dyn (non-dynamic SoA)
Functional variable	PERFORM (performativity)	desc (descriptive use)
		perf (performative use)
Contextual variable	MEDIUM	oral (oral)
		non-oral (non-oral)

6.5 Statistical approach

Most of the hypotheses in Chapters 7 and 8 were tested by means of one or more statistical tools. All statistical procedures were carried out using the open-source statistical programming environment *R* (R Core Team, 2022).

Bivariate analyses relied on typical measures of association for categorical variables, namely those associated with the χ^2-test of independence (see Levshina, 2015, Chapter 9). This test is based on the comparison between observed and expected frequencies, and tells us whether the difference between the proportions of two variables is statistically significant. When reporting the results of the χ^2-test, I will provide (i) the χ^2-statistic, whose size is proportional to the sum of the differences between the observed and the expected frequencies, (ii) the degrees of freedom, (iii) Cramér's *V*, whose absolute values range from 0 (no association) to 1 (perfect association), and (iv) *p*-values, which inform us of the statistical significance of the effect at the level of 0.05 (values above this threshold indicate a not significant effect). *R* package vcd (Meyer et al., 2022) was used to perform the χ^2-test and obtain the associated measures.

Multivariate results were obtained through logistic regression, which allowed me to model the relationships of ADVERB, as a dependent variable, with many of the other categories, which were taken as explanatory factors by the logistic model. Given the number of variables involved and the complexity of the resulting model, I used two complementary approaches to logistic regression. I address the reader to the section where results are reported (§ 7.3) for details on this statistical tool.

CHAPTER 7

Epistemic adverbs
Syntagmatic and paradigmatic properties

This chapter provides an overview of the behavior of epistemic adverbs in written language. It also sheds some light on how adverbs differ from one another by uncovering the usage patterns associated with each of them. After presenting the working hypotheses (§ 7.1), the chapter reports the results of the corpus study, either univariate and bivariate (§ 7.2) or multivariate (§ 7.3). A summary and discussion of the main findings is provided at the end (§ 7.4).

7.1 Variables and hypotheses

Epistemic adverbs were examined in the light of several variables, presented in detail in § 6.4 and summarily in Table 6.1. Some variables are associated with a hypothesis, but most of them are purely exploratory – given the lack of prior studies on epistemic adverbs from a variationist perspective, we do not yet know which variables will yield results. Exploratory variables include VERB, POLARITY, TIME, CONTROL, DYNAM, AUX, MODFUT, SENTENCE, CLAUSE, DISTANCE, and PERFORM. For these, two generic research questions are formulated: "Is there a relationship between ADVERB and this variable?" and "If so, what is that relationship?"

Epistemic modality has been divided into three semantic dimensions relevant to the behavior of adverbs (see (89)). Probability is a continuous dimension, whereas certainty and possibility are not. Therefore, it is expected that probability adverbs have the ability to further modify the epistemic qualification, while the opposite is true for certainty and possibility adverbs. The first hypothesis, regarding MODIF, is as follows:

(99) Hypothesis 1. Only epistemic adverbs conveying a probability value are modified by a grading expression.

Adverbs are known for taking many different positions in a clause. Nevertheless, their position is not random, but guided by information-structural principles, such as their scope over information (Verhagen, 1986, pp. 82–86) and the non-focal character of the epistemic qualification (Nuyts, 2001a, pp. 79–100). According to Nuyts (2001a, pp. 261–272), the syntax of epistemic expressions is determined by the counteraction of two forces: an information-structural force, which favors a non-focal expression for epistemic qualifications (and therefore a sentence-internal position); and an iconic force, which favors the preservation of the status of the qualification as a meta-operator over the SoA (and therefore a sentence-initial position). Nuyts (2001a, p. 94) found that in Dutch, English, and German main clauses "the default placement of the adverb seems to be in sentence-internal position." Similarly, six out of the ten English adverbs examined by Simon-Vandenbergen and Aijmer (2007, pp. 279–282) prefer the sentence-internal position. Nuyts (2001a, p. 265) considers this a compromise between the information-structural force and the iconic force. These considerations are based on the assumption that elements with a special informational status, namely, focal elements, are placed in initial position by default. However, initial position in Galician is focal only in exceptional cases. In fact, final position is the unmarked position for the focus of a sentence in Galician (Álvarez & Xove, 2002, p. 78). Therefore, there are no grounds for this kind of tension between the information-structural force and the iconic force in Galician, since the initial position seems to satisfy the requirements of both. That is the hypothesis related to POSITION that will be tested here:

(100) Hypothesis 2. The initial position is the default placement of epistemic adverbs.

Two classes of possibility adverbs have been distinguished (§ 6.2). Cornillie (2010) shows how Type A adverbs, represented in this study by *quizais*, are less successful in interaction than Type B expressions, represented here by *se cadra*. Oral contexts are likely to reflect, at least partially, the characteristics of spoken conversational (hence interactional) settings. The following hypothesis is made in connection with MEDIUM:

(101) Hypothesis 3. Type B possibility adverbs occur more frequently in oral contexts.

Finally, verbal mood was not included as a variable in the multivariate part of the study, which is modeled taking ADVERB as the dependent variable. Mood distribution depends on epistemic expressions, as shown by previous research (e.g., Deshors & Waltermire, 2019; Hirota, 2021), and not the other way around – the choice between adverbs is not conditioned by the mood of the verb, rather, epistemic adverbs either allow verbal mood to alternate between the indicative and the subjunctive, or they do not. Thus, including MOOD as a factor conditioning ADVERB would be inadequate.

7.2 Univariate and bivariate results

Before the multivariate analysis, let us take a look at the variables individually and pairwise. Given the number of variables, the focus will be on the variable of interest, ADVERB, and its relation to the other variables, but other interesting interactions will also be broached. I will first provide a brief overview of the results, and then focus on some variables that deserve further attention.

7.2.1 A general picture

The results of the corpus study are summarized in Table 7.1, which presents the distribution of the levels of the variables by ADVERB. A preliminary comment of the results for each variable follows.

Table 7.1 Summary of bivariate results

		cert	segu	prob	posi	quiz	seca
MODIF	mod	0	0	15	6	0	0
	non-mod	300	300	285	294	300	300
VERB	estar	13	22	13	16	15	14
	haber	17	14	7	8	8	13
	poder	18	8	11	9	19	18
	ser	104	63	97	90	121	95
	ter	13	21	22	20	19	17
	other	135	172	150	157	118	143
MOOD	ind	300	288	221	185	147	290
	sbjv	0	12	79	115	153	10
POLARITY	aff	231	266	253	257	259	257
	neg	69	34	47	43	41	43
AUX	deber	1	1	0	1	0	0
	haber	0	2	3	1	0	0
	poder	2	0	0	1	5	5
	non-aux	297	297	297	297	295	295
MODFUT	mod	1	27	14	7	5	6
	non-mod	299	273	286	293	295	294
SENTENCE	declar	300	300	300	300	298	294
	inter	0	0	0	0	2	6

Table 7.1 *(continued)*

		cert	segu	prob	posi	quiz	seca
CLAUSE	main	250	219	205	207	239	233
	subord	50	81	95	93	61	67
POSITION	ini	192	211	205	201	207	234
	pre-v	22	46	37	50	59	26
	post-v	67	39	57	48	31	37
	fin	19	4	1	1	3	3
DISTANCE	adj	120	160	163	155	144	149
	near-adj	75	77	67	68	70	81
	non-adj	70	47	50	54	47	51
	distant	35	16	20	23	39	19
TIME	fut	2	40	46	50	22	39
	futpast	5	21	12	22	11	3
	indet	39	32	50	31	51	40
	past	127	122	100	109	93	88
	pres	127	85	92	88	123	130
CONTROL	ctrl	17	59	39	49	41	41
	non-ctrl	283	241	261	251	259	259
DYNAM	dyn	80	133	100	114	80	103
	non-dyn	220	167	200	186	220	197
PERFORM	desc	9	15	16	24	15	10
	perf	291	285	284	276	285	290
MEDIUM	oral	14	42	40	38	40	77
	non-oral	286	258	260	262	260	223

MODIF. Adverb modifiers are very infrequent, and they only occur with *probablemente* and *posiblemente*. Four out of six adverbs in the dataset do not take a modifier on any occasion.

VERB. The five most frequent verb lemmas amount to more than half of finite verbs in the dataset (925/1,800, 51.39%), and, unsurprisingly, all of them are auxiliary verbs. But even among these very frequent verbs remarkable differences arise: almost one in three observations feature *ser* 'be' as their finite verb (570/1,800, 31.67%), whereas each of the other very frequent lemmas occur in less than 7% of observations.

MOOD. The indicative mood occurs in 1,431 observations (79.5%), whereas the subjunctive mood occurs in 369 (20.5%). This distribution is far from being even across adverbs. Some of them have a high share of the subjunctive (*probablemente, posiblemente, quizais*), others combine with the subjunctive only occasionally (*seguramente, se cadra*), and another one only takes the indicative (*certamente*).

POLARITY. 1,523 clauses (84.61%) are affirmative, whereas 277 (15.39%) are negative. Most adverbs feature around 40/300 cases (13.33%) of negation, but *certamente* is an exception, with 69/300 cases (23%).

AUX and MODFUT. The co-occurrence of an epistemic adverb and another (near-)epistemic expression is a very infrequent phenomenon in the dataset. A (near-)epistemic auxiliary co-occurred with an adverb in 22/1,800 cases, that is, 1.22%, while the numbers for epistemic uses of future tenses are higher, with 60/1,800 cases, or 3.33%. Deriving patterns of co-occurrence with auxiliaries from the data is tempting, but the numbers are too small to be on the safe side. As for the modal future, it is worth noting that it co-occurs with all adverbs and that *probablemente* and, especially, *seguramente* are the ones with the highest shares.

SENTENCE. Epistemic adverbs only occur in declarative sentences, with few exceptions: *quizais* and *se cadra* occur twice (0.67%) and six times (2%), respectively, in an interrogative sentence.

CLAUSE. Epistemic adverbs occur more frequently in main clauses than in subordinate clauses (1,353/1,800, 75.17% vs. 447/1,800, 24.83%, respectively). It seems that *seguramente, probablemente,* and *posiblemente* occur more easily (approx. 90/300, 30%) in subordinate clauses than the other adverbs, which range from 50/300 (16.67%) to 67/300 cases (22.33%).

POSITION. All adverbs occur more frequently on the left of the SoA than in any other place. Medial positions are not rare for any adverb, unlike final position, which is very infrequent for all adverbs but *certamente*. A concerning issue in the annotation process was adverb position in subordinate clauses, specifically, whether relative pronouns are considered as part of the SoA and therefore as filling the initial position of the clause. I determined that adverbs immediately preceded by a subordinator, be it a relative pronoun or a conjunction, were considered SoA-initial. Table 7.2 shows the distribution of adverb position by clause type. Main and subordinate clauses share similar proportions of position types, and the statistics reveal no significant association between POSITION and CLAUSE ($\chi^2(3) = 5.8807, p > 0.05$, Cramér's $V = 0.057$), which I take as an indication that the methodological decision was adequate.

DISTANCE. In most cases, adverbs are adjacent to the finite verb. As distance between adverb and verb increases, the number of observations decreases.

Table 7.2 Position distribution by clause type

	main		subord	
	N	%	N	%
ini	931	68.81	319	71.36
pre-v	176	13.01	64	14.32
post-v	218	16.11	61	13.65
fin	28	2.07	3	0.67

Although *certamente* conforms to this general pattern, it is the most deviant in this respect, as it contains the fewest cases of adjacency.

TIME. Observations feature one of five different possible time reference values. 645/1,800 (35.83%) SoAs are located in the present, 639/1,800 (35.50%) are located in the past, 199/1,800 (11.06%) in the future, 74/1,800 (4.11%) in the future-in-the-past, and 243/1,800 (13.50%) have an indeterminate time reference. There seems to be a great degree of divergence between adverbs regarding this variable, which will be better understood by means of the coming multivariate approach.

CONTROL and DYNAM. The unmarked values (non-controlled SoA / non-dynamic SoA) are the most frequent in both cases (1,554/1,800, 86.33%; 1,190/1,800, 66.11%), although controlled SoAs are much rarer than dynamic ones. As one would expect from the prevalence of the unmarked values, non-controlled, non-dynamic SoAs (or: states) represent the majority of observations (1,189/1,800, 66.06%). Non-controlled, dynamic SoAs (or: processes) (365/1,800, 20.28%) and controlled, dynamic ones (or: actions) (245/1,800, 13.61%) are also frequent patterns. However, there is only one case (0.06%) of a controlled, non-dynamic SoA (or: position) (on SoA typology, see Dik, 1997, pp. 114–115).

PERFORM. Epistemic adverbs are used performatively in the vast majority of cases (1,711/1,800, 95.06%). No relevant differences between adverbs seem to exist in this respect.

MEDIUM. 251/1,800 (13.94%) observations are oral. Most adverbs occur around 40/300 times (13.33%) in an oral context, whereas the count goes down to 14/300 (4.67%) for *certamente* and up to 77/300 (25.67%) for *se cadra*.

7.2.2 Adverb modifiers

The general results show that modification of epistemic adverbs is very restricted. In order to obtain a more in-depth view of the phenomenon, I examined the occurrence of adverb modifiers in the whole CORGA database. Thus, adverbs were searched preceded by one of six degree modifiers (*moi* 'very', *bastante* 'quite', *pouco* 'few, small', *case* 'almost', *máis* 'more', *menos* 'less'). This did not change the general conclusion that epistemic adverbs seldom take a degree modifier.

Half of the lemmas considered, namely *certamente, quizais,* and *se cadra,* did not take a modifier in any of their occurrences in the whole CORGA database. *Seguramente, probablemente,* and *posiblemente* were modified by *moi,* to wildly varying degrees: 1/2,179 or 0.05% (*seguramente*[1]), 108/2,380 or 4.5% (*probablemente*) and 27/1,417 or 1.9% (*posiblemente*). The only other case of modification was *máis* preceding *probablemente* on 9 occasions, that is, 0.4%. Some examples follow:

(102) a. Para os maiores, porque o viron anotar, rebotear e facer o seu clásico reverso no vello Sar. E, para os novos, porque *moi* <u>seguramente</u> os seus familiares lles terán falado algunha vez do que significou este coruñés de 1,92 na historia do club.
'For the elderly, because they saw him score, get rebounds, and perform his classic spin move in the Old Sar [arena]. And, for the young, because their family members have very probably told them sometime what this 1.92 m man from A Coruña meant for the history of the club.' (CORGA)
b. *Moi* <u>probablemente</u> a partir de mañá non poderei voltar a ese centro.
'Very probably, starting tomorrow, I will not be able to go back to that center.' (CORGA)
c. Pode parecer complicado, pouco viable e, *moi* <u>posiblemente</u>, imposible.
'It may seem complicated, not very feasible, and, very probably, impossible.' (CORGA)
d. … esta liberación de sustancias tóxicas … podería suceder para evita-la autotoxicidade ou *máis* <u>probablemente</u> para evita-la concorrencia doutras plantas competidoras.
'… such release of toxic substances … could happen to avoid autotoxicity or, more probably, to avoid concurrence of other, competing plants.' (CORGA)

These results confirm the differences between epistemic dimensions in terms of gradability: only probability adverbs are modified by degree expressions, in contrast with certainty and possibility adverbs, which do not take modifiers at all. There are also important differences among adverbs of probability. The prototypical member of the category, *probablemente,* is modified more frequently and by a

---

1. Bear in mind that none of this cases made it into the sample used in the corpus study. That is why I reported above that only *probablemente* and *posiblemente* take modifiers, since those results were limited to the observations randomly selected, none of which feature *seguramente* with a modifier.

larger number of different expressions than more peripheral probability adverbs *seguramente* and *posiblemente*.

However, these possibilities of modification are quite restricted, and pale in comparison with those of epistemic adjectives. According to Rodríguez-Espiñeira's (2010) data, the Spanish adjectives *probable, improbable, posible*, and *imposible* may combine with between 4 and 10 different modifiers each, and in the case of probability expressions they do so very frequently: *probable* is modified in 45.5% of cases, whereas *improbable* is modified in 31.6% of cases. *Posible* and *imposible*, though, are modified in only 0.9% and 5.8% of occurrences, respectively.

In order to compare adverbs to adjectives, I searched for *probable* preceded by the six mentioned modifiers in CORGA. This adjective combines with all but one of the modifiers, the exception being *case* 'almost'. It takes a modifier in 498/1,130 cases, that is, in 44% of cases, which constitutes an almost perfect match with the Spanish cognate. In comparison with the adverb, the adjective is modified roughly ten times as much.

This confirms that adjectives are more easily modified than adverbs, and code very specific epistemic values. This is due to information-structural reasons, namely the fact that adjectives are the preferred form for the focal expression of epistemic modality (see Nuyts, 2001a, Chapter 2). Adverbs, in turn, are "low profile" expressions from the point of view of information structure, suited for the default, non-focal status of the epistemic qualification, so that their epistemic value does not need further specification in the vast majority of cases.

7.2.3 A note on mood

The issue of mood selection is a complex one, and cannot be covered in depth here, so let us just get a general picture of the results. As pointed out above, mood distribution is far from being even across adverbs. Figure 7.1 shows that, if one excludes *se cadra*, mood distribution forms a cline that corresponds to the epistemic scale in (89), with a prevalence of the indicative in the upper sections of the scale and an increasing presence of the subjunctive as one moves down.

An important caveat when considering these data is that the alternation between the indicative and the subjunctive is (assumed to be) impossible when the adverb follows the verb – when the verb precedes the adverb only the indicative is licensed. There is a slight increase of the subjunctive when the data are restricted to pre-verbal occurrences of the adverbs, which is in line with theoretical expectations (for comparison see Tables A.2 and A.3, Appendix A). Nevertheless, there was one case of pre-adverbial subjunctive selection in the dataset, no doubt a very exceptional one:

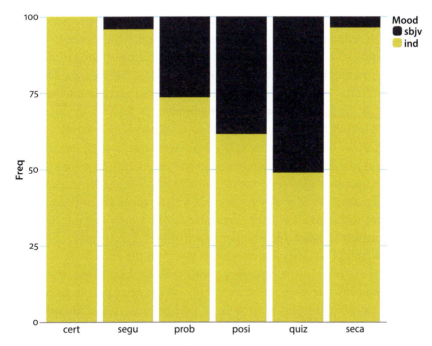

Figure 7.1 Mood distribution across adverbs

(103) A realidade constatable documentalmente é que dende os primeiros do XIX foron creándose orquestras sinfónicas – as primerias [sic] *sexan* <u>posiblemente</u> as de Tenerife e A Coruña, que deron a coñece-la música de Beethoven na vida do autor ...
'The reality that can be verified by documents is that since the beginning of the 19th century symphonic orchestras were created – the first ones are possibly those in Tenerife and A Coruña, which made known Beethoven's music during the author's life ...' (CORGA)

In (103) the utterance qualified by the epistemic adverb is an attributive clause in which the subject is moved to a focal position on the right of the verb – thus enabling relativization – and the non-verbal predicate is topicalized. This atypical word order may explain the occurrence of the unexpected subjunctive. Such an exceptional case does not undermine the general consideration that the alternation is licensed when the adverb precedes the verb – it rather reinforces it – though one cannot dismiss the possibility of finding the subjunctive before the adverb in very marked contexts.

Something that might call the attention of Galician grammarians is the similarity between *seguramente* and *se cadra* in terms of mood distribution. Álvarez and Xove (2002, p.180) point out that *seguramente, posiblemente,* and *quizais,* among other adverbs, license the mood alternation when they precede the verb, whereas with *se cadra* the indicative is the only option – and any native speaker would endorse such claim. Nevertheless, corpus evidence points in a different direction, grouping together *seguramente* and *se cadra*: when considering only these two adverbs, no significant association between ADVERB and MOOD was found, that is, both adverbs are indistinguishable as regards mood selection, according to corpus findings ($\chi^2(1) = 0.047$, $p > 0.5$, Cramér's $V = 0.018$).

The similarity between the two adverbs may be due to both having entered the paradigm of epistemic uncertainty in relatively recent times (see §6.2), but language contact may also play a role. Some linguistic changes in Galician are the result of a situation of prolonged contact with Spanish. Often times, linguists are presented with two alternative explanations, one which sees the change as a result of language contact and another one that sees it as a result of language-internal dynamics (see, e.g., Aguete Cajiao, 2020, on the emergence of an alternative vowel system). In the case of *se cadra* and the subjunctive, the fact that uncertainty adverbs develop mood variability over time as part of grammaticalization (cf. Cornillie, 2016) is in tension with the potential purist attitudes of language users that would drive them to prefer differential forms (*se cadra*) over forms that are common to both Galician and Spanish (*quizais*, *talvez*) when both are perceived as semantically equivalent, thus equating the former to the latter at a morphosyntactic level.

Rather than being mutually exclusive, the two explanations are compatible inasmuch as both argue for the same analogical process as the driver of change. They differ as to the nature of the analogical relationship: between a less grammaticalized form and more grammaticalized forms, in one case, and between a differential form and forms common with Spanish, in the other. There is nothing barring from considering both types of analogical relationships as fueling the process, but further evidence is needed to assess their interplay.

7.3 Multivariate results: Logistic regression

Logistic regression enables us to model the relationships between a dependent categorical variable and two or more explanatory variables or predictors. In our case the dependent variable is ADVERB, which has more than two levels. Therefore, multinomial logistic regression (MLR) is required. The interpretation of the model can be challenging when the number of levels of the dependent variable is high, as in this case. Thus, I combined two complementary approaches to MLR (see Levshina, 2015, Chapter 13). The first approach fits a binary model for every adverb, taking one of the adverbs as the reference level (i.e., the base for comparison). For instance, if we take *probablemente* as the reference level, MLR will compare the outcome for *probablemente* against the outcome for *certamente* and then proceed with the rest of pairwise comparisons (i.e., *probablemente* vs. *seguramente*, *probablemente* vs. *posiblemente*, and so on). R package mlogit (Croissant, 2020) was used to perform MLR in this way. The other approach compares the outcome for each adverb against the outcomes for all other adverbs, and tells us which predictors (dis)favor, say, *probablemente* in comparison with all other adverbs. In this case, the package polytomous (Arppe, 2013) was used. I shall refer to the first MLR type as the "pairwise" approach, and to the second type as the "one vs. rest" approach.

In logistic regression, one must choose a reference level for every predictor. This is the variant that will be compared with every other variant of the same predictor. This choice is not statistically important, but it may influence how the model is interpreted. The most frequent outcome for every predictor was set as the reference level. This seems adequate, since in most cases the most frequent outcome is either the "non-application" value or the less marked variant.

A high number of variables and levels increases the chances of encountering problems with sparse data. The absence of observations for some contexts results in zero values, or knockouts (Paolillo, 2002, p. 30), which may pose a problem for statistical models. In the case of logistic regression, zero values would result in very large standard errors and *p*-values, which would compromise the reliability of the model (Levshina, 2015, p. 273). Given the difficulty in recoding the predictors affected by knockouts (those with at least one zero value in Table 7.1), a decision was made to exclude some variables and levels. The variables excluded are MODIF, AUX, EPIFUT, and SENTENCE. None of these variables could be recoded, either because they already are as simple as they can be (they have exactly two levels), or because grouping the application values would not be adequate, as in the case of AUX.[2]

Another requirement of logistic regression has to do with the number of observations needed. A conservative rule states that the number of "events per parameter" must be approximately 10, but 5–9 events per parameter are usually acceptable (Hosmer et al., 2013, pp. 407–408). In practical terms, this means that the total number of levels in the predictors plus the intercept must not exceed the number of observations for the least frequent outcome of the dependent variable divided by 5–10. In order to comply with this requirement, two models were fitted: a morpho-syntactic model and a lexico-semantic one, summarized in (104).

---

2. The co-occurrence variables are included in order to unravel semantic patterns. Conflating the different auxiliaries into one single level would conceal their semantic differences. These variables will be dealt with from a qualitative perspective in the next chapter.

Note that the variable MEDIUM does not have a clear position in this conceptual divide, so it was fitted in the least saturated model, that is, the morpho-syntactic one. The sum of the levels of all predictors for every model is 12 and 19, respectively, thus obtaining 15–20 events per parameter.

(104) a. Morpho-syntactic model
 ADVERB ~ CLAUSE + POSITION + DISTANCE + MEDIUM
 b. Lexico-semantic model
 ADVERB ~ VERB + POLARITY + TIME + CONTROL + DYNAM + PERFORM

The final regression model was identified through single term deletions of predictors using the Wald test for the pairwise approach (function waldtest() in the mlogit package) and ANOVA for the one vs. rest approach. This allowed me to remove the variables that do not contribute in a statistically significant way to the explanatory power of the model, which are VERB, CONTROL, DYNAM, and PERFORM. The statistically significant variables from the two initial models could be fitted in one final model, available in (105). Both approaches to MLR led to the same relevant predictors, with the exception of DISTANCE, which was only picked by the pairwise approach. No significant interactions were found.

(105) Final model
 ADVERB ~ POLARITY + CLAUSE + POSITION + (DISTANCE) + TIME + MEDIUM

The complete *R* output for the three models can be found in Listings B.1 through B.6 (Appendix B). All coefficients are given in log odds ratios, which are preferred over odds ratios: being centered around zero, log odds ratios offer an easier interpretation (Gries, 2013, p. 187).

7.3.1 The pairwise approach

The first approach to MLR compares the results for *probablemente* with those for every other adverb. *Probablemente* was selected as the reference level on account of its central position on the epistemic scale.

The final regression model includes six predictors. The model is highly significant ($p < 0.000$) and returned a McFadden's R^2 value of 0.053. R^2 values from 0.2 to 0.4 would indicate an excellent fit (Levshina, 2015, p. 280). Thus, our model accounts for a decent amount of the variation, but still leaves a lot of variation unaccounted for. This is expected, since many variables are exploratory, and some important variables, such as adverb meaning, could not be included in MLR. The model identified six relevant predictors, which we will explore down below.

Let us start by comparing *probablemente* with *certamente* with the help of Table 7.3. Note (i) that the leftmost column contains the name of every level in lowercase preceded by the name of their variable in uppercase and (ii) that the reference levels are not shown in the table.[3] The most important measures to interpret the results are the estimates, in log odds ratios, and the *p*-values (i.e., the second and last columns of the table). The former tell us the size and direction of the effect, and take values between -∞ and ∞. The latter inform us of the statistical significance of an effect at the level of 0.05 – values above this threshold indicate a not significant effect.

Table 7.3 Summary of the MLR model for *certamente*. Not statistically significant estimates are in parentheses

	Estimate	Std. Error	z-value	Pr(>|z|)
(intercept)	(0.11890)	0.20613	0.57683	0.56406
POLARITYneg	0.52530	0.24499	2.14419	0.03202
CLAUSEsubord	−0.72070	0.20969	−3.43699	0.00059
POSITIONpre-v	(−0.17441)	0.30178	−0.57794	0.56330
POSITIONpost-v	0.47966	0.23537	2.03794	0.04156
POSITIONfin	2.85437	1.04576	2.72947	0.00634
DISTANCEnear-adj	(0.34221)	0.24972	1.37033	0.17058
DISTANCEnon-adj	0.52427	0.25379	2.06580	0.03885
DISTANCEdistant	0.78425	0.33165	2.36469	0.01804
TIMEfut	−3.34510	0.73817	−4.53163	0.00001
TIMEfutpast	−1.16979	0.56231	−2.08034	0.03749
TIMEindet	−0.67130	0.26207	−2.56148	0.01042
TIMEpast	(−0.12099)	0.19864	−0.60910	0.54246
MEDIUMoral	−1.25969	0.33578	−3.75154	0.00018

The results show that POLARITY has a significant effect in distinguishing between *certamente* and *probablemente*. The positive estimate indicates that negative contexts increase the odds of *certamente* against *probablemente* in comparison with the reference level (i.e., affirmative polarity). The estimate for subordinate clauses is preceded by a minus sign, which reveals that these contexts decrease the odds of *certamente* against *probablemente* vis-à-vis main clauses. Post-verbal and final position favor *certamente*, the effect being much stronger in the case of final position. A greater distance between the adverb and the finite verb favors *certamente* (see the effect of non-adjacent and distant contexts), whereas the difference between adjacent and near-adjacent distance is not significant. *Cer-*

---

3. The reference levels are: POLARITY = aff; CLAUSE = main; POSITION = ini; TIME = pres; CONTROL = non-ctrl; MEDIUM = non-oral (see Table 6.1).

tamente has a reluctance to scope over SoAs with a future, future-in-the-past, or indeterminate time reference, and is disfavored by oral contexts.

Table 7.4 offers the results corresponding to the comparison with *seguramente*, which reveal minor differences between this item and *probablemente*. The only statistically significant result is in terms of polarity: *seguramente* is disfavored in negative contexts, that is, it shows a pattern opposite to *certamente*. *Probablemente* and *seguramente* do not differ significantly as to the other predictors.

Table 7.4 Summary of the MLR model for *seguramente*. Not statistically significant estimates are in parentheses

	Estimate	Std. Error	z-value	Pr(>|z|)
(intercept)	(0.07824)	0.20006	0.39109	0.69573
POLARITYneg	−0.57473	0.27173	−2.11511	0.03442
CLAUSEsubord	(−0.31328)	0.18672	−1.67781	0.09338
POSITIONpre-v	(0.19794)	0.24989	0.79211	0.42830
POSITIONpost-v	(−0.41407)	0.24419	−1.69570	0.08994
POSITIONfin	(1.24900)	1.12881	1.10648	0.26852
DISTANCEnear-adj	(0.23983)	0.23031	1.04133	0.29772
DISTANCEnon-adj	(−0.11757)	0.24933	−0.47154	0.63726
DISTANCEdistant	(−0.32475)	0.36644	−0.88621	0.37551
TIMEfut	(−0.07108)	0.26665	−0.26657	0.78980
TIMEfutpast	(0.71402)	0.39968	1.78646	0.07402
TIMEindet	(−0.34286)	0.27704	−1.23760	0.21586
TIMEpast	(0.30779)	0.20587	1.49511	0.13489
MEDIUMoral	(0.03645)	0.24446	0.14910	0.88147

Probablemente and *posiblemente* are identical in terms of the variables considered here. Table 7.5 shows that the predictors did not yield any statistically significant difference.

Probablemente and *quizais* (Table 7.6) differ in terms of CLAUSE, POSITION, DISTANCE, and TIME. Subordinate clauses are preferred by *probablemente*. As for placement, *quizais* prefers the pre-verbal position, whereas the post-verbal is preferred by *probablemente*. *Quizais* is favored by contexts where there is a greater distance between the adverb and the verb, and disfavored by future time reference.

Table 7.7 shows that *se cadra*, being at the lower end of the scale, has many differences with *probablemente*. Subordinate clauses are again preferred by *probablemente*. *Se cadra* has a reluctance to appear in the post-verbal position and to scope over SoAs with a future-in-the-past temporal location. The oral medium favors *se*

Chapter 7. Epistemic adverbs   135

Table 7.5 Summary of the MLR model for *posiblemente*. Not statistically significant estimates are in parentheses

	Estimate	Std. Error	z-value	Pr(>|z|)
(intercept)	(−0.08312)	0.20157	−0.41236	0.68008
POLARITYneg	(−0.20229)	0.25885	−0.78150	0.43451
CLAUSEsubord	(−0.07265)	0.18265	−0.39777	0.69080
POSITIONpre-v	(0.39664)	0.24687	1.60666	0.10813
POSITIONpost-v	(−0.04039)	0.23553	−0.17146	0.86386
POSITIONfin	(−0.05452)	1.42173	−0.03835	0.96941
DISTANCEnear-adj	(0.09289)	0.23673	0.39240	0.69476
DISTANCEnon-adj	(0.17683)	0.24462	0.72286	0.46976
DISTANCEdistant	(0.23669)	0.34087	0.69437	0.48745
TIMEfut	(0.09028)	0.25551	0.35332	0.72385
TIMEfutpast	(0.65871)	0.39495	1.66782	0.09535
TIMEindet	(−0.47874)	0.27692	−1.72878	0.08385
TIMEpast	(0.11630)	0.20660	0.56293	0.57348
MEDIUMoral	(−0.07758)	0.24837	−0.31238	0.75475

Table 7.6 Summary of the MLR model for *quizais*. Not statistically significant estimates are in parentheses

	Estimate	Std. Error	z-value	Pr(>|z|)
(intercept)	(0.34475)	0.19450	1.77251	0.07631
POLARITYneg	(−0.25340)	0.26425	−0.95891	0.33760
CLAUSEsubord	−0.52454	0.19699	−2.66280	0.00775
POSITIONpre-v	0.58191	0.24278	2.39688	0.01654
POSITIONpost-v	−0.56141	0.26055	−2.15468	0.03119
POSITIONfin	(0.96172)	1.16613	0.82471	0.40954
DISTANCEnear-adj	(0.22510)	0.23903	0.94169	0.34635
DISTANCEnon-adj	(0.02090)	0.25264	0.08272	0.93407
DISTANCEdistant	0.67390	0.31513	2.13847	0.03248
TIMEfut	−1.05560	0.29793	−3.54309	0.00040
TIMEfutpast	(−0.29288)	0.44810	−0.65360	0.51337
TIMEindet	(−0.32370)	0.24938	−1.29801	0.19428
TIMEpast	(−0.37201)	0.20396	−1.82388	0.06817
MEDIUMoral	(−0.05606)	0.24814	−0.22593	0.82125

cadra. POLARITY and DISTANCE are not relevant in distinguishing *se cadra* from *probablemente*.

Table 7.7 Summary of the MLR model for *se cadra*. Not statistically significant estimates are in parentheses

	Estimate	Std. Error	z-value	Pr(>|z|)
(intercept)	0.38833	0.19215	2.02098	0.04328
POLARITYneg	(−0.27076)	0.26143	−1.03570	0.30034
CLAUSEsubord	−0.40672	0.19324	−2.10472	0.03532
POSITIONpre-v	(−0.45979)	0.28198	−1.63056	0.10298
POSITIONpost-v	−0.56334	0.24759	−2.27529	0.02289
POSITIONfin	(0.73660)	1.16856	0.63034	0.52847
DISTANCEnear-adj	(0.28134)	0.23308	1.20707	0.22741
DISTANCEnon-adj	(−0.09411)	0.24797	−0.37951	0.70431
DISTANCEdistant	(−0.14933)	0.35439	−0.42137	0.67348
TIMEfut	(−0.47754)	0.26166	−1.82504	0.06799
TIMEfutpast	−1.54122	0.66498	−2.31769	0.02047
TIMEindet	(−0.36648)	0.25888	−1.41565	0.15688
TIMEpast	(−0.37033)	0.20467	−1.80942	0.07039
MEDIUMoral	0.64915	0.22254	2.91705	0.00353

Let us now sum up the above findings taking the predictors as a reference. The most important predictors are CLAUSE, POSITION, and TIME. Subordinate clauses increase the odds of *probablemente* against three of the other adverbs, the exceptions being the most similar ones, *seguramente* and *posiblemente*. The final position is only relevant in differentiating *probablemente* from *certamente*, whereas the difference between the initial and the pre-verbal position is significant in the case of *quizais*, which is favored by pre-verbal placement. The post-verbal position plays a greater role, favoring *certamente* and disfavoring *quizais* and *se cadra*. Future-oriented time references are also important discriminators. Future time reference favors *probablemente* over *certamente* and *quizais*, while the future-in-the-past disfavors *certamente* and *se cadra*. Indeterminate time reference plays a role in distinguishing between *probablemente* and *certamente*.

The other variables play a more marginal role. POLARITY has opposite effects on *certamente* and *seguramente*, which are the adverbs that deviate significantly from what is the norm in terms of polarity distribution. DISTANCE singles out *certamente* and *quizais* as adverbs with a stronger preference for appearing far away from the verb. Finally, MEDIUM discriminates between *certamente* and *se cadra*, on the one hand, and *probablemente*, on the other: the oral medium boosts the chances of *se cadra* while reducing those of *certamente*.

7.3.2 The one vs. rest approach

Our second approach to MLR compares the outcome for every adverb with all other possibilities. Thus, no reference level is needed for the dependent variable. The model identified five significant predictors, and returned a McFadden's R^2 value of 0.048. This value is very similar to the one obtained in the previous model, so we are faced again with a limited account of the variation. A difference with the previous approach is the exclusion of DISTANCE from the final model, which leaves us with five significant predictors, instead of six.

Table 7.8 gathers the MLR coefficients, whereas *p*-values can be found in Table A.4 (Appendix A). The table of coefficients includes the results for every adverb. Thus, we can see that most adverbs do not differ in terms of POLARITY, but *certamente* and *seguramente* have a positive and a negative bias, respectively, towards negative contexts. This matches the results from the previous approach.

Subordinate clauses decrease the odds of *certamente* and increase those of *probablemente* with respect to the rest of the adverbs, which did not yield significant results. In the previous approach there was a significant negative effect of subordinate clauses on *quizais* and *se cadra*, which is lost in the present approach. It seems that that effect is due to pairwise comparisons with *probablemente*: the present approach reveals that *probablemente* has a bias towards subordinate contexts, whereas *quizais* and *se cadra* do not yield significant effects when compared with all other adverbs.

POSITION offers a complex picture. *Seguramente, probablemente,* and *posiblemente* make no difference between, on the one hand, the initial position, and, on the other hand, pre-verbal, post-verbal, and final positions. The pre-verbal position increases the odds of *quizais* and decreases those of *certamente* and *se cadra*, while the post-verbal increases the chances of *certamente* and decreases the chances of *quizais* and *se cadra*. The final position has a strong positive effect on *certamente*. This picture is very similar to the one offered by the pairwise approach. In fact, the current picture matches all patterns provided by the previous approach, and adds new ones, namely the negative effect of the pre-verbal position on *certamente* and *se cadra*.

The one vs. rest approach uncovered a number of patterns concerning TIME that were missing in the previous approach. Future time reference has a significant effect on all adverbs but *se cadra*. It increases the odds of *seguramente, probablemente,* and *posiblemente*, while decreasing the chances of *quizais* and, especially, *certamente*. The future-in-the-past has a negative effect on *certamente* and

Table 7.8 Estimates of the MLR model (one vs. rest approach). Not statistically significant estimates are in parentheses

	cert	segu	prob	posi	quiz	seca
(Intercept)	−1.38487	−1.82787	−1.90177	−1.89686	−1.32265	−1.42496
POLARITYneg	0.82808	−0.48521	(0.03963)	(−0.14768)	(−0.17840)	(−0.11561)
CLAUSEsubord	−0.56844	(0.05094)	0.40958	(0.27726)	(−0.27940)	(−0.05601)
POSITIONpre-v	−0.53095	(0.15069)	(−0.13963)	(0.28473)	0.51281	−0.63502
POSITIONpost-v	0.55426	(−0.19790)	(0.27149)	(0.13179)	−0.54264	−0.39770
POSITIONfin	2.20039	(−0.27342)	(−1.62838)	(−1.64124)	(−0.73444)	(−0.85886)
TIMEfut	−3.04447	0.47482	0.56487	0.69404	−0.71194	(−0.02872)
TIMEfutpast	−1.27834	0.97163	(0.04155)	0.89029	(−0.29476)	−1.64882
TIMEindet	(−0.33971)	(−0.00689)	0.42708	(−0.13866)	(0.06944)	(−0.04471)
TIMEpast	(−0.02923)	0.44772	(0.07460)	(0.22676)	−0.33686	−0.36308
MEDIUMoral	−1.44237	(0.06274)	(−0.00590)	(−0.11227)	(−0.08558)	0.87388

se cadra and a positive one on *seguramente* and *posiblemente*. Indeterminate time reference only affects the odds of *probablemente*, which are favored by timeless SoAs. The past disfavors *quizais* and *se cadra*, while favoring *seguramente*. The only pattern yielded by the pairwise approach that is missing in the one vs. rest approach is a significant effect of indeterminate time reference on *certamente*, but again this is a result of a comparison with *probablemente*, which has a preference for indeterminate time reference.

The two approaches agree completely with each other as far as MEDIUM is concerned: oral contexts favor *certamente* and disfavor *se cadra*. The rest of the adverbs are not influenced by this factor.

The previous approach took *probablemente* as its reference level. Judging from the results of the current approach, this seems to have been an adequate decision, since *probablemente* turned out to be neutral in terms of most of the variables when compared with the rest of the adverbs. Yet, *posiblemente* is even less deviant, so it might also constitute a suitable midpoint.

7.4 Summary and discussion

This chapter has analyzed a number of factors in relation to epistemic adverbs. Some of the variables were purely exploratory, aimed at finding relationships between epistemic adverbs and possibly relevant factors. Other variables were used to test specific hypotheses. This closing section will report and discuss the main findings.

7.4.1 How epistemic adverbs are alike

The focus of the chapter has been on finding what makes adverbs different from one another in order to explain their internal diversity. However, what adverbs have in common is also an important issue.

No relation between epistemic adverbs and the finite verb of the clause they scope over was found. This is not surprising, since adverbs scope over whole predications rather than particular predicates. Clauses qualified by an epistemic adverb have auxiliaries as their finite verb very frequently, but this is probably a trend of clauses in Galician at a general level.

Epistemic adverbs occur almost always in a declarative sentence. The few exceptions are two and six occurrences of possibility adverbs *quizais* and *se cadra*, respectively. Performative uses of epistemic expressions only happen in declarative clauses. Since most of the occurrences of *quizais* and *se cadra* in interrogative sentences do not correspond with descriptive uses, the only remaining alternative is that they express non-epistemic meaning. Discussion of these cases is left for the next chapter, where the meanings of the adverbs will be dealt with (see §8.2.2.3).

Even though relevant differences between adverbs in terms of POSITION were found, all adverbs occur most frequently before the finite verb and, particularly, before the SoA. The initial position is the most common placement for all adverbs. This confirms our second hypothesis (100), according to which the initial position is the default placement for epistemic adverbs.

In the paradigmatic approach laid out by Nuyts (2001a), adverbs are expected to occur in an internal position, as that position is considered to be non-salient from an information-structural point of view. This is the case of (106), where *quizais* is placed between the subject, which functions as the topic, and the predicate, which functions as the comment.

(106) Unha interpretación en tal sentido *quizais* fose válida para o período inmediatamente anterior.
'Such an interpretation maybe was valid for the immediately preceding period.'
(CORGA)

Thus, *quizais* in (106) is a "comment modifier" that precedes the constituent it scopes over, which is usually newly asserted or focal information (see Verhagen, 1986, pp. 82–86). Some authors have linked the medial position to epistemic meaning in the context of adverbs. For instance, Hoye (1997, p. 197) observes that "modal environments tend to favour the interpolation [i.e., medial position] of adverbs which express dubitative meanings," and Suzuki (2018, p. 46) argues that "the occurrence in the medial is the clear evidence that a given adverb is used for epistemic marking." However, this seems to be a property of English and other

Germanic languages. Examples such as (106) are not the norm in Galician, where adverbs have a strong preference for the initial position. A more representative example would be (107).

(107) *Quizais* a miña ollada foi dura de máis.
'Maybe my look was too hard.' (CORGA)

Quizais appears in (107) as the leftmost element of the utterance, preceding the SoA. In the paradigmatic approach, adverbs are not expected in initial position, since such position is taken to be very sensitive to information-structural factors, and adverbs are low-profile expressions from the point of view of information structure. Nevertheless, the initial position is by far the most frequent placement for epistemic adverbs in Galician. This is because the initial position is non-salient, and sentence focus tends to be placed in final position. The initial position allows epistemic adverbs to function as modal themes, different from topical (i.e., predication-internal) themes, setting the modal qualification they express as the point of departure for the message. Epistemic adverbs are "ideal scene-setters" (Hoye, 1997, p. 185) that advance the speaker/writer's judgment of the matter, and serve as a guide to the hearer/reader for interpreting linguistic content. Even in English, the existence of modal themes is widely recognized (e.g., Halliday, 2014, pp. 105–112; Hoye, 1997, pp. 148–152).

These findings question the interaction between the iconic force and the information-structural force as regards the syntax of epistemic adverbs (see §7.1). In Galician there are no grounds for the purported tension between the two forces: epistemic adverbs in initial position satisfy both alike, as they occupy a non-salient position, consistent with their low informational profile, and, by preceding the SoA, reflect the status of the qualification as a meta-operator over the SoA. Hence, the overwhelming prevalence of the initial position in the data.

Adverbs differ significantly in terms of DISTANCE, according to the first MLR approach. Nevertheless, most adverb occurrences are adjacent to the finite verb, and as the distance increases the number of observations decreases, for all adverbs. Therefore, epistemic adverbs are strongly attracted to the finite verb of the clause.

DISTANCE and POSITION are correlated ($\chi^2(9) = 269.19$, $p < 0.000$, Cramér's $V = 0.223$). The probabilities of finding an adverb in initial position and adjacent to the finite verb are the highest: 27.76% of all occurrences. Table 7.9 shows that almost 40% of adverbs in initial position are also adjacent to the verb. It is likely that many of such cases correspond to instances of subject omission. Thus, the syntactic ability to omit the subject may account for this major pattern (i.e., initial, adjacent contexts), but an influence over the initial position at a general level does not follow.

Table 7.9 Bivariate results for DISTANCE and POSITION

	ini N	ini %	pre-v N	pre-v %	post-v N	post-v %	fin N	fin %
adj	498	39.84	155	64.58	234	83.87	4	12.90
near-adj	329	26.32	67	27.92	33	11.83	9	29.03
non-adj	278	22.24	12	5.00	12	4.30	17	54.84
distant	145	11.60	6	2.50	0	0.00	1	3.23

Near-adjacency in initial position is the hardest context to assess. There are many different 1–3-syllables-long linguistic elements that may occur before the verb, some of which are participants in the SoA, thereby topical themes (noun phrases in subject or object function, temporal and spatial adverbs, etc.), whereas others are not (clitics, negative particles, etc.). Without further scrutiny, it is hard to tell whether the 26.32% of initial adverbs in near-adjacent contexts are cases of subject omission. Non-adjacent and distant contexts (> 3 syllables between the adverb and the verb) amount to around a third of the adverbs in the initial, and are likely to contain a topical theme, since the number and length of non-topical elements is limited. Hence, a considerable portion of initial adverbs (33.84% corresponding to non-adjacent and distant contexts) is probably independent from the syntactic ability of Galician to omit the subject noun phrase.

On account of these observations, the strong preference of Galician adverbs for the initial position seems to be (at least partially) independent from the ability to omit the subject or the absence of a more suitable thematic element.[4]

Additional results come from the semantics of the SoA. Adverbs do not differ significantly from one another in terms of either CONTROL or DYNAM, with all adverbs scoping more frequently over states than over any other SoA type. As regards performativity, epistemic adverbs are used performatively in roughly 95% of occasions. This is hardly surprising, since adverbs lack the structural features that enable descriptive uses.

To sum up, a typical occurrence of an epistemic adverb in Galician has the following properties:

- It does not take a degree modifier.
- It occurs in declarative sentences and main clauses.
- It fills the initial position of the clause, performing a thematic function (i.e., it is chosen by the speaker/writer as the point of departure for their message).

---

4. Nuyts (2001a, p. 95) argues that the need of filling the initial position of the clause may account for a number of occurrences of adverbs in initial position in Dutch and German.

- It occurs at a short distance from the finite verb.
- It scopes over non-controlled, non-dynamic events located in the past or the present time.
- It performs an epistemic qualification (i.e., it expresses the speaker/writer's point of view at the moment of speech).

7.4.2 How epistemic adverbs differ from one another

Galician has a sizable number of epistemic adverbs, six of which have been considered here. They span over the whole epistemic scale. The current investigation has shed some light on the factors that underlie the diversity of epistemic adverbial forms.

The ability to take degree modifiers sets apart *seguramente*, *probablemente*, and *posiblemente* from the rest of the adverbs. This is explained on semantic grounds: these three adverbs encode probability, which is a gradual dimension, whereas the other adverbs convey either certainty or possibility, which are not gradual. This confirms our first hypothesis (99). Among the three probability expressions, *probablemente* seems to be more developed in terms of its modification capabilities, since it occurs more frequently and with a higher number of different modifiers than *seguramente* and *posiblemente*. These differences are subtle, but they reveal a higher entrenchment of *probablemente* as a probability adverb, as a result of diachrony – *seguramente* and *posiblemente* have come to encode a probability epistemic value only in recent times (see § 6.2).

MOOD divides adverbs into three groups that do not match the epistemic semantic dimensions. *Certamente* only combines with the indicative, in contrast with the rest of the adverbs, which allow for verbal mood to alternate between the indicative and the subjunctive. Yet, there are differences between the adverbs that license the alternation. *Seguramente* and *se cadra* have a very small share of the subjunctive (approx. 4%), being indistinguishable from one another in terms of mood choice. The proportion of subjunctive selection for *probablemente*, *posiblemente*, and *quizais* ranges from approx. 26% to approx. 50%. Therefore, mood alternation is only licensed by uncertainty adverbs. This underscores the view of epistemic adverbs as irrealis operators over the verbal irrealis marker (i.e., the subjunctive) (Givón, 2001, pp. 313–315). There seems to be a cline according to which subjunctive selection increases as epistemic certainty decreases. The behavior of *se cadra* contradicts this observation: being a possibility adverb one would expect it to have higher rates of subjunctive selection. Diachrony might be a factor explaining this deviance, though. Both *se cadra* and *seguramente* have very low rates of subjunctive selection because they have come to encode epistemic uncertainty only in recent times: the first documented occurrences of *se cadra* are from the second half of the 19th century (see §6.2.3), whereas *seguramente* showed signs of the certainty semantics until the early 20th century (Míguez, 2019). The mood alternation seems to be a morphosyntactic pattern characteristic of uncertainty adverbs, so it is expected that emerging uncertainty adverbs take some time to develop the pattern – note that *seguramente* evolved from encoding certainty, and *se cadra* developed out of a conditional clause, both of which preceding conditions license exclusively the indicative.

Epistemic adverbs scope over negative SoAs in approx. 15% of cases. This is a ratio similar to the one found by Nuyts (2001a, p. 86) for Dutch and German adverbs (approx. 12%). Nevertheless, significant differences concerning polarity were found among Galician adverbs. Whereas the share of negative SoAs revolves around 15% for most adverbs, *certamente* and *seguramente* are deviant in opposite directions, with 23% and approx. 11%, respectively. The reasons for this divergence are unclear. Since these adverbs are opposed in terms of (inter)subjectivity, one could think of the subjective/intersubjective contrast as causing different rates of negation, but then one would have to explain why (subjective) possibility adverbs and (intersubjective) probability ones do not deviate significantly from one another. I have no explanation for these results as of yet, but the coming pragmatic analysis of the adverbs in Chapter 8 may clarify this point.

The initial position is the preferred placement for all adverbs, yet *se cadra* has the strongest preference. This is no doubt related to the diachronic trajectory of the adverb: it originated from a conditional protasis, which by default precedes the main clause or apodosis. Parenthetical (medial) uses are a further step in the development path towards an epistemic adverb. Thus, the strong preference for the initial must be seen as the preservation of a preexisting syntactic pattern, which in itself is a sign of the recent emergence of this linguistic string as an epistemic marker.

Certamente is the adverb in the sample that more easily takes a post-verbal position, either medial or final. This deviant pattern may be related to its epistemic meaning of certainty. Since the default expression for certainty in language is an unqualified assertion, explicitly marking certainty is anomalous by virtue of the Gricean maxim of quantity. As a consequence, it may be the case that markers of certainty, more often than expressions conveying other epistemic values, perform textual or interactional functions along with or instead of epistemic marking. This may explain why *certamente* takes the final position more easily than any other adverb: the right periphery of the clause has been related to discourse functions (Beeching & Detges, 2014). I will challenge this hypothesis in the next chapter.

Post-verbal medial position deserves further attention. According to the MLR study, *certamente* is the only adverb that is favored by this position when compared with the other adverbs. In turn, *quizais* and *se cadra* are disfavored by this syntactic slot, whereas the probability adverbs seem to represent a middle ground between the two former patterns. It is worth noting that the post-verbal position is more strongly associated to adjacency to the verb than any other position (see Table 7.9). It would seem that the post-verbal adjacent position is a sweet spot for -*mente* adverbs, at least sweeter than for non-*mente* forms. This may be due to the length of -*mente* adverbs (4–5 syllables), which might make them too salient so as to be inserted between a topical element and the verb, and may also be a consequence of retention of their original use as manner adverbs, which are placed right after the verb in Galician. The fact that *certamente* is especially sensitive to this restriction might be related to its higher rates of negation, which adds another, possibly salient element (i.e., the negator) to the pre-verbal slot. *Quizais* is favored by pre-verbal medial position when compared with the other adverbs, and this may be a consequence of it being free from the restrictions of -*mente* adverbs and of the preference of *se cadra* for the initial slot.

Interesting patterns have arisen with regard to time reference. *Certamente* is present- and past-oriented, and hardly ever occurs with a time reference with a future component (i.e., future or future-in-the-past). Certainty and the past have been linked in philosophical terms: "If experience is the ground of our certainty, then naturally it is past experience" (Wittgenstein, 1969, §275). It seems, however, that the connection between the explicit marking of certainty and time reference can be extended to include both the past and the present, since *certamente* makes no difference between these two time frames.

Probability adverbs have the strongest preference for the future among epistemic adverbs, although they are most likely to be found in the past, and show up more frequently in the present than in the future. The two possibility adverbs in the dataset prefer the present over the past, and differ as to their relation with the future: *quizais* is disfavored in future contexts whereas the difference between the future and the present is not relevant in predicting the occurrence of *se cadra*. This, again, is due to differences in historical development: the original SoA expressed by the protasis *se cadra* has a future time reference ('if the chance will arise'), which demands a future time reference in the apodosis.[5] Although *se cadra* is well into the grammaticalization path, as shown by its frequent occurrence with past and present time references, which would render the original construction ungrammatical, the high rates of the future compared with *quizais* are a reminder of its origins. Additionally, the fact that *se cadra* is a Type B adverb

---

5. Note that the verbal form *cadra* corresponds to the present tense, since the expression of present and future time references are neutralized in Galician conditional clauses (Álvarez & Xove, 2002, p. 156). Note also that the very close Portuguese form *se calhar* (see Pinto de Lima, 2008) features a future subjunctive form, and that this tense is virtually lost in Present-Day Galician (see Freixeiro Mato, 2000/2006a, pp. 359–370).

that yields an open perspective on the SoA is likely to be connected to the factual openness of future time reference.

Epistemic adverbs have a strong preference to comment on non-future (i.e., present and past) information. When they do scope over future facts a value of probability is usually preferred. Certainty is non-future-oriented, whereas possibility is present-oriented. The connection between past time reference and epistemic dimensions might be epistemological. A past SoA is more likely to be known and reflected upon by the speaker/writer than a non-past SoA, since there is generally more time to process past information. This explains why expressions with a stronger epistemic value, that is, certainty and probability adverbs, qualify past SoAs more often than the weaker possibility expressions do – there is usually more grounds to be sure about the past. This would also explain the association between *seguramente*, the strongest probability adverb, and past time reference. The relation between possibility and the present, on the one hand, and probability and the future, on the other, seems harder to account for in these terms.

Finally, this study has found that contextual variation exists in terms of MEDIUM. Our third hypothesis (101), has been confirmed: *se cadra* is associated with oral contexts.[6] This furthers the idea that more recent epistemic (possibility) adverbs are more interaction-focused than long-established epistemic markers. Cornillie (2010) obtained comparable results when contrasting Spanish *a lo mejor* with *quizá(s)* and the *-mente* adverbs. From a diachronic perspective, these findings support the idea – present in Cornillie (2008) and Míguez (2021) – that epistemic adverbs and close expressions (viz. evidential (semi-)auxiliaries) do not conform to unidirectional (inter)subjectification. In Traugott and Dasher's (2002) framework meanings change in the direction of increased (inter)subjectivity, that is, non-subjective > subjective > intersubjective, but not the other way around. Adverbs such as *certamente* and *seguramente* developed intersubjective (i.e., discourse-oriented) meaning early on, and only later did their subjective (i.e., epistemic) meaning emerge (Míguez, 2021). The present survey has found evidence that suggests that *se cadra* might be undergoing a similar development.

The other adverb that has been found to be sensitive to medium variation is *certamente*, which is highly associated with non-oral contexts. This is in apparent contradiction to the aforementioned idea that *certamente* has a higher discourse (i.e., interactive or textual) load. The coming pragmatic analysis of the adverb may clarify this issue.

---

[6]. I would like to remind the reader that the corpus of study is mainly composed of written language and that oral contexts often correspond to written representations of orality, that is, fictional dialogues and transcriptions of interviews.

CHAPTER 8

Epistemic adverbs
A pragmatic approach

This chapter is concerned with the pragmatics of the six epistemic adverbs previously investigated. It has two major goals. The first goal is to draw the line between epistemic modality, on the one hand, and discourse strategies, namely mitigation and strengthening, on the other hand, using Galician epistemic adverbs as a case study. Epistemic modality was previously characterized as an indication of the degree of likelihood of occurrence of the SoA, as performed by the speaker (§5.2). In this view, epistemic modality is a scalar semantic category that ranges from possibility to certainty, with an intermediate area of probability. Mitigation and strengthening are discourse strategies that modify the illocutionary force of the speech act, downplaying the utterance or reinforcing it, respectively (Holmes, 1984). In §4.2, I argued against the widespread direct association of epistemic values and strategic ones, on the grounds that it leaves the notion of discourse strategy void of meaning. The pragmatic analysis carried out in this chapter will provide empirical evidence to support that view.

The preceding chapter has revealed patterns of variation that seem to be due to the epistemic value encoded by the adverbs: the stronger adverb *certamente* is deviant in many respects (polarity, position, time reference…), whereas probability expressions differ from one another only in minor details, and possibility adverbs have particularities of their own. The second goal of this chapter is to shed light on these contrasts between adverb types by studying their meaning. Thus, attention will be paid to the combination of adverbs with other (near-)epistemic expressions and their occurrence in different contexts.

The chapter is organized as follows. First, the variables and hypotheses are presented (§8.1). A thorough pragmatic analysis of the corpus data is carried out in §8.2. §8.3, §8.4, and §8.5 are devoted to explore the connections of adverb meaning and other factors, namely co-occurring (near-)epistemic expressions and variables such as POSITION and MEDIUM. A summary and discussion of the main findings is offered at the end of the chapter (§8.6).

8.1 Variables and hypotheses

This part of the study uses a number of previously introduced variables, such as POLARITY, AUX, MODFUT, SENTENCE, POSITION, and MEDIUM (see Table 6.1). Its main interest, though, lies in the variable MEANING, whose values are defined and illustrated in the next section. MEANING is interesting by itself, but its relation to other variables cannot be disregarded. Exploring the links between the semantics of epistemic adverbs and factors such as negation or co-occurring expressions may shed new light on the workings of the epistemic modality system. In these particular cases (POLARITY, AUX, MODFUT), the variables are purely exploratory. Nevertheless, the other variables are accompanied by a working hypothesis.

The previous chapter advanced the idea that an epistemic meaning of certainty may not be as viable as other epistemic values. The main reason for this is that explicitly marking certainty is redundant (i.e., it flouts the maxim of quantity), but other pragmatic reasons may be at play too (e.g., marking certainty might be perceived as conveying the speaker's cognitive superiority, thus as threatening for the interlocutor). As a consequence, one would expect that epistemic certainty rarely occurs in discourse and that other pragmatically more viable meanings take its place. Our fourth hypothesis is as follows:

(108) Hypothesis 4. The epistemic meaning in *certamente* is marginal and vulnerable to ambiguity with (an)other, more viable meaning(s).

We have also seen before that epistemic adverbs occur in non-declarative sentences, namely interrogative ones, and that these are not cases of descriptive uses of the adverbs. Since performative epistemic modality only happens in declarative sentences, these cases must correspond to non-epistemic uses. More specifically, it is likely for such uses to pertain to the level of discourse, rather than modality or other domains, given that questions are usually addressed to an audience. The following hypothesis will be tested:

(109) Hypothesis 5. Epistemic adverbs in interrogative contexts fulfill a discourse function.

Finally, oral contexts are assumed to reflect the interaction between interlocutors, or at least to do so more often than non-oral contexts. Accordingly, they must be related to discourse meaning:

(110) Hypothesis 6. Oral contexts are associated with discourse-oriented uses of the adverbs.

8.2 Pragmatic analysis[1]

The analysis consists of a classification of every instance of an adverb into one or more meaning categories. Such categories have been established through observation of the data, that is, by finding differences and similarities between occurrences. Thus, the process was a constant round trip between data and definitions. This procedure, exclusively based on semantic criteria, was followed by Byloo et al. (2007) in their analysis of Dutch *zeker* and English *certainly*. Some authors (e.g., Simon-Vandenbergen & Aijmer, 2007) have used other analytical devices, such as paraphrases, to establish meaning categories, but these are problematic. For instance, if we used *de verdade* 'seriously, honestly' or *efectivamente* 'indeed' to detect the non-epistemic uses of *certamente*, it would soon become obvious that such expressions do not provide a complete match, but rather alter the context where *certamente* originally occurred, and that they possess complex meaning patterns of their own. As a consequence, the use of paraphrases as a methodological tool was dismissed.

Another noteworthy observation has to do with the fact that, on many occasions, assigning a single value to a particular occurrence was not possible. In these cases, all the values observed were reflected in the annotation. These are instances of ambiguous contexts, which are *critical* from a diachronic point of view (Diewald, 2002): ambiguities can offer insights into the origin of a linguistic unit, and may signal future paths of development.

The different meanings are classified in terms of Traugott's (inter)subjectivity, using the unambiguous labels introduced at the end of § 4.3, that is, modality (subjectivity), discourse (intersubjectivity), and other (objectivity/non-subjectivity). Here is a brief preliminary definition of each category:

- Modal uses: *epistemic modality*. The adverb qualifies the SoA in terms of likelihood.
- Discourse-oriented uses
  - *Mitigation*. The adverb downplays the force of the assertion for face-saving purposes.
  - *Strengthening*. The adverb reinforces the assertion.
  - *Tendency*. The adverb provides an orientation to an otherwise neutral polar question.

---

1. An earlier version of this analysis was published in Míguez, V. (2022). On epistemic modality and discourse strategy: evidence from Galician adverbs. *Journal of Pragmatics, 201,* 32–42. https://doi.org/10.1016/j.pragma.2022.09.003

- Other uses
    - *Conditionality*. The linguistic string *se cadra* functions as a conditional protasis.
    - *Situational dynamic possibility*. The adverb expresses a potential inherent in the SoA.

8.2.1 Modal uses

Modal epistemic uses involve an expression of the speaker's assessment of likelihood of the SoA. Adverbs usually convey diverging epistemic values, corresponding to one of three dimensions: certainty, probability, or possibility (see §6.1). Certainty and possibility are conceptually simple, consisting of one discreet semantic value, whereas probability is potentially gradable.

In its epistemic use *certamente* expresses certainty that the (positive or negative) SoA applies. (111) gathers examples of this use.

(111)   a.   Foi esta indeterminación o que o induciu a non dicir nada á policía. Esto e os reberetes fantásticos do sucedido, que *certamente* farían pensar á policía nunha historia de drogas ou alcohol.

'It was this lack of resolution what led him not to tell anything to the police. That and the fantastic details of what had happened, which would certainly lead the police to think of a story of drugs or alcohol.' (CORGA)

b.   Chámanlle imposición e compárana coa que se fixo do castelán outrora. A falacia do argumento evidénciase cun símil que pode parecer antigo: Non é o mesmo destronar un rei lexítimo que repoñelo no seu trono. *Certamente* non leron a Paulo Freire na súa *Pedagoxía do oprimido*, perfectamente aplicábel ao caso do galego.

'They call it imposition, and compare it with what was done with Castilian in the past. The fallacy of the argument is made evident by a simile that may seem old: dethroning a legitimate king is not the same as putting him back in his throne. They certainly did not read Paulo Freire's *Pedagogy of the Oppressed*, fully applicable to the case of Galician.' (CORGA)

The explicit marking of certainty flouts the maxim of quantity, raising pragmatic by-effects, such as signaling that the speaker is not really sure about what they are saying or that there is some reason to doubt it – why would they otherwise *insist* on an element that needs not be marked explicitly? This is the certainty paradox (see §4.2.3), which explains why (111a) and (111b) sound less certain than their unqualified counterparts.

In these examples, what *certamente* does is signal the existence of the epistemic assessment, something that a bare assertion does not do. In (111a) *certamente* expresses an epistemic qualification by the protagonist. However, it is the narrative voice who is producing this piece of language. For an omniscient narrator like this one, it would be strange to utter an epistemic judgment, which would question their unlimited knowledge of events. Thus, the presence of *certamente* forces the reader to interpret the utterance as an epistemic judgment made by the protagonist. The epistemic adverb turns the clause into a prediction by the protagonist (an assessment of likelihood from a past temporal anchor), whereas without the adverb the clause could be interpreted as a report of facts by the omniscient narrator (what *will* happen in the protagonist's time frame, what *has* happened from the point of view of the narrator).

In (111b) *certamente* is used in a similar way, with different effects. This example is part of an article where the author calls for the restoration of all social uses of the Galician language. In this particular excerpt, she argues against the idea that Galician is being imposed, and concludes that the supporters of such "fallacy" do not know Paulo Freire's work. Such supporters are unspecified (their referent is unknown), so the conclusion is introduced by *certamente* to denote an epistemic qualification, thus signaling that the SoA is the product of a reasoning process (rather than, say, world knowledge or hearsay): their ignorance of Freire's ideas is a logical conclusion of the preceding discourse. *Certamente*, conveying the degree of likelihood of the SoA, invites an inferential reading, since the context explicitly mentions the evidence (i.e., the "evident fallacy") leading to the epistemic judgment. This inferential nuance of *certamente* is due to the context and absent in most of its epistemic uses.[2]

Seguramente, *probablemente*, and *posiblemente* convey probability in their epistemic uses, that is, they present the SoA as the preferred hypothetical scenario. The following examples illustrate this.

(112) a. A relación antre espacio e tempo é inequívoca. *Seguramente* foi Aristóteles o primeiro que tentou aprofundar, dentro do pensamento occidental, no concepto de espacio e tamén o primeiro en tentar de establecer a súa relación co tempo.

'The relationship between space and time is unequivocal. Aristotle was probably the first one, in Western thought, who tried to look into the concept of space and also the first one who tried to establish its relationship with time.' (CORGA)

---

2. We must bear in mind that epistemic modality and inferential evidentiality refer to different aspects of the same reasoning process (see § 4.1.4). Therefore, it may be the case that they often implicate one another, although in a way much weaker and more indirect than that of (111b).

b. Segundo a STS de 2 de abril de 2001, a importación de obras lícitas non se podía sancionar conforme ao artigo 270 do CP. Polo tanto, xurisprudencialmente negábase esta posibilidade. O lexislador, sen embargo, en 2003 decántase pola posición contraria e reforma o artigo 270.2 da forma que expuxo. E iso permite pensar que *probabelmente* o que pretende o lexislador penal é precisamente sancionar a importación das copias lícitas e non as ilícitas, xa que esta última conduta xa sería de por si delituosa.

'According to the STS [Supreme Court Judgment] of 2 April 2001, import of legal works could not be punished in accordance with CP [Criminal Code] article 270. Therefore, this possibility was denied in terms of jurisprudence. The legislator, however, opts for the opposite stance in 2003, and reforms article 270.2 in the way they presented. And that allows (one) to think that what the legislator probably intends is precisely to punish the import of legal copies rather than illegal ones, since the latter behavior would already be a criminal act by itself.' (CORGA)

c. Mentres o home dependeu da caza para vivir non puido medrar de maneira notable, xa que non podía facer acopio de alimentos que lle permitiran enfrentarse a épocas de escaseza na caza. É coa aparición da agricultura, no neolítico, cando os alimentos poden acumularse e almacenarse e as poboacións medrar en número. Así, cara ó ano 8.000 antes de Cristo, a humanidade alcanza *posibelmente* unha cifra preto dos 5 millóns de persoas.

'As long as man depended on hunting to survive, he could not grow in a remarkable way, since he could not store up the food that would enable him to deal with periods of game scarcity. It is with the emergence of agriculture, in the Neolithic, when food can be accumulated and stored up, and populations can grow in number. Thus, around the year 8000 BC, humanity probably reaches a figure close to 5 million people.' (CORGA)

The adverbs denote decreasing degrees of probability. (112a) puts forward a stronger hypothesis than that of (112b), which is in turn stronger than the one contained in (112c). Moreover, the epistemic judgment in (112a) is exclusively ascribed to the writer, whereas the ones in (112b) and (112c) are presented as shared between the writers and others – they are opposed in terms of (inter)subjectivity. Example (112b) is especially remarkable in this connection, because it features a syntactic pattern that makes it obvious that the judgment is conceived of as impersonal or not exclusive to the writer (*E iso permite pensar que* 'And that allows (one) to think that...').

Finally, *quizais* and *se cadra* express a neutral stance towards the occurrence of the SoA (i.e., possibility), when used as epistemic markers. Examples are from dialogical contexts – a newspaper interview and a fictional conversation.

(113) a. –¿Roberto Blanco Torres vende máis cós escritores doutros anos?

–*Quizais* estea vendendo máis. Pode deberse á figura e ó espírito que crea Blanco Torres pola forma en que morreu.

'–Does Roberto Blanco Torres sell more than writers from previous years?

–Maybe he is selling more. It may be due to the character and spirit that Blanco Torres creates because of the way he died.' (CORGA)

b. –Era bandida.

–¿Boa ou mala?

–Nunca me parara a pensalo, pero, *se cadra*, era boa –sorriu–. Coma Robin Hood.

'–She was a bandit.

–Good or evil?

–I had never given it any thought, but, perhaps, she was good

–she smiled–. Like Robin Hood.' (CORGA)

In strictly semantic terms a qualification of epistemic possibility expresses that the SoA is not barred by evidence. However, expressions of epistemic possibility are often more than professions of ignorance, and must rely on positive evidence (see Przyjemski, 2017; von Fintel & Gillies, 2008). When the speaker puts forward a particular hypothesis, they are highlighting it as a good candidate to explain some aspect of reality. In fact, reporting on any possibility that may be compatible with what the speaker knows – anything that is not barred by evidence – potentially flouts the cooperative principle, and hinders effective communication. (113) contains examples where the epistemic judgment is (i) relevant on account of a previous intervention by the interlocutor and (ii) based on the speaker's knowledge, which is made explicit in (113a).

These examples also illustrate the distinction between Type A and Type B possibility adverbs (see §6.2). In (113a), *quizais* introduces a hypothesis that was put forward by the interviewer in the preceding utterance; the interviewee is supposed to have knowledge of the topic under discussion and a stance on this particular issue. By contrast, in (113b), the hypothesis is presented as produced at the moment of speech, and there is explicit mention by the speaker to a lack of previous thought on the question. Examples such as these reinforce the idea that *quizais* conveys epistemic possibilities which are (presented as) the result of a careful reflection, while epistemic possibilities introduced by *se cadra* are implied to be improvised while speaking, but further evidence is needed to reach a final conclusion on this matter.

I have previously discussed so-called "concessive uses" of epistemic modal expressions, and concluded that they should not be considered separate meanings, since they do not (exclusively) depend on the epistemic marker, which conveys an epistemic or strengthening meaning, but are rather a property of the bigger context – see the discussion around Example (61). Epistemic adverbs may also play a (key) role in other discourse strategies, such as irony, illustrated in (114).

(114)   Pasaron dous anos desde as últimas eleccións en Galicia. Xa poucos recordan a trasfega das sacas retidas en Caracas ou en Bos Aires. Algúns conxuráronse en desterrar dunha vez por todas tales feitos e irregularidades. Nada se fixo, nada se fará. Parece que o censo exterior cobrará aínda máis peso e transcendencia. *Quizais* en Arxentina siga habendo, milagrosamente, máis de catrocentos galegos centenarios. Só se puido demostrar que vivían 25 deles á hora de votar. Misterios, misterios que non interesa resolver.

'It has been two years since the last elections in Galicia. Very few remember now the transfer of sacks retained in Caracas or in Buenos Aires. Some have come together to eradicate once and for all such actions and irregularities. Nothing has been done, nothing will be done. It seems that the external census will acquire even more importance and significance. Maybe in Argentina there still are, miraculously, more than 400 hundred-year-old Galicians. Only 25 of them could be proved to be alive at the time of voting. Mysteries, mysteries that no one is interested in solving.'   (CORGA)

Ironic uses have been found for *certamente, posiblemente, quizais,* and *se cadra.* In (114) *quizais* conveys an epistemic evaluation, and irony is derived from context, particularly from the writer's knowledge of the electoral fraud and his skepticism on it being solved. The writer even adds evidence against the hypothesis introduced by *quizais* (*Só se puido demostrar que vivían 25 deles á hora de votar* 'Only 25 of them could be proved to be alive at the time of voting'). Thus, it is strongly implied that the epistemic qualification is not put forward as a serious hypothesis by the writer, but it rather serves his discourse goals, namely remarking the scale of the fraud. Ironic uses of epistemic adverbs are aimed at showing the absurdity of the opposite stance. The epistemic adverb enables the ironic reading of the utterance, but, strictly speaking, it does nothing more than conveying an epistemic judgment. In other words, this epistemic qualification in this specific context is interpreted as ironic, but this is not something the adverb does by itself. The same is true for all other cases of ironic readings in the data. Therefore, I have not considered irony as a separate category.

8.2.2 Discourse-oriented uses

This section discusses a range of meanings concerned with interaction management and discourse organization. This is a very broad area that, as will be seen, encompasses a variety of uses of the adverbs. I will occasionally mention textual functions of the adverbs, such as concession, exemplification, and polyphonic triggering, but these are not the focus of this book (see, e.g., Jarrett, 2022, pp. 101–113).

8.2.2.1 *Mitigation*

With the exception of *certamente*, all epistemic adverbs feature mitigating uses. Mitigation is a discourse strategy whose aim is to reduce the force of the assertion, for face-saving purposes, as established in § 4.2.1. In essence, mitigation is a way of sounding less aggressive in order for the message to come across as less unfavorable towards someone – usually, but not necessarily, the hearer/reader. Some examples follow.

(115) a. Traballos coma o de DKTC, Lamatumbá, The Homens, Loretta Martin, Zënzar, Compañía do Ruido, Marful, Galegoz... demostran que a música ferve en cada recuncho, cadaquén co seu carácter propio, por iso recoméndolles ás persoas que se ocupan de facer crítica musical que teñan coidado e sexan respectuosos. *Se cadra* non convén falar de mundos que non se coñecen antes de condenalos.

'Works such as those by DKTC, Lamatumbá, The Homens, Loretta Martin, Zënzar, Compañía do Ruido, Marful, Galegoz... show that music swarms every corner, everyone with their own character, that is why I recommend people concerned with musical review to be careful and respectful. Perhaps it is not convenient to talk about worlds that are unknown for oneself before condemning them.' (CORGA)

b. Apurei a repeti-lo último número do teléfono. Equivoqueime polas présas. *Posiblemente* tampouco nos poderiamos ver hoxe, sentíao. Por moito que insistía e repetía a palabra *sentir*, non me servía de consolo.

'I rushed to repeat the last telephone number. I failed because of the hurry. Possibly we could not see each other today either, he was sorry. No matter how much he insisted on and repeated the word *sorry*, it did not offer me any consolation.' (CORGA)

These are some of the few unambiguously mitigating examples in the data. The adverbs do not convey here an epistemic qualification, but rather downplay the force of the assertion. In (115a) the writer uses *se cadra* to mitigate his deontic judgment, thus sounding less aggressive towards "people concerned with musical review." In (115b) *posiblemente* introduces an indirect speech passage where the first person narrator represents the words of her telephonic interlocutor. The juxtaposition of the sentence led by *posiblemente* and the one containing the apology reveal that the use of the epistemic adverb is purely mitigating, as not being able to meet is not a hypothesis but a fact to be sorry about. An epistemic reading, that is, a judgment about the likelihood of the SoA, does not seem feasible in either case.

It is no surprise that mitigating uses are common in interactional settings: mitigation is often aimed at saving the hearer's face. A typical case involves a directive speech act, which inherently threatens the interlocutor's negative face, that is, the desire of "freedom of action and freedom from imposition" (Brown & Levinson, 1987, p. 61). (116) is such an example.

(116) De súpeto Eva advertiunos que estábamos sós; "*se cadra* deberiamos pedi-la conta". Pero esta circunstancia foi interpretada doutro xeito polo persoal do restaurante, que, na figura da propietaria ..., se achegou a nós, saudou a Nano e, con toda naturalidade, sentou na nosa mesa.

'Suddenly, Eva warned us that we were alone; "perhaps we should ask for the bill." But this situation was interpreted in a different way by the staff of the restaurant, particularly the owner ... who approached us, greeted Nano, and, taking all in stride, sat with us at the table.' (CORGA)

In this example, the quoted speaker uses *se cadra* to introduce her order, thus mitigating the directive speech act. The use of the *pospretérito* or conditional form *deberiamos* 'we should' instead of the present indicative *debemos* 'we must' is also telling, since this is a well-known mitigating strategy (Álvarez & Xove, 2002, p. 281; Freixeiro Mato, 2000/2006a, p. 353).

However typical conversational examples are, mitigation is found in other contexts as well. Examples (115a) and (117) instantiate cases in which, despite a lack of a direct interlocutor, a mitigating discourse strategy is present in the use of the adverbs.

(117) Había só dúas semanas, eu dixera que a moza do Bruto era unha estreita co gusto no cu, e dixérao a voz en grito, un sábado pola noite que todo o mundo anda por aí, e por riba mentres mexaba nunha farola. Ben, algo borracho *quizais* fose, pero agora ía pagalo a prezo de ouro.

'Just two weeks before, I had said that the Brute's girlfriend was prudish and had an awful taste, and I had said so shouting, a Saturday night when everybody is out, and, on top of that, while I was pissing on a streetlight. Well, I was maybe a little bit drunk, but now I was about to pay through the nose for it.' (CORGA)

What is special about (117) compared with the previous examples is that mitigation is used here to save the speaker/writer's (in this case, the first person narrator) own face. Not only does the narrative voice use the possibility adverb *quizais* to reduce the force of an assertion that would compromise him, but he also alters the semantics of the clause by means of the quantifier *algo* 'a bit', a typical example of a *bush*, that is, a mitigator that acts on conceptual (i.e., non-procedural) meaning (see Caffi, 2007, pp. 98–102).[3]

Mitigating uses of *seguramente* deserve a separate mention. There is a recurring pattern in the data that involves the use of *seguramente* with a second person subject and a modal future form. This pattern is common to both mitigating and strengthening uses of the adverb (see Example (124) below). Some of the mitigating examples are the following.

(118) a. Nesta altura do estudio, o lector *seguramente* terá ben claro que a viúva non só está sometida ás tensións que nacen dentro de si senón a todo un cúmulo que provén do entorno social en que se move.

'At this point of the study, the reader probably knows that the widow is subject not only to the tensions arising within herself, but also to all those stemming from the social context she lives in.' (CORGA)

b. *Seguramente* comprobarías que na inmensa maioría de libros de ciencia ou de historia da ciencia a penas podemos atopar algún nome de muller.

'You have probably noted that in the vast majority of science or history of science books we can hardly find any woman's name.' (CORGA)

In these examples, *seguramente* functions as a mitigating device that saves the reader's face. The writer's intentions are to build solidarity with the reader, which is why they explicitly mention the information they assume to be known for the reader, solving the risk of the reader ignoring it. Not using *seguramente* (nor the modal future form) in these cases would be assuming too much on the reader's part, whereas using a possibility adverb would be assuming too little – both options being face-threatening for the reader. The high probability conveyed by *seguramente* seems to provide the perfect fit for these contexts.

If one excludes (115), all of the above cases allow an epistemic reading along with the mitigating one, that is, the adverbs assess the SoA as possible or probable, and, in doing so, downplay the force of the assertion in order to sound less aggressive.

---

3. Quantifiers, just like epistemic expressions, should not be readily considered mitigators: there is no strategic discourse planning when they correspond to the actual state of mind of the speaker/writer (in the example, if one was actually just a little bit drunk). Only if they are used to "minimize" the content in order to save someone's face should they be considered mitigating devices.

8.2.2.2 *Strengthening*

In this use, *certamente* reinforces the assertion it occurs in. This assertion is often some kind of assessment, as in (119), where the speakers/writers express an aesthetic and a quality judgment, respectively.

(119) a. Cunqueiro, que escribe, *certamente*, moi ben non nos agrada moitas veces.

'Cunqueiro, who certainly writes very well, does not please us in many cases.' (CORGA)

b. –Luís Seoane, que naceu en Bos Aires e era fillo de emigrantes, foi probablemente o galego máis universal de todos eses anos … ¿Coñeceuno vostede? ¿Como o recorda?

–Coñecino en Bos Aires a través de Rodolfo Prada. Era un home excepcional, *certamente*.

'–Luís Seoane, who was born in Buenos Aires the child of expatriates, was probably the most universal Galician of those years …

Did you know him? How do you remember him?

–I met him in Buenos Aires thanks to Rodolfo Prada. He was an exceptional man, certainly.' (CORGA)

In (119), *certamente* bolsters the point of view of the speakers/writers, emphasizing their commitment to the assessment (i.e., Cunqueiro's quality as a writer and Seoane's exceptionality as a man). This is a very frequent reason to use *certamente* in its strengthening function. Nevertheless, this use of the adverb is also found with 'neutral' descriptions of facts, as in (120).

(120) a. Unha loba! A tarefa non era doada, máis ben era imposible. *Certamente*, as lobas, para parir e sacar adiante os seus lobetos, afástanse dos seus conxéneres, co que o fillo do ferreiro non tería que enfrontarse a toda unha manda.

'A she-wolf! The task was not easy, it was rather impossible. Certainly, she-wolves get away from their fellow wolves to carry forward their pups, so the blacksmith's son wouldn't have to deal with a whole pack of wolves.' (CORGA)

b. O problema radica en que restan dous asentos para tres grupos, o que de entrada deixa o BNG sen practicamente ningunha posibilidade de manter a vicesecretaría que ocupou Carme Adán no anterior mandato … *Certamente* o regulamento do Parlamento permitiría que o PSdeG quedase cos dous postos, sen ceder ningún nin a AGE nin ao BNG. Esta posibilidade, malia que resta representatividade e pluralidade á Mesa, cobra cada vez maior forza …

'The problem is that there are two seats left for three groups, which at first glance leaves the BNG [Galician Nationalist Bloc] with virtually no chance of keeping the Vice-Secretariat held by Carme Adán in the previous term ... Certainly the regulation of the Parliament would allow the PSdeG [Socialists' Party of Galicia] to retain the two seats, without giving any of them either to AGE [Galician Alternative of the Left] or to the BNG. This possibility, despite it undermines the representativeness and plurality of the Bureau, becomes ever stronger ...' (CORGA)

In (120), *certamente* strengthens utterances that do not convey the personal view of the writer but general information about the world, that is, a description of reality rather than an interpretation thereof – in the above cases, she-wolves habits and Parliament regulation. While the rhetorical usefulness of strengthening one's point of view as in (119) is obvious, the reasons for highlighting "objective" information are less clear at first glance. However, underlining particular pieces of information has more to do with the purported relevance of the latter in the discourse context than with their "(non-)neutrality" or "objectivity." Thus, *certamente* in (120) highlights information that, despite (supposedly) being generally known, is key to understand the situation under discussion. By using the adverb, the writer marks the content of the utterance as part of the common ground between the writer and the reader, thus recognizing the reader as equally knowledgeable and avoiding sounding naive by presenting as new information that is, or might be, widely known – English *of course* works in a similar way (see the discussion around Example (38); Simon-Vandenbergen & Aijmer, 2007, p. 205). The use of *certamente* in the previous Examples (119) is also due to this type of contextual relevance: the aesthetic judgment is strengthened in (119a) in order to downplay the force of the negative view expressed in the main clause, whereas the quality assessment in (119b) is strengthened to show that it is in agreement with the interlocutor's perspective.

The strengthening use is often aimed at triggering a polyphony that enables the speaker/writer to show agreement with an external source. Such source may be explicit, typical instances being the direct interlocutor in a conversation, as in the interview in (119b), and a referred work in an essayistic text, or implicit, as in (120b). This shows that *certamente* codes intersubjectivity, which allows it to evoke different voices in discourse and plays a key role in triggering polyphony, especially when the external source is implicit. Thus, *certamente* in its strengthening uses serves a discourse-structuring function, connecting the assertion it occurs in with other pieces of information, be they preceding or following utterances or implicit expectations. Pietrandrea (2008) found Italian *certamente* to behave in a very similar way.

This ability of the adverb to evoke different voices in discourse may be the underlying cause of the association found between *certamente* and negation in the previous chapter. Negation is inherently contrastive (Nuyts, 2001a, p. 80): a negative expression does not show up for its own sake, but reacts to the corresponding positive view present in or retrievable from the context, which is comparable to what *certamente* as a strengthener often does. The next examples feature cases of strengthening uses in negative polar sentences.

(121) a. Pode parecer unha digresión gratuíta a insistencia en suliñar a viaxe simbólica dos homes de "Nós" dende a cultura europea ata a cultura galega. Mais non o é, *certamente*, para os obxectivos do presente traballo ...

'Insisting on underlining the symbolic journey of the "Nós" generation from European culture to Galician culture may seem a gratuitous digression. But it certainly is not for the goals of the present work ...' (CORGA)

b. Ben é certo que houbo viaxeiros, como a americana Ruth Anderson, que se achegaron con outro coidado e respecto á nosa terra e á nosa xente, e os testemuños dos cales son hoxe obxecto de culto. Pero a realidade foi que, cada vez máis, o movemento gregario das viaxes colectivas e ás présas foise impoñendo e que o que hoxe se pode considerar como unha das fontes de riqueza máis importante do país non derivou, *certamente*, nunha mellora da súa educación na valoración estética e medioambiental.

'It is true that there were travelers, such as American Ruth Anderson, who approached our land and our people with a different care and respect, and their testimonies are today the object of worship. But the reality was that, ever more, the gregarious movement of collective and hasty travels gradually established itself and that what today can be considered one of the most important sources of wealth in the country certainly did not result in an improvement of its education on aesthetic and environmental estimation.' (CORGA)

The negative sentence where *certamente* occurs in (121a) is an adversative clause that negates the immediately preceding utterance. In (121b) what the negative expression does is reject what the writer assumes should be the case in a normal situation, namely that a big source of wealth would improve the country's education in key respects. Negation thus reacts to an opposing positive view in the context. As for *certamente*, in these negative contexts the adverb functions in the same way as in the preceding examples: it marks the content as something widely known and shared between the speaker/writer and the hearer/reader – the solidarity is even greater as both participants are "united" against an opposing stance. These contextual effects are not inherent in the strengthening use, and may be found in the epistemic use as well – although they are clearly more prominent in the former – in examples such as (111b).

Given the tendency of the adverb to interact with (contrasting) contextual information and co-occur with negation, it is no wonder why it is often found in concessive contexts. A typical instance is (122).

(122) O vocabulario, *certamente*, foi enriquecido por un certo número de expresións novas, pero nin o fondo esencial do léxico nin o sistema gramatical, que constitúen o fundamento dunha lingua, foron liquidados ou reemprazados ...

'The vocabulary was certainly enriched by a number of new expressions, but neither the essential lexical pool nor the grammatical system, which constitute the foundation of a language, were erased or replaced.' (CORGA)

In this example, the adverb strengthens the first clause, which is then contrasted with the following clause, introduced by *pero* 'but'. *Certamente* thus reinforces the conceded part of the utterance, flagging that particular piece of information as known and shared. As already noted (§ 4.2.2), there is no reason to classify concessive cases into a separate category. In fact, the adverb's ability to appear either in the conceded clause, as in (122), or in the contrasting clause, as in (121a), makes it obvious that it plays no role in the definition of this syntactic pattern. The adverb may certainly be taken as a signal of a concessive discourse strategy when it scopes over the concession, as it announces the forthcoming contrast, but at any rate the adverb retains its strengthening value – it reinforces agreement, usually in order to render the upcoming disagreement less aggressive.

Strengthening uses are often ambiguous with epistemic uses. In cases such as (123), *certamente* allows both interpretations: it conveys either that the speaker considers it 100% likely that the SoA applies (i.e., epistemic modality), or that they strongly ascertain that what they say is true (i.e., strengthening).

(123) a. Pois tampouco pagaba a pena vivir se tiña de facelo en permanente anguria. Diante de todo contaba a súa tranquilidade. E *certamente* un crime non sería o que mellor lla aportaría.

'Living was not worth it if it had to be done in permanent anguish. His peace of mind was first. And a crime would certainly not be the best thing to give him it.' (CORGA)

b. A solución podia ser un intento de desbloquear o proceso autonómico galego, pero *certamente* non supoñia unha mellora do proxecto.

'The solution might be an attempt to unblock the Galician autonomic process, but it certainly did not constitute an improvement of the project.' (CORGA)

Finally, there is a special case of strengthening that involves the use of *seguramente*, which assesses as highly likely an assumption that threatens the interlocutor's face. Formally, this use is very similar to mitigating uses of the adverb, see (118), since it involves a second person subject and a modal future form. However, context reveals that the intention of the speaker is to challenge their interlocutor, rather than build solidarity with them, and formal differences also exist as regards intonation patterns – the mitigating use has an unmarked intonation, while the challenging use has the intonation typical of declarative sentences preceding tag questions. (124) is the only example of this use in the dataset.

(124) – … Pero, ¿como sabe vostede tanto de nós se nunca viñemos aquí?

–¡Ai, meu neno! –salaiou a Metralla–. Eu sonche soa e o meu único divertimento é falar coa xente, e falando sábense cousas. Ademais aquí na aldea o tempo non corre igual que nas cidades. Aquí temos máis tempo para falar. Gústanos saber o que lle sucede á xente que está connosco, e saber que foi da que xa non está connosco.

–*Seguramente* saberá quen foi Leonel –espetou de pronto Ana, sorprendendo tamén a Miguel.

–¿Leonel? ¿Quen é? Non sei… Non é unha persoa da parroquia, ¿pois non? Anque…, ai si, esperade, algo me soa ese nome, pero non consigo lembrar… ¿Para que o queredes saber?

'– … But, how do you know so much about us if we never came here?

–Oh, my boy! –sighed "the Metralla"–. I am alone, and my only form of entertainment is talking to people, and by talking one gets to know things. Besides, here in the village time does not go by as in cities. Here we have more time to talk. We like to know what happens to people who are with us and what happened to people who are no longer with us.

–Surely you know who Leonel was –suddenly blurted out Ana, surprising Miguel too.

–Leonel? Who is that? I don't know… He's not a person from the parish, is he? Although… oh yes, wait, that name is somewhat familiar, but I can't remember… Why do you want to know?' (CORGA)

In (124), *seguramente* conveys an epistemic evaluation about whether the interlocutor knows someone called Leonel. However, the utterance does more than just put forward a hypothesis: the speaker challenges the interlocutor, since she highly expects that the SoA applies, that is, that the hearer knows Leonel, which needs not be the case. This challenging use crucially depends on the high epistemic assurance encoded by *seguramente*: the absence of an epistemic marker – note that the modal future is also present in the example – would render the sentence a description of facts, whereas the presence of a weaker epistemic adverb, such as *quizais* or *se cadra*, would not threaten the interlocutor's face – it would rather be a polite way of asking for information.

This example illustrates the use of strengthening in conflict settings, where this pragmatic strategy is used to threaten the interlocutor's face for impoliteness purposes. Situations of conflict where these challenging uses arise are not frequent in written language, but they are often found in spoken discourse, as shown in the work of Brenes Peña (2011), focused on television talk shows.

8.2.2.3 *Tendency*

The impossibility of questioning an epistemic evaluation expressed by an adverb is a well-established fact that is explained by the non-availability of (structural) descriptive uses for epistemic adverbs (see Nuyts, 2001a, pp. 57–59). Therefore, epistemic adverbs occurring in interrogative sentences do not express performative epistemic modality, but they may convey epistemic modality descriptively. (125) is an example – the only one in my data – where an epistemic adverb occurring in a question describes an epistemic qualification.

(125) Hai uns meses, dende a Asociación chegouse a afirmar que a sanidade galega podería perder 200 millóns de euros. Agora que a crise parece confirmada, e que mesmo o Ministerio de Economía recoñece a deriva negativa das cifras macroeconómicas, é posíbel afirmar que *quizais* esa cantidade sexa maior?

'Some months ago, the association stated that the Galician healthcare system could lose 200 million euros. Now that the crisis seems confirmed, and even the Ministry of Economy recognizes the negative drift of macroeconomic figures, is it possible to say that maybe that number is bigger?' (CORGA)

This example corresponds to a non-structural descriptive use. The adverb is part of an embedded clause, and is not the questioned constituent – the questioned constituent is rather the adjective *posíbel*, which in this case expresses a deontic judgment. This only confirms our previous assumptions on the limits of finding epistemic qualifications expressed by adverbs in questions.

Epistemic adverbs occurring in interrogative sentences are known to modify the tendency of the question (Bellert, 1977, p. 344; Nuyts, 2001a, p. 58), and the ones found in this study are no exception. *Quizais* and *se cadra* occur in polar questions to achieve special effects in discourse, as in the next examples.

(126) a. –¡¿O meu home?! ¡¿Que deixa a Olimpio dono de todo?! –exclamou Leonor.

–Exacto –confirmou a xuíz. ... –Debe ter moito tino cando lle dea a noticia ó seu home –aconsellou–. Por certo, ¿onde me dixo que estaba?

Chapter 8. Epistemic adverbs   163

E sen agardar resposta, lanzoulle: "Porque... desculpe a indiscreción pero, ¿non morrería?" ...

–¿Está enfermo *quizais*? –aventurouse a dici-la xuíz.

–Non, non, enfermo que eu saiba non –respondeu Leonor.

E antes de que a señoría interrogase de novo, afirmou:

–Está de viaxe.

'–My husband?! He left everything to Olimpio?! –exclaimed Leonor.

–Exactly –confirmed the judge. You must be very careful when telling the news to your husband –she advised–. By the way, where did you say he is?

And without waiting for a response, she blurted out: "Well ... sorry for the indiscretion, but he is not dead, is he?" ...

–Is he sick, maybe?–ventured the judge.

–No, no, he is not sick, as far as I know –replied Leonor.

And before her ladyship could interrogate her again, she stated:

–He is on a trip.'   (CORGA)

b. –¿Por que me observades con tanta curiosidade? –preguntou Hassefus ao universitario– ¿*Se cadra* xamais vistes un estranxeiro?

'–Why are you observing me with so much curiosity? –Hassefus asked the university student– Have you perhaps never seen a foreigner?' (CORGA)

In these examples, the adverbs turn a neutral polar question into a tendentious one, that is, the speakers use the adverb to show that they are biased towards one of the alternatives posed by the question. Specifically, the speakers imply that what is asked is true (in the above cases: 'your husband is sick'; 'you have never seen a stranger'), and this has different effects depending on context. In (126a), it indicates that the speaker suspects that her interlocutor has knowledge about the SoA, thus suggesting that the latter is withholding information from her. In (126b), the concealed affirmation threatens the hearer's face as a reaction to his curious and, one supposes, annoying way of looking. It is obvious that in neither of these examples the epistemic component is the focus of concern.

Interestingly, some Iberian Romance languages (namely, Galician, Portuguese, and Spanish) have a dedicated "epistemic" adverb for questions, *acaso* (see Gerards & Kabatek, 2018, pp. 149–151; Sučić, 2019),[4] which works in a way similar to *quizais* and *se cadra* in the previous examples, but (typically) emphasizing the opposite of what is asked (i.e., adding a negative bias to the question).

---

4. Given the low occurrence of *acaso* in declarative sentences its epistemic character is questionable.

8.2.3 Other uses

Epistemic adverbs were found to convey two different meanings excluded from the realm of modality and discourse: situational dynamic possibility and conditionality. Dynamic possibility is usually characterized as the ascription of an ability to the first argument participant in the SoA (see §2.1.1). A typical example includes the use of the modal auxiliary *can* in a sentence like *She can swim 10 km in a row*. Two types of dynamic possibility are often distinguished, depending on whether the ability is seen as inherent to the participant or as imposed on them. A third type of dynamic possibility is sometimes included (see §2.1.2.1), namely a situational one that expresses possibilities or potentials not related to any participant, but inherent in the SoA. In my sample of Galician adverbs, situational dynamic possibility is conveyed by *posiblemente, quizais,* and *se cadra*. This meaning is always ambiguous with an epistemic modal qualification. In fact, the epistemic reading seems more likely in all cases, but the dynamic interpretation is still feasible. Examples are the following:

(127) a. Eran os animais desta raza os que compoñían o groso das expedicións dirixidas aos matadeiros de fora da Galiza, lugares onde ao efectuar as pesaxes, *posibelmente*, se confundisen os caracteres dunha e outra estirpe.

'It was animals of this breed that comprised the bulk of the shipments headed for slaughterhouses outside Galiza, places where, at the moment of weighing, the traits of both breeds were possibly confounded.' (CORGA)

b. Sempre había que cear ás horas máis dispares. Se cadra un día xantaba ás doce da mañá e ceaba ás once da noite; outro tiña que xantar ás catro da tarde e xa non ceaba; e ó día seguinte había que pasar sen almorzar, e *quizais* xantase ás once da mañá e cease ás cinco da tarde.

'Dinner always had to be had at the most disparate hours. Perhaps one day he had lunch at noon and dinner at 11 p.m.; another day he had to lunch at 4 p.m. and did not have dinner; and on the next day breakfast had to be forgone, and he maybe had lunch at 11 a.m. and dinner at 5 p.m.' (CORGA)

c. Pasou a ser unha rapariga normal, que ía á escola, xogaba cos nenos da rúa e o día das Angustias, *se cadra*, levaba o cadaleito dun meniño salvado ao pé da morte ...

'She became a normal child, who attended school, played with the kids on the street, and on the Día das Angustias [Day of Anguish], perhaps, carried the coffin of a little child saved at death's door ...' (CORGA)

In these examples, the epistemic adverbs can be read as expressing either a potential inherent in the SoA (i.e., dynamic modality) or a possibility/probability based on the speaker's knowledge (i.e., epistemic modality). Some of these examples, particularly (127b) and (127c), can also be viewed as cases of what others have referred to as fictional uses (Pic & Furmaniak, 2012, p. 27) or exemplification (Jarrett, 2022, pp. 101–104), where the adverbs provide concrete examples of what is being discussed in the larger discourse context.

The second non-modal, non-discourse-oriented meaning is conditionality. This use is only found in *se cadra*, which originated from a conditional clause. The availability of this use is a sign of the recent emergence of this epistemic adverb. In the conditional use, the meaning of the expression is compositional, *se* being the conditional subordination marker and *cadra* the present indicative third person singular form of the verb *cadrar*. The expression thus conveys a condition based on chance ('if it happens to be') or convenience ('if it is convenient'). In my samples, the conditional use is always ambiguous with an epistemic modal reading.

(128) a. Pero, se estudiar non lle leva idea, mándao ao conservatorio, que, *se cadra*, acaba na Nacional, dando concertos polo mundo adiante...

'But, if he does not want to study, send him to the music school, since, perhaps/if the chance arises, he ends up in the National [Orchestra], giving concerts around the world...' (CORGA)

b. Ben podemos recapitular agora os principais pontos xa tratados denantes de enfrentármonos ó epilogo deste traballo, a desamortización. Cando tentemos de explicala poderemos, *se cadra*, recoller algún froito de todo o que aquí levamos exposto.

'We may well now summarize the main points discussed, before heading towards the epilogue of this work, the *desamortización* [ecclesiastical confiscation]. When we try to explain it, we will be able, perhaps/if the chance arises/if it suits us, to reap benefits from what we have presented thus far.'
(CORGA)

(128a) exemplifies the most frequent scenario, where the epistemic meaning is ambiguous with a chance conditional. By contrast, (128b) is the only case in the samples where the epistemic meaning coexists with the convenience conditional – note, though, that the chance conditional also seems a feasible reading.

Finally, there is one case of triple semantic ambiguity – the only one found in the samples, besides (128b) – involving *se cadra*: in (129) this linguistic string allows the epistemic modal meaning, the dynamic meaning, and the conditional meaning.

(129) A conclusión de todo isto é que non existen primeiro cousas que despois, *se cadra*, forman relacións, senón que, pola contra, as cousas non son máis que froitos desa esencial relación que constitúe a realidade.

'The conclusion of all this is that there do not first exist things that later, perhaps/possibly/if the chance arises, form relationships with one another, but rather, on the contrary, things are nothing else than products of that essential relationship that reality is.' (CORGA)

8.2.4 Results

Table 8.1 shows the absolute frequency of each use or combination of uses by adverb. The unambiguous epistemic use is the most frequent for all adverbs but *certamente*. Whereas for the rest of the adverbs unambiguous epistemic modality represents between 81% and 99% of their uses, for *certamente* the share goes down to 6%. All instances of ambiguity involve the epistemic meaning. Many ambiguous uses represent a very small fraction of the semantics of an adverb (< 1%), but some are notable, such as the epistemic/strengthening use in *certamente* (19%), the epistemic/conditional use in *se cadra* (9%), or the epistemic/mitigating use in *quizais* and *se cadra* (approx. 5%). Unambiguous non-epistemic uses are rare, such as the mitigating and tendentious ones, with the exception of the strengthening use in *certamente*, which is the main meaning of the adverb (75%).

Table 8.1 Absolute frequency of uses by adverb

	cert	segu	prob	posi	quiz	seca
epist.	18	292	299	292	282	243
epist./cond.	0	0	0	0	0	27
epist./cond./dynamic	0	0	0	0	0	1
epist./dynamic	0	0	0	3	1	4
epist./mitigating	0	7	1	4	15	17
epist./strengthening	57	1	0	0	0	0
mitigating	0	0	0	1	0	2
strengthening	225	0	0	0	0	0
tendentious	0	0	0	0	2	6

In addition to providing the figures on occurrences of each use or combination of uses, I grouped the uses according to the three categories used above (modal, discourse-oriented, and other). The presence of ambiguous instances in the data is problematic in this respect, and requires the use of a particular way of counting when using these labels. Thus, conservative and progressive counts are used. The former favors modality, whereas the latter favors non-modal (i.e., discourse-oriented and other) meanings.[5] In the conservative count, cases ambiguous between a modal reading and a non-modal one are counted as modal; in the progressive count, contexts that yielded both a modal interpretation and a non-modal one are counted either as discourse-oriented or as other, depending on the meanings present – note that no ambiguities between *discourse-oriented* and *other* uses were found. This way of counting will be instrumental in testing our hypotheses. The results are displayed in Tables 8.2 and 8.3.

Table 8.2 Results for MEANING. Conservative count (favors modality)

	cert	segu	prob	posi	quiz	seca
modal	75	300	300	299	298	292
discourse	225	0	0	1	2	8

Table 8.3 Results for MEANING. Progressive count (disfavors modality)

	cert	segu	prob	posi	quiz	seca
modal	18	292	299	292	282	243
discourse	282	8	1	5	17	25
other	0	0	0	3	1	32

8.3 Adverb meaning and co-occurrence with (near-)epistemic expressions

An important concern for functional linguistics regarding the qualifications of SoAs is their ordering or relative scope (see §3.1). Determining the scope of modal categories, such as deontic or epistemic modality, relative to situational categories, such as space and time, is uncomplicated, as the combination of expressions of these qualifications in one clause shows that modal markers are not restricted by situating expressions, as in the examples in (86). However, the scope of modal categories relative to one another and the very possibility of combining two performative modal qualifications in one clause raise a number of issues.

Nuyts (2009) has proposed a "one-commitment-per-clause" principle (see §3.1.3), arguing that speakers are not concerned with expressing their commitment to the SoA in different ways at the same time and that doing so would be too intensive for the processing capabilities of the human conceptual system. He

---

5. Nuyts and Byloo (2015) also use "conservative" and "progressive" counts, but their use of the labels has diachronic connotations which are not intended here.

concludes that "combinations of performative deontic and epistemic, deontic and evidential, or epistemic and evidential expressions in one clause are very hard to find" (Nuyts, 2009, p. 155), and groups problematic cases into four patterns, three of which are compatible with his explanation. In the first pattern, one of the expressions is used performatively and the other descriptively; in the second pattern, both expressions behave as an idiomatic unit which cannot be compositionally analyzed; in the third pattern, both forms are performative, but they occur with an important time lag in between, so that the fact that they appear in the same clause is questionable. The fourth pattern is the only (apparent) actual exception to the principle, since both forms are performative, occur in the same clause, affect the same SoA, and the same lemmas reoccur in several observations, being unlikely that they are mere mistakes. Most of the examples discussed in this section correspond to the latter pattern, specifically, to combinations of an epistemic adverb and a (near-)epistemic (i.e., epistemic or inferential) verb form (i.e., an auxiliary and/or a future tense).

Co-occurrence of adverbs and (near-)epistemic auxiliaries is scarce. The modal verb *deber (de)* 'must' occurs three times in the dataset with an inferential value (once each with *certamente*, *seguramente*, and *posiblemente*). Examples follow.

(130) a. Que teñen en común os técnicos que traballan durante xeiras ilimitadas porque lles apaixona o traballo que realizan e as maquiladoras que realizan xeiras extenuantes para gañar un mísero soldo, os milleiros de obesos do mundo occidental cos milleiros de famentos do mundo enteiro ou o fundamentalismo e o multiculturalismo? Aparentemente nada, pero <u>certamente</u> algunha relación *deberá* existir en tanto en canto son produto dunha mesma sociedade: a da globalización capitalista.

'What do they have in common, the technicians who work for endless sessions because they are passionate about their job and the maquiladoras who work exhausting sessions to earn a miserable salary, the thousands of obese people in the Western world and the thousands of hungry people in the whole world, or fundamentalism and multiculturalism? Apparently nothing, but some relation must certainly exist as far as they are products of the same society: that of capitalist globalization.' (CORGA)

b. É Parménides, antes que Platón –e Nietzsche ten moita razón en velo así– o verdadeiro fundador da filosofía e da racionalidade, de aí que a intuición do sen sentido do mundo conleve a condena radical do pensador eleático: Parménides dixo: "non se pode pensar o que non é". Nós estamos no outro estremo e dicimos: "o que pode ser pensado *debe* ser <u>seguramente</u> unha ficción".

'It is Parmenides, before Plato – and Nietzsche is quite right in seeing it like this – the true founder of philosophy and rationality, hence why the intuition of the nonsense of the world leads to the radical condemnation of the Eleatic thinker: Parmenides said: "what is not cannot be thought." We are in the opposite end, and say: "what can be thought must probably be a fiction."' (CORGA)

c. Non sei exactamente de que argumentos bota man pero *imaxino* que, <u>posibelmente</u>, se *debe* remitir ao socorrido exemplo de Xaime Quintanilla.

'I do not know exactly what arguments he uses, but I imagine that, probably, he must be referring to the frequent example of Xaime Quintanilla.' (CORGA)

In these examples, both the adverb and the modal auxiliary are no doubt used performatively, and affect the same SoA. In two of the examples there are not just two but three qualificational expressions for the same target – note the future tense form of the modal auxiliary in (130a) and the verb form *imaxino* 'I imagine' in (130c). The example featuring *certamente* offers some doubts as a relevant instance of a combination of an epistemic adverb and a modal auxiliary, since the most likely value for the adverb in this context is strengthening – combining the '100% likelihood' value of *certamente* with the weaker reliability of *deber* yields a contradiction. The other two cases are not so easily dismissed, though. In these, the two (or three) expressions work together to convey the writer's hypotheses/suspicions, being therefore harmonious or, at least, not contradictory in semantic terms. The question arises then as to what semantic value(s) the combined expressions convey – epistemic modality, inferentiality, or both? I will address the possible answers to this question after going through some examples featuring the auxiliary *haber (de)* and modal future forms.

The auxiliary *haber (de)* with an inferential value combines with all probability adverbs. It occurs once with *posiblemente*, twice with *seguramente*, and three times with *probablemente*. These are some of the examples.

(131) a. De brigada non pasaría, como así foi, e con esta graduación e as difamacións recaídas sobre a súa persoa *haberia de* morrer, <u>seguramente</u>.

'He would not be promoted beyond warrant officer, as it happened, and with such rank and the defamation fallen upon his person he would die, probably.' (CORGA)

b. Alí, no cume coñecido como Faro de Entenza recibe ese nome [cadeira do rei mouro] un escano situado baixo unha laxe, onde <u>probabelmente</u> o rei mouro *haberia de* sentar, da mesma maneira que o faría no castro de Flores, en Feás, no concello de Aranga.

'There, in the peak known as Faro de Entenza, that name [seat of the Moor king] is bestowed to a bench under a big rock, where the Moor king would probably seat, as he would do in the *castro* [fort] of Flores, in Feás, in the municipality of Aranga.' (CORGA)

c. Nos mobles –cadeiras, sillas, mesas– descansaban follas de periódicos, que, por abandono, non se botaran, e <u>probablemente</u> non se *habían* botar nunca, nas papeleiras.

'On the furniture – stools, chairs, tables – there lied newspapers sheets, which, as a result of abandonment, were not thrown in the bin, and would probably never be.' (CORGA)

d. Ó doutor Livesey <u>posiblemente</u> a fortuna adquirida lle *había de* servir para mercar novos aparellos e libros actualizados da ciencia médica, novas menciñas…, ou para adquirir unha boa colección de pipas, escravo como era do tabaco.

'Doctor Livesey would probably use the fortune obtained to buy new devices and updated medical science books, new medicines… or to acquire a nice collection of pipes, being a slave of tobacco as he was.' (CORGA)

The Romance morphological future is known to have originated from the merging of the infinitive and the present tense forms of Latin *habeo* (e.g., *cantare habeo* > *cantarei*), whereas the conditional stems from the combination of the infinitive and the imperfect forms of *habeo* (e.g., *cantare habebam* > *cantaría*).[6] Thus, the morphological future tenses and the modal *haber (de)* in Galician originated from the same Latin construction, and their formal similarity is still perceivable (compare synthetic *cantarei* and analytic *hei (de) cantar*). There are also parallels in the semantic domain, as the modal resembles the morphological future in that a form in the present tense may indicate either future temporal reference or present temporal reference with an inferential reading: as Freixeiro Mato (2000/2006a, p. 472) points out, *serán as dez* (future tense) is synonymous with *han (de) ser as dez* (modal *haber (de)*), both meaning 'it must be 10 o'clock'. These parallels notwithstanding, the periphrasis *haber (de)* + infinitive often has a future, rather than present, temporal value, relative to either a present or a past reference point – what we have been calling future and future-in-the-past time references. With a future temporal value, the morphological future and the periphrasis are different in that the latter always has a modal component which is not necessarily present in the former. Therefore, using the periphrasis exclusively as a future marker sounds hardly acceptable: *o gañador recibirá/??ha (de) recibir 5000 euros* 'the winner will earn 5,000 euros' (cf. Álvarez & Xove, 2002, p. 356). The same

---

6. See Ferreiro (1999, pp. 300–304) for a Galician account.

relations exist between the morphological conditional or *pospretérito* and the auxiliary in its past forms (*había/habería (de)* + infinitive).

In the dataset, no instance of inferential *haber (de)* with a present time reference was found. In all of the above Examples (131) *haber (de)* conveys an inferential value concerning a future-in-the-past SoA. Thus, *haber* occurs in the conditional (*habería*) in the first two examples and in the imperfect (*había*) in the last two instances. The temporal and modal values of these two alternative tenses are equivalent, and both forms seem interchangeable in these contexts. Again, we are facing in these examples the combination of an epistemic adverb and an inferential verb form.

As for the modal future, it is by far the most frequent co-occurring form, combining with all adverbs on 60 occasions in total. The adverbs most attracted to the modal future are *seguramente* (27 cases) and, to a lesser extent, *probablemente* (14 cases). *Posiblemente*, *quizais*, and *se cadra* co-occur with modal uses of the future in between 5 and 7 cases each. *Certamente* only co-occurs once with the modal future, see (130a).

(132) a. Son dúas as plantas deste tipo que se producen: o liño e o sirgo. O primeiro *tería* <u>seguramente</u> unha importancia maior, por ser o seu uso máis común, e del temos cinco citas, a última xustamente de 1400.

'Two plants of this type are produced: flax and silk. The former had probably greater importance, as its use was more widespread, and we have five quotes thereof, the last one precisely from 1400.' (CORGA)

b. Quen non concorde con isto <u>probablemente</u> tampouco *aturará* a Warhol (e quen non atura a Warhol non entende case nada da arte contemporánea).

'Whoever does not agree with this probably does not withstand Warhol either (and whoever does not withstand Warhol understands next to nothing about contemporary art).' (CORGA)

c. un exemplo desto témolo por exemplo en Narón donde, como xa vimos, existia un Sindicato Agrario de Oficios Varios, sendo difícil poñer os límites entre as actividades de oficio e as propiamente agrarias, que <u>posibelmente</u> *estarían* interrelacionadas en maior ou menor medida.

'We have an example of this in Narón, where, as we have already seen, there was a union of farmers and various trades, being difficult to establish the limits between trading activities and actual farming activities, which were probably interrelated to a greater or lesser extent.' (CORGA)

d. <u>Quizais</u> *será* esta penuria de medios a razón de vender tódolos utensilios dous anos despois do seu establecemento, segundo lemos no libro de notas da "Unión Obrera" na súa sesión inicial.

'Maybe this scarcity of means is the reason to sell all utensils two years after its establishment, according to what we read in the notebook of the "Unión Obrera" [Workers Union] in its initial session.' (CORGA)

e. Un tampouco entende como estes pequenos países chegaron a un equilibrio xusto de poboación urbana e rural, de desenvolvemento agrario e industrial, e aquí nin de lonxe podemos pensar en algo semellante. *Serán* máis intelixentes, digo eu. Ou *terán* mellores políticos, <u>se cadra</u>.

'One does not understand either how these small countries reached a fair balance between urban and rural population, between agricultural and industrial development, whereas we are far from conceiving something similar here. They are more intelligent, I guess. Or they have better politicians, perhaps.' (CORGA)

The examples above feature cases of an epistemic adverb and one (and sometimes two) inferential expressions. I suggested earlier (at the end of § 4.1.4) that a corpus analysis could shed light on the problematic semantic status of these expressions and serve as a complement to judgments based on intuitions. According to the semantic interpretation of the examples, the three expressions of interest (auxiliaries *deber (de)* and *haber (de)* and the modal future) convey inferential, rather than epistemic, values. In the above examples, *deber (de)*, *haber (de)*, and modal future forms are concerned with the degree of reliability of the inference of the SoA. Arguments in support of this interpretation are the presence of the inferential cognitive verb *imaxinar* in (130c) and the behavior of the modal future in questions: in contrast with epistemic adverbs, which modify the tendency of the question, as seen above (§ 8.2.3), or epistemic adjectives, which, allowing descriptive uses, question the epistemic qualification (Nuyts, 2001a, p. 76), modal uses of future forms in interrogative contexts behave differently. Consider the following examples from Italian and Galician:

(133) a. Dove sarà la chiave?

'Where is the key I wonder?'

b. Gianni sarà di Amburgo?

'Is Gianni from Hamburg I wonder?'

(Eckardt & Beltrama, 2019, p. 148, their translation)

(134) a. Distraída, miraba polas fiestras os movementos privados dos veciños. É un vicio que teño dende sempre, imaxino as vidas das persoas que viven tras os cristais. Como *serán*? *Terán* libros? Plantas? Canciños de porcelana?

'Distracted, I looked the private movements of the neighbors through the windows. It is a vice I have always had; I imagine the lives of the people who live behind the glasses. What are they like? Do they have books? Plants? Little porcelain dogs?' (CORGA)

b. O primeiro que lle chamou a atención foi o feito de que David non estivese alí, ela dixéralle que despois das sete o agardaba na rocha. Pero non se vía o seu vehículo por ningures. ¿Por onde *andaría*? O mellor xeito de saír de dúbidas era mirar na pantalla do seu aeromóbil, alí podería ver se David se atopaba preto ou lonxe.

'The first thing that caught her eye was the fact that David was not there; she had told him that she would wait for him at the rock after 7. But his vehicle was nowhere to be seen. Where was he? The best way to find out was to look at her aeromobile screen; there she could see whether David was close or far away.' (CORGA)

In these interrogative contexts, the modal future forms in Italian and Galician behave like inferential expressions of languages with grammatical systems of evidentiality, yielding "conjectural questions," which "convey[s] the speaker's curiosity about a certain issue" (Eckardt & Beltrama, 2019, p.125) and do not require the addressee to answer. In fact, the Galician examples are verbal representations of thought, where an answer from an interlocutor is not even feasible. Their sole purpose is to convey the wondering about a situation.

The modal verb *deber (de)* contrasts with *haber (de)* and the inferential future in terms of the degree of reliability of the inference – the former encodes high reliability, the latter convey low reliability. Squartini (2008) shows that the equivalent devices in French and Italian differ as to the types of informational bases they are compatible with. In Galician, the picture is roughly the same as that reported by Squartini (2008): *deber (de)* allows circumstantial inferences, of a sensory basis, and generic inferences, of a cognitive basis, but not conjectures, which lack an informational basis; whereas *haber (de)* and the future are compatible with generic inferences and conjectures, but infelicitous with circumstantial inferences (see § 4.1.4). Written language favors generic inferences, based on speaker's knowledge and experience, over circumstantial inferences and conjectures. Thus, all the examples above excluding (133) and (134) correspond to generic inferences, with the arguable exception of (132e), where the future forms convey conjectures. The functional overlapping of *deber (de)* and the inferential future with respect to generic inferences might explain why both devices occur in the same clause – actually, in the same word, *deberá* – in (130a).

At this point, we must address the main concern regarding the previous examples: what is the meaning of epistemic adverbs and inferential expressions in their performative uses when they affect the same SoA? According to Nuyts's (2009) principle, only one qualification can be present in the same clause, so both expressions together should convey either epistemic modality or inferential evidentiality. This option seems hardly satisfactory, as it raises the thorny issue of which domain would prevail, and why. Epistemic adverbs are clearly epistemic, while inferential expressions have a disputed semantic status (see §4.1.4). Thus, one could argue that the latter are actually epistemic, rather than inferential, and that both expressions convey in fact the same qualification. However, the presence of unambiguously inferential forms, such as *imaxino*, in perfectly acceptable examples, such as (130c), challenges this account. Similarly, it is far-fetched to argue that *posiblemente* loses the epistemic semantics or that *imaxino* is deprived of its inferential meaning because the other marker is present in the clause. The only alternative is to accept the combination of two qualifications in one clause, as Cornillie (2009) proposes. From this perspective, the inferential expression reflects the reliability of the reasoning process leading to the SoA, whereas the epistemic adverb assesses the likelihood of the SoA resulting from that reasoning process. In other words, "[e]vidential expressions indicate that there are reasons for the assumption made by the speaker and epistemic expressions evaluate that assumption" (Cornillie, 2009, p. 57).

The results of the corpus study show that the combination of inferential forms and epistemic adverbs in the same clause is, in general, very rare. Therefore, they support Nuyts's (2009) "one-commitment-per-clause" principle, if considered a general tendency of language, rather than a categorical rule. However, the most frequent case of co-occurrence, that of *seguramente* and the inferential future, accounts for 9% of the total occurrences of the adverb, which, despite being modest, suggests that the pattern has some degree of entrenchment and is far from being exceptional.

The last case of co-occurrence is that of the auxiliary *poder* 'can/may', which has an epistemic meaning in 13 observations of the dataset. It co-appears five times with *quizais*, five times with *se cadra*, twice with *certamente*, and once with *posiblemente*.

(135) a. Eva Comín afirma nun artigo (*Aten Primaria* 2007; 39 (11): 587–9) que nos países desenvolvidos, con incidencias baixas da doenza e programas de cribado poboacionais, "o impacto da vacinación será bastante menor que nos países en vías de desenvolvemento, onde o cribado de lesións de colo uterino está pouco estendido". <u>Certamente</u>, neses países a vacinación de adolescentes antes do inicio da actividade sexual *podería* ter unha repercusión importante na redución da incidencia do cancro de colo de útero, cunha boa relación custo-beneficio.

'Eva Comín argues in an article (*Aten Primaria* 2007; 39 (11): 587–9) that in developed countries, with a low incidence of the disease and population screening programs, "the impact of the vaccine will be much lower than in

b. Unha boa idea realizada por un empresario con poucos recursos de todo tipo non sae. Compartida cun ou con varios pode ser un éxito. <u>Posiblemente</u>, a relación co Norte de Portugal *poida* ir, nun próximo futuro, por este camiño.

'A good idea put into practice by a businessman with few resources of all sorts does not work out. Shared with one or several others it may be a success. Possibly/probably, the relation with North Portugal might go this way in the near future.' (CORGA)

c. O salario no campo sería mesmo unha axuda para cidadáns en mala posición, que acudían desa forma ó pluriemprego. Johan, zapateiro, traballa nunhas viñas de Mor Rodrigues, xunto con outros catro labradores "da dita Mor Rodrigues", expresión que parece indicar que tales xornaleiros non eran temporeiros, senón que dispuñan dun contrato máis firme. A situación destes *podía* ser, <u>quizais</u>, a dunha categoría asimilada ou próxima á de criados.

'The salary in the countryside was even a way of assistance for citizens in a bad position, who thus resorted to moonlighting. Johan, a shoemaker, works in the vineyards of Mor Rodrigues, together with other four plowmen "of said Mor Rodrigues," an expression that seems to indicate that such laborers were not seasonal workers, but had a more stable contract. They might have had, perhaps, a category assimilated or close to that of servants.' (CORGA)

d. … logo, no xuicio, pode ser que o culpable non mereza privación de libertade, nin alonxamento, nin traballo temporal nunha granxa; a sanción *pode* consistir, <u>se cadra</u>, en mandalo a unha escola, ou talvez amonestalo, diante dos veciños ou dos seus compañeiros de labor.

'… then, at trial, it may be that the culprit does not deserve deprivation of liberty, nor estrangement, nor temporal labor in a farm; the punishment may consist, perhaps, in sending him to a school, or maybe admonishing him in front of his neighbors or workmates.' (CORGA)

In (135a), *certamente* strengthens the epistemic judgment expressed by *poder*. This is a very good illustration of the intersubjective, polyphonic character of the adverb, which serves the writer to align himself with the previously quoted author, whose words are taken as a point of departure for the subsequent discourse. An epistemic reading in this case is not feasible, since the differing degrees of likelihood encoded by *certamente* (certainty) and *poder* (possibility) would yield a contradiction.

The interpretation of *posiblemente* and *poder* in (135b) is problematic in part precisely because of this type of semantic clash. A non-epistemic value for *poder* seems hard to obtain, be it dynamic or deontic. In fact, the role of *posiblemente* as the modal theme of the clause sets an epistemic tone that is hard to cancel. There are two alternative valid interpretations of this example. In the first one, the adverb and the modal verb convey a harmonious qualification, that is, both express epistemic possibility. This is not unreasonable, since *posiblemente*'s meaning has shifted from possibility to probability (see §6.2.2). Semantic changes do not spread instantly nor uniformly across the language community, so synchronic availability of competing meanings is to be expected – thus, finding speakers with different semantic representations of the same item would not be surprising. In the second valid interpretation, the writer includes *posiblemente* at the beginning of the utterance, and, when producing the SoA, rethinks its likelihood in terms of a (slightly) different value. This alternative is probably less likely, given that writing usually provides enough time to plan one's utterance carefully, although production errors are possible even in very controlled settings.

Finally, *quizais* and *se cadra* co-occur with epistemic *poder* in the last two examples of (135). The adverbs and the modal verb convey the same epistemic value, so their co-occurrences can be considered harmonic. Although infrequent, these cases show that speakers may feel the need to mark the same content in different ways in the same clause. Marking the same epistemic, or, generally, modal, meaning in several ways in the same utterance is probably related to a desire of being very explicit about one's attitudes. Moreover, the redundant marking of particular semantic values may also be a natural tendency of language production, especially in spontaneous contexts – think of how common expressions such as *subir arriba* 'go-up upward' are in informal speech, and how hard to find they are in more formal contexts.

In summary, co-occurrence of epistemic adverbs and (near-)epistemic expressions is rare in written language at a general level. However, some particular patterns are recurrent, and deserve further attention, especially on account of the semantic particularities of the combined expressions.

8.4 Adverb meaning and position

The previous chapter has revealed that epistemic adverbs in Galician have a strong preference for the initial position, occupy the medial position in some cases, and very rarely occur in final position. In turn, the current pragmatic analysis shows that modal meaning is predominant among epistemic adverbs. *Certamente* is the most deviant member of the paradigm, as it occurs in final position more frequently than any other adverb and conveys discourse-oriented meaning in most of its occurrences.

Beeching and Detges (2014) put forward the idea that the left and right peripheries of the utterance (LP and RP, respectively) are functionally asymmetric. In particular, they claim that items at LP are usually subjective (modal, for our purposes), while those at RP are likely to be intersubjective (discourse-oriented, in our terms). A first concern when dealing with these notions is their characterization. Typically applied to spoken discourse, LP and RP are located either at the beginning or at the end of the turn. Thus understood, the notions are hardly useful for the analysis of our data, since the vast majority of observations are from written language, where turns are usually absent. A model that permits greater granularity is the one proposed by Degand (2014), which distinguishes between the peripheries of the turn and the peripheries of the clause.

At the peripheries of the turn 31/195 oral examples (28/190 at LP, 3/5 at RP) are relevant. At LP most examples perform a modal function: 20 observations correspond to unambiguous epistemic uses, five to uses that allow a modal or a discourse reading, namely, epistemic possibility and mitigation, whereas three are unambiguously discourse-oriented, corresponding to strengthening and challenging meanings. Several of these examples are found in journalistic interviews, one of the most common types of interactional contexts in the dataset. In such situations, interviewers often present a hypothesis as a way of bringing up a particular topic, prompting the interviewee's comment on the issue. We have such an example in (136a). On other occasions, it is the interviewee who uses an epistemic adverb to begin their turn, either to introduce a mitigated reply that nuances their interlocutor's stance, as in (136b), or to strengthen their assertion, confirming the interviewer's claims, as in (136c) – an additional example is (113a) above.

(136) a. ENTREVISTADOR: Moitas competencias das comunidades autónomas do Estado Español están a ser conculcadas co pretexto de Bruxelas.

ENTREVISTADO: Pero tamén hai parcelas de soberanía dos estados que están sendo cedidas a Bruxelas, ás veces inconstitucionalmente.

ENTREVISTADOR: *Quizais* a palabra do futuro sexa "integración"…

ENTREVISTADO: Eu creo que o obxectivo histórico dos nacionalismos foi a reformulación radical do Estado, é dicir, das relacións entre as distintas nacións ou comunidades, ou como se queiran chamar. E eso segue aí…

'INTERVIEWER: Many competences of autonomous communities of the Spanish State are being infringed with the pretext of Brussels.

INTERVIEWEE: But there are also areas of the sovereignty of States that are being handed over to Brussels, sometimes unconstitutionally.

INTERVIEWER: Maybe the word of the future is "integration"...

INTERVIEWEE: I think that the historical goal of nationalist movements was the radical reformulation of the State, that is, of the relations between the different nations or communities, or however they want to be called. And that is still there...' (CORGA)

b. ENTREVISTADOR: Pero os teléfonos de gama alta xa rozan os 700 euros e tamén están afectados pola obsolescencia funcional. Non podemos gastar esa cantidade cada dous anos...

ENTREVISTADO: *Quizais* non sexa necesario tanto. Dende o 3G, comercializáronse catro versións máis de iPhone. Eu, por exemplo, pasei do 3G ao iPhone 4 e, de momento, síntome satisfeito. Cando cambie de teléfono fareino pensando en termos de durabilidade.

'INTERVIEWER: But high-end smartphones are close to 700 euros, and are also affected by functional obsolescence. We cannot spend that amount of money every two years...

INTERVIEWEE: Maybe that much is not necessary. Since 3G, four more versions of iPhone have been commercialized. For instance, I went from 3G to iPhone 4, and, to date, am satisfied. When I replace my phone I will do so thinking in terms of durability.' (CORGA)

c. ENTREVISTADOR: ... ¿non sería a influencia de Dámaso e de Lapesa o que vos condicionou, aínda que a ti de forma eventual, cara ós estudos filolóxicos?

ENTREVISTADO: *Certamente* cando estudiabamos en Madrid, tanto Lorenzo, coma Bernardino, coma min, fomos conscientes de que tiñamos que aproveita-la Escola de Filoloxía Española para cando chegásemos a Galicia funda-la Escola de Filoloxía Galega.

'INTERVIEWER: ... wasn't the influence of Dámaso and Lapesa what led you [plural], although in a temporary way for you [singular], to philological studies?

INTERVIEWEE: Certainly, when we studied in Madrid, Lorenzo, Bernardino, and I were aware that we had to take advantage of the Spanish Philological School so as to found the Galician Philological School when we came to Galicia.' (CORGA)

These examples by no means exhaust adverb uses at the LP of the turn. Such uses are common in fictional dialogues as well, such as (124), and (116), where we find discourse-oriented functions.

As for the turn's RP, the three examples are two tendentious uses (*quizais* and *se cadra*) and one epistemic use (*seguramente*). Tendentious uses have already been analyzed, and an example at RP can be found in (126a). (137) is a case of an epistemic use at the RP of the turn.

(137) – ... Volve a Madrid inmediatamente. Onte deixaches a auga do baño aberta, inundaches o piso e caeu para o de abaixo. Xa ves o irresponsábel que es, que vas facer por aí ti soa, acabarás a mercé de calquera. Volve á casa inmediatamente e obedece ao teu pai. Quero falar contigo.

–Xa que o sabes non cho teño que dicir, vou de viaxe. É un asunto persoal, chamoume unha amiga, volverei a Madrid o luns *seguramente* –improvisou.

–¿Pensas que chupo o dedo? Sei perfectamente onde vas e con quen vas. Seguro que está el agora contigo.

'– ... Come back to Madrid immediately. Yesterday you left the water in the bathroom running, you flooded the floor, and it fell downstairs. You see how irresponsible your are; what are you going to do out there alone? You will end up at the mercy of anyone. Come back home immediately, and obey your father. I want to talk to you.

–Since you know it I don't have to tell you, I'm going on a trip. It's a personal matter, a [female] friend called me, I'll be back in Madrid by Monday, probably –she improvised.

–Do you think I was born yesterday? I perfectly know where you go and who you go with. Surely he is with you right now.'　　　　　　　　　　(CORGA)

The occurrence of the epistemic use at the end of the turn in (137) is to do with the improvised character of the SoA, explicitly mentioned in the text. The speaker does not start the sentence announcing her stance, as it frequently happens, but adds the adverb as an afterthought. Given that the epistemic qualification operates over the SoA, it cannot be thought before the SoA has been conceived of. Since this SoA was devised while speaking, its meta-operator was produced after the SoA itself, constituent order thus reflecting the order of the conceptualization processes.

At the peripheries of the clause we find all observations with an initial or a final adverb – this also includes the ones at the peripheries of the turn, just discussed. Tables 8.4 and 8.5 contain the distribution of meanings by position in the conservative and the progressive count, respectively (see §8.2.4 on this counting system). Both modal and discourse-oriented meaning show a consistent pattern across counts. Both types of meaning occur far more frequently in initial position (at least > 64% of cases). Modal meaning makes no difference between pre-verbal and post-verbal medial positions, whereas discourse-oriented meaning clearly prefers the post-verbal over the pre-verbal medial position. Discourse-oriented meaning has a higher share of final placement vis-à-vis modal meaning (<1% vs. >6%). The final position is the least frequent placement overall, only surpassing pre-verbal medial position of discourse-oriented meaning in the conservative count. The observations with an adverb in final position correspond to nine unambiguous epistemic uses (*se cadra*: two; *quizais*: one; *posiblemente*: one; *probablemente*: one; *seguramente*: four), two epistemic/strengthening uses (*certamente*), 17 unambiguous strengthening uses (*certamente*), and three tendentious uses (*quizais*: two; *se cadra*: one).

Table 8.4 MEANING by POSITION. Conservative count

	modal		discourse	
	N	%	N	%
ini	1098	70.20	152	64.41
pre-v	224	14.32	16	6.78
post-v	231	14.77	48	20.34
fin	11	0.70	20	8.47

Table 8.5 MEANING by POSITION. Progressive count

	other		modal		discourse	
	N	%	N	%	N	%
ini	29	80.56	996	69.89	225	66.37
pre-v	6	16.67	206	14.46	28	8.26
post-v	1	2.78	214	15.02	64	18.88
fin	0	0.00	9	0.63	22	6.49

A statistically significant association between MEANING and POSITION exists: $\chi^2(3) = 85.752$, $p < 0.000$, Cramér's $V = 0.218$ (conservative count); $\chi^2(6) = 71.006$, $p < 0.000$, Cramér's $V = 0.140$ (progressive count). This involves a positive association between discourse-oriented meaning and the final position (or: RP) and a negative association between the latter and modal meaning. The initial position (or: LP) makes no significant contribution to the χ^2-statistic, according to the standardized residuals. A look at Tables 8.4 and 8.5 reveals that adverbs occur at LP in the vast majority of cases, even when they perform a discourse function. Thus, strictly speaking, a functional asymmetry between LP and RP does not hold. This is in accordance with Beeching and Detges's (2014, p. 18) own conclusion that the peripheries hypothesis "cannot be upheld in a 'strong' and exclusive way." Nevertheless, our results show that discourse-oriented meaning is more attracted to RP than any other type of meaning and that most adverb occurrences at RP are discourse-oriented (20 discourse-oriented vs. nine modal vs. two ambiguous). RP is strongly disfavored at a general level by epistemic adverbs, but discourse-oriented meaning significantly improves the chances of finding such expressions at RP.

A word of caution must be added. There is no reason, at first glance, to think that the diverging patterns of *certamente* in terms of POSITION are independent from its semantic peculiarity – the fact that it is the only adverb in the sample with a majority of discourse-oriented uses. This is an important consideration, since we rely solely on this linguistic expression to argue for a (weak) association between discourse-oriented meaning and RP. For the rest of the adverbs, discourse-oriented meaning follows a distribution similar to that of modal meaning – with the exception of the two clause-final tendentious uses of *quizais*. It is also true, though, that unambiguous epistemic uses are extremely rare in final position (only 9/1425 or 0.63% in the whole dataset) and that discourse-oriented uses of adverbs different from *certamente* are too scarce so as to make cautious claims.

8.5 Adverb meaning and orality

Another dimension that was hypothesized to be related to discourse-oriented meaning is MEDIUM. In particular, oral contexts, unlike non-oral contexts, reflect conversational interaction, and are therefore likely to be home to discourse-oriented meaning – recall our sixth hypothesis in (110). However, precisely the opposite seems to be the case in our data: Tables 8.6 and 8.7 show that around 14% of modal meaning occurs in oral contexts, whereas for discourse-oriented uses the percentage goes down to 11.5% in the progressive count and 8.05% in the conservative count. These differences are statistically significant: $\chi^2(1) = 7.7403$, $p < 0.01$, Cramér's $V = 0.066$ (conservative count); $\chi^2(2) = 9.9983$, $p < 0.01$, Cramér's $V = 0.075$ (progressive count).

Table 8.6 MEANING by MEDIUM. Conservative count

	modal		discourse	
	N	%	N	%
non-oral	1333	85.23	217	91.95
oral	231	14.77	19	8.05

Table 8.7 MEANING by MEDIUM. Progressive count

	other		modal		discourse	
	N	%	N	%	N	%
non-oral	25	69.44	1225	85.96	300	88.50
oral	11	30.56	200	14.04	39	11.50

The previous chapter (§ 7.3) revealed associations between *certamente*, on the one hand, and the final position and non-oral contexts, on the other hand. This chapter has shown that this adverb is also associated with discourse-oriented meaning. Thus, looking into the relations between discourse-oriented meaning, POSITION, and MEDIUM using *certamente* as a proxy for discourse-oriented meaning is problematic, something that must be borne in mind when assessing the above results.

Certamente has a reluctance to appear in oral contexts. This is not due, though, to its discourse-oriented meaning, but rather to it being a very formal linguistic expression. Most oral contexts in the dataset are informal, whereas *certamente* can be considered a learned form tied to formal (written) registers. Since *certamente* accounts for most observations of discourse-oriented uses, the unexpected negative association between oral contexts and discourse-oriented meaning is a reflection of the negative association between *certamente* and oral contexts.

8.6 Summary and discussion

This chapter has focused on the meaning of epistemic adverbs and its relations with factors such as negation, co-occurring modal expressions, adverb placement, and oral contexts. Some hypotheses have been tested, but most of the chapter has been of an exploratory nature.

8.6.1 Main findings

Epistemic adverbs were found to express an array of meanings that correspond to different values along the (inter)subjectivity (in Traugott's sense) spectrum. Modal (subjective) meanings match the three epistemic values that the adverbs were assumed to encode (§ 6.2): possibility, probability, and certainty. Discourse-oriented (intersubjective) meanings are mostly interaction-oriented, used by speakers/writers to manage the interlocutors' faces and pursue particular rhetorical goals, but to some extent they are also concerned with discourse-structuring – think of the ability of strengthening uses to refer to other pieces of information in the context or announce forthcoming disagreement. Other (objective/non-subjective) meanings are scarce, and often raise diachronic implications, since they are often linked to the source construction for the adverb (e.g., the conditional use in *se cadra*).

Adverbs of uncertainty (*seguramente, probablemente, posiblemente, quizais,* and *se cadra*) are primarily epistemic: more than 80% of their uses correspond to unambiguous epistemic modality. Mitigation is the only non-epistemic use shared by all of them, although it has little quantitative significance (<7%). In this use, the adverbs downplay the force of the assertion in order for the speaker/writer to sound less aggressive. Typical uses arise in spoken interaction, but the data shows that mitigation is not uncommon in written language either. *Posiblemente, quizais,* and *se cadra* have dynamic modal uses, that is, they can be interpreted as expressing a potential inherent in the SoA, in a few cases (<1.7%). *Quizais* and *se cadra* are the only adverbs in the sample that appear in interrogative sentences, where they modify the tendency of the question, implicitly asserting that what is asked is true, with various contextual effects. *Se cadra* is used as a conditional protasis (always ambiguously with epistemic modality) in a relevant portion of cases (approx. 9%), which is a consequence of its particular diachronic development.

Certamente is the most deviant epistemic adverb in the sample, as it does not have epistemic modality as its primary meaning. In fact, unambiguous epistemic modality accounts for only 6% of its uses, whereas ambiguous epistemic uses represent 19%. *Certamente* is essentially a strengthener that also acts as an intersubjective marker, namely as a polyphonic trigger, reinforcing the assertion and relating it to contextually retrievable information. This confirms our fourth hypothesis (108), according to which the epistemic meaning in *certamente* is marginal and very vulnerable to ambiguity. Another peculiarity of this adverb, spotted in the previous chapter, is that it has significantly higher rates of negation than the other members of the epistemic adverbial paradigm. I suggested that this may be related to a functional alignment between *certamente* and negation: a negative SoA occurs as a reaction to the corresponding positive situation, and the polyphonic character of the adverb is often used to address contrasting contextual information.

The main conclusion of the semantic analysis of epistemic adverbs is the existence of an asymmetry between the epistemic value encoded by the adverb and the discourse strategic goals it serves: whereas possibility adverbs feature a variety of strategic uses, of little quantitative significance, and probability adverbs are close to being purely epistemic expressions, an adverb of certainty is used strategically on most occasions. This asymmetry stems from the divergent communicative status of certainty and uncertainty. The former does not require linguistic marking, unlike the latter, which must be explicitly marked. This makes adverbs of certainty less viable than other epistemic markers, because they flout the maxim of quantity (i.e., they are redundant, since a bare assertion already conveys certainty), and may pose a risk of threatening the interlocutor's face by asserting the speaker's cognitive superiority – they are a way of saying 'I know more than you'. The reason why the strategic use is so prominent in an adverb like *certamente* is that strengthening avoids the pragmatic problems of certainty, so that the adverb aligns with the rhetorical goals of the speaker/writer, becoming a useful tool to show agreement – in concessions, and beyond – or acknowledge the contribution of others to one's discourse.

Although the main contrast is between certainty and uncertainty adverbs, the latter do not constitute an homogeneous group. Possibility adverbs are clearly more versatile than probability adverbs in terms of strategic meaning. They are used as mitigators more often, and have tendentious uses, which probability adverbs lack. As for mitigation, this difference is likely to be down to the epistemic dimensions themselves. Epistemic possibility provides the ideal semantic value to downgrade the force of the assertion, as it qualifies the SoA with the lowest degree of likelihood, turning it into the weakest hypothesis possible. Epistemic probability, however, would yield too strong an assertion in many cases, making this epistemic value a less viable source of mitigating uses in most contexts. Probability adverbs do work as mitigators, though, since a stronger epistemic value may be more effective in some particular situations. For instance, *seguramente* occurs with a second person subject to build solidarity with the addressee when something is assumed to be known by the latter, as seen in (118).

Our fifth hypothesis, (109), has been confirmed: epistemic adverbs perform discourse functions in interrogative sentences. In particular, possibility adverbs modify the tendency of the question, turning it into a biased one. Interrogative sentences provide an ideal breeding ground for discourse-oriented meaning, as they inherently involve the existence of an audience the discourse is addressed towards.

Epistemic adverbs co-occur with inferential verbal expressions, namely auxiliaries *deber (de)* and *haber (de)* and the morphological future. This is overall a marginal phenomenon in the data, but some entrenchment exists in the form of a recurrent pattern: probability adverb + inferential future. Thus, the expression of two different modal qualifications affecting the same SoA seems perfectly acceptable, something that stands in contradiction with Nuyts's (2009) "one-commitment-per-clause" principle. The harmonious co-occurrence of possibility adverbs with epistemic *poder* has a lower incidence than the pattern probability adverb + inferential expression, which leads to the idea that speakers/writers find some usefulness in conveying different aspects of the reasoning process that led to conceive of the SoA, that is, the likelihood of occurrence or epistemic modality plus the reliability of the inference or inferentiality.

The relation between the types of meaning conveyed by adverbs and their placement in the clause has yielded interesting results. An association between discourse-oriented meaning and the final position was found, suggesting that there is some room to argue for a functional asymmetry between LP and RP. Nevertheless, discourse-oriented uses of the adverbs, like modal and other uses, occur more often in initial position than anywhere else in the clause. Thus, the peripheries hypothesis can only be upheld in a very weak way.

Finally, the hypothesis that oral contexts are associated with discourse-oriented uses of the adverbs (110) was rejected by the data. However, such counterintuitive results can be considered spurious, since *certamente*, accounting for most discourse uses, is negatively associated with spoken language. Therefore, an appropriate answer to this research question is still pending.

8.6.2 Diachronic implications

Even though this study has made use of synchronic data, the annotation of several semantic values for the same observation (i.e., ambiguities) raises diachronic implications, because of the *critical* character of such contexts in the development of new meanings (Diewald, 2002): ambiguous contexts are critical from a diachronic perspective because they provide an opportunity for new meanings to arise out of previously encoded meanings through invited inferences (Traugott & Dasher, 2002). Epistemic modality is ambiguous with most other semantic values of epistemic adverbs. Thus, it would seem reasonable to assume that most non-epistemic meanings detected developed out of the epistemic meaning. In many cases, there is even good reason to believe so. However, as I will argue, this is not always the case.

Most mitigating uses are ambiguous with an epistemic modal use (41 ambiguous vs. 3 unambiguous). Some authors argue that mitigating expressions do not form a paradigm of their own, but rather parasitize preexisting linguistic expressions (e.g., Albelda Marco & Estellés Arguedas, 2021b, p. 81; see § 4.2.1). Members of some linguistic paradigms often act as mitigators by virtue of their semantic characteristics. Typical examples are modal expressions, such as uncertainty and inferential markers, and quantifiers, such as *un pouco* 'a little'. These expressions alter the semantics of the utterance in a way that can be easily exploited to downplay the force of the assertion for face-saving purposes (e.g., by turning a problematic affirmation into a hypothesis or minimizing a negative attribute of the addressee). This naturally entails that mitigation is achieved in context through the strategic exploitation of semantic dimensions encoded by particular linguistic expressions and, from a diachronic point of view, that mitigation is a context-dependent meaning of epistemic adverbs. Of course, mitigation can generalize across contexts, and eventually become part of the semantics of an expression. However, judging from the data, where less than 7% of mitigating uses are unambiguous, and from the fact that mitigation can be productively derived from the main meaning of the analyzed expressions, this is far from being the case of epistemic adverbs, as far as our data can tell.

The strengthening use labeled as challenging is susceptible of a similar analysis. This strategic meaning is clearly dependent on the epistemic semantics, particularly, the semantics of high probability, which are key in performing the confrontational strategy illustrated in (124). Although only one example was found in the data, it clearly points in this direction. Moreover, the challenging use resembles an older use of the adverb. In the early 20th century, *seguramente* had a "pragmatic use" in which, instead of modifying the semantics of (some part of) the utterance, it changed the nature of the speech act (Míguez, 2021). The same use was detected in cognate forms from Dutch (*zeker*, Byloo et al., 2007) and English (*surely*, Simon-Vandenbergen & Aijmer, 2007, pp. 136–137). In this use, the adverb occurred in interrogative sentences, yielding a hybrid sentence type – Byloo et al. (2007) call it a "declarogative" (cf. Sadock, 1971) – aimed at seeking confirmation from the interlocutor, and comparable to a tag question. Examples are the following.

(138) a. Mar.: –¿Xa pensas botarlle o lazo?

    Mer.: –Como poida atrapá-lo… Non é fácil atopar un bon partido non saíndo d'aquí, de sorte que se algún aparece por casualidá, hai que tratar de cazá-lo… Inda que teña que correr atrás del, como cando andamos perseguindo as bolboretas.

    Mar.: –¿E *seguramente* irá hoxe ao baile do Casino?

    Mer.: –Por eso vou eu.

    Mar.: –Daquela é mellor para o éisito dos teus proieitos que m'eu quede na casa (rindo).

    'Mar.: –Are you already thinking of snaring him?

    Mer.: –If I could catch him… It isn't easy to find a good catch without getting out of here, so if one appears by chance, you must try to catch him… Even if you have to run after him, like when we chase butterflies.

    Mar.: –And surely he will go today to the ball at the Casino?

    Mer.: –That's why I'm going.

    Mar.: –Then it will be best for the success of your plan that I stay at home [laughing].' (TILG)

b. Hij zal wel weten wat ie kan *zeker*?
'He'll know what he can do, won't he?'
(Byloo et al., 2007, p. 52, their translation)

c. Of course the chaos when the Supreme Being was discovered tied up, and concussed on the floor would be indescribable, but *surely* they would need to be more than just lucky to win much more time out of mere chaos?
(Simon-Vandenbergen & Aijmer, 2007, p. 136)

In the Germanic languages, these interrogatives retain declarative syntax, as Byloo et al. (2007) point out, which is a clear indication that they cannot be considered true questions: the adverb functions in this context as a signal of this particular kind of speech act. In the Galician example, Mar. seeks confirmation of a fact that she assumes to be the case, and introduces *seguramente* in her apparently interrogative sentence to make clear that she has high expectations that the SoA applies. It is significant that Mer.'s reply does not answer the question but elaborates on the topic, thus treating Mar.'s question as a declarative clause.

This pragmatic use and the challenging use are similar in that both are addressee-oriented and encourage the interlocutor to agree with the speaker, so it is possible that they are related from a diachronic point of view. Specifically, it may be the case that the epistemic meaning of *seguramente* favors this kind of strategic use, since it is frequently addressee-oriented – we have also seen this pattern in mitigating uses and in combinations with the modal future, such as (118).

The diachronic development of the tendentious use is a little thornier. An adverb cannot be used to question an epistemic qualification, and the lack of observations ambiguous between the tendentious and the epistemic use provides no reason to establish a diachronic relation. However, possibility adverbs (*quizais, se cadra, acaso*...) consistently give rise to tendentious uses, which suggests that epistemic possibility plays a role in the emergence of this meaning – Nuyts (2001a, p. 58) even claims that the latter "is no doubt derived from the epistemic use." A scenario that allows for the emergence of tendentious uses out of epistemic ones requires, in principle, critical contexts where both coexist. The only cases where adverbs express an epistemic qualification in an interrogative sentence seem to be non-structural descriptive uses. These, though, can hardly be considered candidates for the source construction of the tendentious use, since they can only be achieved through very particular syntactic patterns (complement clauses, *according to*-phrases) that are unable to yield tendentious interpretations. Note that in the descriptive reading the adverb expresses a qualification by someone different from the speaker and the hearer at the time of speech, so it cannot be also interpreted as a speech act modifier – it is rather part of the embedded information.

Epistemic adverbs, lacking structural descriptive uses, are not susceptible to the interrogative flip, a deictic movement that shifts the origin of the qualification from the speaker to the hearer. The interrogative flip has been discussed in relation with epistemic and evidential expressions (e.g., Eckardt & Beltrama, 2019; San Roque et al., 2017), and is illustrated in the following example:

(139) Where might the key be?
'What are possible locations of the key, according to what *you* believe?'
(Eckardt & Beltrama, 2019, p. 124)

In the flip reading, the modal (evidential or epistemic) qualification is not performed by the speaker, but rather described and questioned taking the hearer as the reference point – it is essentially a way of asking about the interlocutor's epistemic or evidential insight on the SoA. Epistemic adverbs do not yield this interpretation, and, furthermore, restrict their occurrences in interrogative contexts to *yes/no* questions, which, unlike *wh*-questions, are prone to tendentious readings.

With no other way to introduce adverbial epistemic meaning in a question, an avenue worth exploring is considering the tendentious use as a systematic result of the combination of epistemic possibility and the semantics of questions, in a vein similar to the one proposed by Littell et al. (2010) for conjectural questions (see (133) and (134)). Since ordinary questions are a request for information unknown to the speaker, introducing a declarative element (viz. an epistemic adverb) has the potential to raise a number of implicatures: (i) the use of a possibility adverb in a question implies that the speaker has some (rudimentary) knowledge of the SoA, hence that they have a (slight) preference for one of the answers; (ii) with stronger epistemic values, such as that of *seguramente*, the speaker is implying that they have a good grasp of the questioned SoA and that their interrogative sentence is not an ordinary request for information, but rather a search for confirmation. This diachronic avenue could explain the lack of critical contexts for tendentious uses in the data and the difficulty to conceive of them.

In the diachrony of auxiliary verbs, epistemic modality is known to have developed out of earlier dynamic and deontic meanings (e.g., Nuyts & Byloo, 2015; Traugott & Dasher, 2002, Chapter 3), showing an evolution in terms of subjectification (see § 4.3). An adjective like *posible* is analogous to its auxiliary counterpart, *poder*, as far as modal meaning is concerned: both expressions carry epistemic, deontic, and dynamic values. Thus, a parallel evolution is highly expected, although it is also highly speculative. Developed out of *posible*, *posiblemente* is also a good candidate for the classic development path dynamic > deontic > epistemic. In fact, diachronic sources reveal the existence of a situational dynamic meaning in previous stages of the adverb (§ 6.2.2). However, there is no evidence of the deontic meaning, and at an intuitive level it is not obvious how such value could be conveyed by the adverb. This is not a problem for a diachronic account, though, since the adverb was compositionally linked to its adjectival base, whose evolution possibly conforms to said pattern.

Adverbs such as *quizais* and *se cadra*, with historical trajectories very different from that of *posiblemente*, feature dynamic uses but not deontic ones, just like the *-mente* adverb. The origins of the dynamic meaning in these adverbs are hard to make out without turning to epistemic possibility. For example, the development of the epistemic meaning in *se cadra* has a straightforward diachronic origin (see § 6.2.3), whereas this is not the case of dynamic possibility. On account of its marginal presence in these two epistemic adverbs, the dynamic use is probably a byproduct of epistemic possibility.[7]

The most prominent non-epistemic meaning among epistemic adverbs turned out to be the strengthening use in *certamente*. An evolution in terms of (inter)subjectification, that is, from a manner adverb, to an epistemic marker, and, finally, a strengthener, is plausible. From this perspective, the current distribution of meanings in the adverb would correlate with their purported age: the predominant strengthening use would be the most recent development, whereas the very marginal epistemic use would be older, and the extremely rare manner use would be even older.[8] However, research shows that the most likely diachronic path is one where the emergence of the epistemic meaning of certainty followed the development of the strengthening meaning, which, in turn, evolved out of manner uses (Míguez, 2021). This consideration stems from the observation that critical contexts in the medieval language correspond to functional ambiguities between manner and strengthening, on the one hand, and strengthening and epistemic modality, on the other hand, thus suggesting that the currently dominant meaning originated from the original manner uses and led to epistemic certainty. According to this view, the epistemic meaning of certainty has remained a marginal, but constant, part of the semantics of *certamente* for a long period of time. Moreover, *seguramente* was found to have had the same evolution, being a strengthener and a certainty marker in Old Galician, hence a near-synonym of *certamente*. Thus, these certainty adverbs instantiate counterexamples to the

---

7. This suggestion contradicts, at first sight, what modal auxiliaries tell us about the diachronic relation between dynamic and epistemic modality. It is worth noting, though, that situational dynamic modality (the one conveyed by adverbs) has a more obvious relation with epistemic modality than its participant-related counterparts, as it describes properties of the situation itself (see Nuyts & Byloo, 2015), which may facilitate a bidrectional diachronic path, similar to the one found for modal and conditional constructions by Kuo (2022).
8. According to Míguez (2021), only 3% of uses of *certamente* in Present-Day Galician are manner uses, all of which correspond to collocations with the verb *saber* 'know', probably the fossilization of a medieval construction.

alleged unidirectionality of (inter)subjectification (see §4.3). This is relevant insofar as the most prominent collection of counterexamples to the unidirectionality principle come from the realm of epistemic and evidential expressions, such as Spanish evidential (semi-)auxiliaries *resultar* and *parecer* and epistemic adverbs *tal vez* and *quizás* (Cornillie, 2008, 2016), a list of exceptions that is joined by Galician *certamente* and *seguramente*.

Finally, *se cadra* offers us a case of grammaticalization in progress.[9] Examples (128) and (129) contain cases where *se cadra* is ambiguous between an epistemic reading and one or more conditional readings. Such ambiguous cases, or critical contexts,[10] amount to 9% (27/300) of the uses of the adverb, and all but one of them correspond to the chance conditional. This supports Rodríguez-Espiñeira's (2019) claim that the chance meaning of *cadrar* was the one leading to the emergence of the epistemic meaning of *se cadra*, contrasting with the proposal by Pinto de Lima (2008) for Portuguese *se calhar*, who argues that the convenience meaning is the source of the epistemic marker.

Even though critical contexts for *se cadra* are found in present-day language, there are clear signs of the development of an independent epistemic meaning in the form of contexts that allow the new meaning but not the older one – "isolating contexts" in Diewald's (2002) terminology. For instance, in (113b), the verb form of the original protasis remains fossilized in the present tense whereas the verb in the main clause takes a past tense form, making the epistemic reading the only feasible one – such "tense disagreement" would be ungrammatical in a conditional construction, since a present tense form in the protasis requires a verb form with future time reference in the apodosis. Another example is (140) below, where *se cadra* has scope over a present subjunctive form, which not only is a case of tense disagreement – the present subjunctive is not found in conditional constructions – but also signals the development of the mood alternation typical of uncertainty adverbs (see §7.2.3).

(140) Se a cultura occidental pasa hoxe por un período patolóxico que *se cadra* lle provoque a morte definitiva, é natural que adoeza de enfermidades diversas.

---

9. Grammaticalization is "the change whereby lexical items and constructions come in certain linguistic contexts to serve grammatical functions and, once grammaticalized, continue to develop new grammatical functions" (Hopper & Traugott, 2003, p. 231). This morphosyntactic development entails a semantic shift from contentful to procedural meaning, that is, "abstract meaning that signals linguistic relations, perspectives and deictic orientation" (Traugott & Trousdale, 2013, p. 12). Thus, the development of an epistemic marker qualifies as a case of grammaticalization, as epistemic meaning is procedural.

10. This situation where an older and a newer meaning of the same expression coexist has been described as divergence or layering in the grammaticalization literature (e.g., Hopper, 1991).

'If Western culture is today in a pathological period that will perhaps cause its final death, it is natural for it to suffer a variety of conditions.' (CORGA)

Other good illustrations of *se cadra*'s independence from the conditional meaning are its occurrence in the apodosis of a conditional construction in (141a) and its scope over the protasis in (141b). These examples show that *se cadra* is not interpreted as a conditional clause, but rather behaves like other epistemic adverbs with regard to conditional constructions – this is especially obvious in (141b), where the structure introduced by *se cadra* is parallel to the one introduced by the epistemic possibility adverb *igual* in the previous sentence.[11]

(141) a. Os historiadores profesionais non parecían estar moi de acordo co asunto, porque pensaban que se a historia acabou, *se cadra* eles ían quedar sen emprego …

'Professional historians did not seem to agree with that point, since they though that if history ended, perhaps they would lose their jobs …' (CORGA)

b. Igual se procuraba ter a casa máis limpa, e aprendía a facer algunha sobremesa rica, *se cadra* se fose máis guapa, máis intelixente, se tivese un traballo mellor, se tivera algún título universitario, igual mañá estaba contento.

'Maybe if she tried to keep the house cleaner, and learned to prepare some tasty dessert, perhaps if she were prettier, more intelligent, if she had a better job, if she had a university degree, maybe tomorrow he will be happy.' (CORGA)

In addition, there are a number of other properties that inform us on the adverbial character of *se cadra* (Rodríguez-Espiñeira, 2019, pp. 202–205): it is syntactically autonomous, as it may stand alone as a reaction to a previous utterance; it scopes over a variety of syntactic units (clauses and phrases of several kinds); it can take different positions in the utterance, and even occur between a main verb and its auxiliary or between the subject and its predicate; and it co-occurs with other expressions that show the speaker's self-doubt.

---

11. What bars the conditional reading in (141b) is the past temporal anchor, rather than the occurrence of the adverb in the apodosis, since conjoining several protasis (i.e., *se a historia acabou* + *se cadra*) seems perfectly fine, as (141b) itself demonstrates. In any case, it is obvious that in this example *se cadra* cannot be interpreted as a conditional clause, despite there being many, which underscores its development as an epistemic adverb.

PART IV

Conclusion

CHAPTER 9

General summary and discussion

Modality is an understudied topic in Galician linguistics. This book concerned itself with modality, with a focus on epistemic adverbs, in order to provide an initial approach to a previously unexplored area of the Galician language. Given the lack of previous studies on the matter from a Galician perspective, the focus was not only on unraveling patterns of variation in the data but also on reviewing the main linguistic approaches to modality.

9.1 Theoretical findings and implications

Part II of the book focused on the concept of modality. Several approaches were examined, including the traditional classes, the possible worlds model, the factuality scale approach, the force dynamics model, the typological perspective, and different functional grammar and interactional approaches. Epistemic modality was also discussed in relation with close categories such as tense, aspect, mood, and evidentiality, as well as (inter)subjectivity, mitigation, and strengthening, and an alternative proposal for understanding modal categories was put forward.

Chapter 2 surveyed the main approaches to modality, and concluded that modality is not coherent as an analytical linguistic notion nor as a cognitive category. The possible worlds model defines modality relying on the discrete notions of necessity and possibility, which cannot account for the scalar character of modal categories such as epistemic modality. The factuality scale approach overcomes these limitations, but fails to provide a unifying principle, that is, a coherent semantic substance for the global concept of modality. Resorting to non-factuality as a way to characterize modality seems arbitrary, since it separates values that clearly belong to the same semantic area: this is the case of certainty, which is factual as well as epistemic. Force dynamics deserves a similar consideration, as it does not provide a conceptual definition that singles out modality from other domains.

The success of modality as a linguistic notion was linked to the existence of modal auxiliaries, that is, grammatical devices that express all or most meanings associated with modality. However, these formal devices are very rare outside Europe, according to typological findings. Thus, there is no reason to maintain modality as a paramount analytical category, since it is not semantically coherent nor can it account for the grammatical behavior of most languages of the world.

Regarding the boundaries of modality vis-à-vis other linguistic categories, dealt with in Chapter 4, the relationship with evidentiality and mitigation is of special interest. Epistemic modality and (inferential) evidentiality are often linked to one another in terms of overlap or inclusion. A conclusion was drawn that epistemic modality and inferentiality are clearly distinguished in the conceptual domain. They are logically connected in that both refer to the same cognitive process, although they describe different aspects of the latter. Even when they occur in the same utterance (an issue that was dealt with in Part III), they convey different, albeit complementary, meanings.

The relationship between epistemic modality and mitigation is even more problematic than the one between epistemic modality and evidentiality. A widespread view is that epistemic modality entails mitigation. Such an approach was deemed inadequate on the grounds that it assumes that the semantics of uncertainty always involve a particular pragmatic strategy, which need not be the case, as shown in the empirical approach in Chapter 8. When an uncertainty expression (only) reflects the mental state of the speaker (i.e., a doubt), no special effects are sought by the speaker, therefore there is no gain in speaking of mitigation. In fact, doing so jeopardizes the usefulness of the notion of strategy, which is then directly linked to particular linguistic forms and semantic values. For an epistemic expression to convey mitigation it must play a role in face management, particularly, it must contribute directly to avoiding a face-threatening act.

Many authors acknowledge the difficulty of defining modality in simple terms, but few have proposed alternatives. Based on Nuyts (2005, 2017), Chapter 5 tried to provide a framework that overcomes the limitations of traditional approaches to modality. Such a framework is based on the idea that the different classes of modality are actually quite divergent semantic areas, each of which should be considered as a basic linguistic category in its own right. Thus, each modal category corresponds to some kind of attitudinal qualification of the SoA on the part of the speaker. The types of semantic categories that can be considered modal are restricted by a number of factors, namely, scalar semantic structure, wide semantic scope, and performative flexibility. These features distinguish modal categories from other semantic domains that modify SoAs (such as time and aspect), and are in line with the prominent role of the speaker in the expression of modality. This approach results in the exclusion of some of the traditional modal categories, such as dynamic modality, and the inclusion of domains that are often excluded from modality, such as inferential evidentiality and affective stance. The proposal was illustrated with Galician examples of different expression types for each modal category, and revealed the particular internal structure of each modal class.

9.2 Empirical findings and implications

In Part III six adverbs were analyzed by means of a corpus study: *certamente, seguramente, probablemente, posiblemente, quizais,* and *se cadra*. Spanning over the whole epistemic scale – i.e., from certainty (*certamente*), through probability (*seguramente, probablemente, posiblemente*), to possibility (*quizais, se cadra*) – they provide a representative picture of the adverbial expression of epistemic modality. A corpus study was carried out where these adverbs were analyzed considering a large number of variables pertaining to levels of analysis that range from the adverbial phrase to the extra-linguistic context. In order to accommodate all the variables, a number of restrictions were imposed on the data, leading to the exclusion of observations where adverbs have non-sentential scope or where they scope over a non-finite verb. A total of 1,800 observations (300 per adverb) were analyzed and manually annotated for 17 variables. The annotated samples were statistically analyzed following a number of procedures, including measures of association, tests of independence, and logistic regression. I summarize below the most important findings and implications of the corpus study.

- The *typical* epistemic adverb. The corpus study showed that the vast majority of occurrences of epistemic adverbs is characterized by a number of syntagmatic properties: they occur in declarative sentences and main clauses; they fill the initial position of the clause; they occur at a short distance from the main verb; they scope over non-controlled, non-dynamic SoAs located in the present or the past; they are performative, expressing the point of view of the speaker/writer at the moment of speech.
- Degree modifiers. Only adverbs encoding probability (*seguramente, probablemente, posiblemente*) take modifiers such as *moi* 'very' and *máis* 'more'. This restriction was linked to the fact that probability is a gradual dimension that can be altered in quantitative terms, unlike certainty and possibility, the values encoded by the three remaining adverbs. *Probablemente* showed up as the most developed expression as for modification capabilities, which I suggested is due to its longer history as a probability adverb. Comparison between adverbs and adjectives revealed that the latter are modified ten times as much, which underscores the role of adjectives as the preferred form for the focal expression of epistemic modality (Nuyts, 2001a).
- The mood alternation. Epistemic adverbs differ in their ability to combine with the subjunctive mood. *Certamente* only combines with the indicative, *seguramente* and *se cadra* have very low rates of subjunctive selection (around 4%), and *probablemente, posiblemente,* and *quizais* select the subjunctive quite frequently (on over 25% of occasions). There is an obvious link between

an adverb conveying uncertainty and it licensing the subjunctive in the main verb. The ability of *se cadra* to combine with the subjunctive is generally rejected by grammarians and native speakers alike, but I suggested that the documented occurrences, rather than being mere mistakes, might be a consequence of both an ongoing development as an uncertainty adverb and the pressure of purist attitudes that favor differential linguistic forms.

- Modal themes. All adverbs occur most frequently in initial position, that is, before the SoA they scope over. Galician epistemic adverbs function primarily as modal themes, advancing the speaker/writer's perspective on the message. This has important implications for the paradigmatic approach to epistemic modality (Nuyts, 2001a), insofar as it contradicts the assumption that an internal position is the default placement for adverbs in accordance with their non-salient informational status. The occurrence in the medial is a characteristic of English and other Germanic languages, but cannot be granted cross-linguistic status. In line with this, it was also found that RP is strongly disfavored at a general level by epistemic adverbs, but discourse-oriented meaning significantly improves the chances of finding such expressions at RP.

- Epistemic modality and time. All of the adverbs examined occur more frequently in contexts with a present or a past time reference than in contexts with a future time reference. The past and the present are more knowable than the future, which explains why stronger epistemic judgments are easier to find in non-future contexts. *Certamente* is the only adverb with a strong reluctance to scope over SoAs with a future component (either the future or the future-in-the-past), whereas probability adverbs have the strongest preference for the future. Conveying a higher degree of probability, *seguramente* is associated with past time reference. Possibility adverbs have a negative association with past time reference, and differ in their preference for non-past temporal frameworks, with *quizais* favoring the present over the future and *se cadra* showing no bias towards either the present or the future. I suggested the existence of links between certainty and the non-future, probability and the future, and possibility and the present, accounting for the deviation of *se cadra* from this pattern in diachronic terms.

- Adverb meaning and discourse strategy. Adverbs of uncertainty convey epistemic modality in most of their occurrences. All of them have non-epistemic, strategic meanings, mitigation being the only one they all share. *Quizais* and *se cadra* also have tendentious uses which arise in interrogative sentences. The most deviant adverb in the sample is *certamente*, since epistemic modality is not its primary meaning. In most cases this adverb functions as a strengthener with a polyphonic overtone, reinforcing the assertion it occurs in and relating it to other pieces of information and points of view different from the speaker/writer's. There exists an asymmetry between epistemic adverbs in terms of how they are used strategically: possibility adverbs feature some strategic uses, of little quantitative significance; probability adverbs are almost purely epistemic; and certainty adverbs take on strategic functions most often. These results have some cross-linguistic validity, as they are in agreement with findings for Dutch and English by Byloo et al. (2007). I accounted for this asymmetry on the basis of the particular communicative status of certainty: expressing certainty flouts the maxim of quantity, and may threat the interlocutor's face, while these problems do not arise when expressions of certainty are aligned with speaker/writer's goals (i.e., when they are used strategically).

- Co-occurrence of modal expressions. Epistemic adverbs and inferential verbal expressions (auxiliaries *deber (de)* and *haber (de)* and the morphological future) occur in the same utterance modifying the same SoA. Although not a frequent phenomenon overall, the pattern probability adverb + inferential future shows some entrenchment. Importantly, the observations examined seem perfectly acceptable in semantic terms, which contradicts the idea of "one commitment per clause" proposed by Nuyts (2009). The expressions convey different modal qualifications, one reflecting the reliability of the cognitive process (inferential) and the other assessing the likelihood of the SoA (epistemic), in line with Cornillie's (2009) ideas.

- The grammaticalization of *se cadra*. Although the book focused on synchronic data, some diachronic implications were raised, especially regarding *se cadra*, which was included in the sample partly because of its recent emergence as an epistemic adverb. This expression originated from a conditional clause, and the semantic analysis revealed the preservation of critical contexts where both the epistemic meaning and the original conditional reading are present. The conditional readings correspond to the 'chance' meaning of the verb *cadrar*, supporting Rodríguez-Espiñeira's (2019) claim that this is the meaning that led to the emergence of an epistemic adverb. Nevertheless, most occurrences of *se cadra* do not allow a conditional reading. This and other pieces of evidence signal the advancement of an independent epistemic meaning, which is, in turn, a sign of an ongoing grammaticalization process.

On a more general level, these findings unraveled, at least partially, the internal structure of the epistemic adverbial domain. Adverbs make up a rich semantic scale that ranges from certainty to possibility, with increasing degrees of probability in between. Such a high degree of semantic specificity is a major factor motivating their internal diversity. Additionally, epistemic possibility consists of two types of expressions. The first type groups adverbs that present the epistemic judgment as the result of a more careful reflection and that have been part of the language for a long time. The second type includes adverbs that introduce hypotheses as devised by the speaker at the moment of speech and that have only entered the language recently. I have argued that *quizais* and *se cadra*, respectively, instantiate these two expression types.

9.3 Future lines of research

This book has taken a first step in the study of modality in Galician. Modality is a vast domain, and the present work has at times only touched on issues that deserve further attention, possibly raising more questions than it answered. In the last paragraphs of this book I would like to highlight a number of avenues that remain open for future research.

The theoretical discussion on modality and related categories has been relentless since linguists took an interest in the topic. This work has argued that modality is not a coherent notion, and has proposed an alternative framework for studying modal meaning. This proposal is not exhaustive, and must be tested and developed in several ways. One of the most interesting challenges this framework presents is the explanation of the co-existence of a wide range of formal devices for the expression of basically the same meaning. Why, for instance, can Galician speakers express epistemic probability by means of either the adjective *probable*, the adverb *probablemente*, or the verb *creo*? A convincing answer was offered in Nuyts's (2001a) seminal work, which laid out a paradigmatic approach to epistemic modality according to which the choice of formal alternatives is determined by a number of functional factors. However, Nuyts (2001a) focused on epistemic modality in West Germanic languages, and this approach must be expanded to other modal categories and replicated in different languages.

In Part III a sizable number of adverbs was considered, but many expressions could still not be studied given the in-depth nature of the analysis. Possibility adverbs are remarkably numerous in Galician, and include expressions such as *talvez*, *igual*, *o mesmo*, and *ao mellor*, in addition to *quizais* and *se cadra*. This astonishing case of synonymy raises further questions on the internal structuring of epistemic adverbs and, on a more general level, on the motivations for linguistic variation. It also provides an interesting object of study for contact linguistics, as some of the expressions (or some of their usage patterns) might be affected by the contact between Galician and Spanish, as discussed in relation with *se cadra* and the subjunctive.

Another limitation of the present work is the rather narrow syntactic contexts in which epistemic adverbs were investigated and the scarcity of spoken data. This provided the study with the uniformity needed for a quantitative approach, but future studies should look at adverbs in other linguistic and extra-linguistic contexts, and delve into their role in conversational settings, as this book has shown that these expressions are very sophisticated from a pragmatic perspective.

An aspect that could not be addressed comprehensively in this book was the alternation between the indicative and the subjunctive when the finite verb is preceded by an adverb of uncertainty. This has been a topic of Romance linguistics for decades (at least since Woehr, 1972), and today attracts the attention of quantitative approaches (e.g., Deshors & Waltermire, 2019; Hirota, 2021). Galician is one of several Iberian Romance languages that allow the alternation, which has only been studied in depth in Spanish so far. Given the synchronic and diachronic implications of this phenomenon, it seems a promising avenue for future investigations.

Bibliography

Abraham, W. (2020). *Modality in syntax, semantics and pragmatics*. Cambridge University Press.

Aguete Cajiao, A. (2020). Contacto de linguas e variedades na emerxencia de novos modelos de vocalismo galego. In F. Dubert-García, V. Míguez, & X. Sousa (Eds.), *Variedades lingüísticas en contacto na Península Ibérica* (pp. 155–193). Consello da Cultura Galega.

Aijmer, K. (2016). Modality and mood in functional linguistic approaches. In J. Nuyts & J. van der Auwera (Eds.), *The Oxford handbook of modality and mood* (pp. 495–513). Oxford University Press.

Aikhenvald, A. Y. (2004). *Evidentiality*. Oxford University Press.

Aikhenvald, A. Y. (2012). The essence of mirativity. *Linguistic Typology*, 16(3), 435–485.

Aikhenvald, A. Y. (2016). Sentence types. In J. Nuyts & J. van der Auwera (Eds.), *The Oxford handbook of modality and mood* (pp. 141–165). Oxford University Press.

Albelda Marco, M. (2010). ¿Cómo se reconoce la atenuación? Una aproximación metodológica basada en el español peninsular hablado. In F. Orletti & L. Mariottini (Eds.), *(Des)cortesía en español: espacios teóricos y metodológicos para su estudio* (pp. 47–70). Università degli Studi Roma Tre / EDICE.

Albelda Marco, M. (2016). Estableciendo límites entre la evidencialidad y la atenuación en español. In R. González Ruiz, D. Izquierdo Alegría, & Ó. Loureda Lamas (Eds.), *La evidencialidad en español: teoría y descripción* (pp. 75–100). Iberoamericana / Vervuert.

Albelda Marco, M. (2018). La variación genérico-discursiva de la atenuación como resultado de la variación de la imagen. *Spanish in Context*, 15(2), 346–368.

Albelda Marco, M., & Cestero Mancera, A. M. (2011). De nuevo, sobre los procedimientos de atenuación lingüística. *Español actual*, 96, 9–40.

Albelda Marco, M., & Estellés Arguedas, M. (2021a). De nuevo sobre la intensificación pragmática: revisión y propuesta. *Estudios Románicos*, 30, 15–37.

Albelda Marco, M., & Estellés Arguedas, M. (2021b). Mitigation revisited. An operative and integrated definition of the pragmatic concept, its strategic values, and its linguistic expression. *Journal of Pragmatics*, 183, 71–86.

Álvarez, R. (2019). Galician linguistics: between Hispanic philological tradition and visibility in the Luso-Brazilian sphere. In G. Rei-Doval & F. Tejedo-Herrero (Eds.), *Lusophone, Galician, and Hispanic linguistics: bridging frames and traditions* (pp. 92–112). Routledge.

Álvarez, R., Regueira, X. L., & Monteagudo, H. (1986). *Gramática galega*. Galaxia.

Álvarez, R., & Xove, X. (2002). *Gramática da lingua galega*. Galaxia.

Ameka, F. K., & Kropp Dakubu, M. E. (Eds.). (2008). *Aspect and modality in Kwa languages*. John Benjamins.

Arppe, A. (2013). *Polytomous: polytomous logistic regression for fixed and mixed effects [0.1.6]*. R Foundation for Statistical Computing. https://cran.r-project.org/src/contrib/Archive/polytomous/

Arregui, A., Rivero, M. L., & Salanova, A. (Eds.). (2017). *Modality across syntactic categories.* Oxford University Press.

Austin, J. L. (1962). *How to do things with words.* Oxford University Press.

Ayoun, D., Celle, A., & Lansari, L. (Eds.). (2018). *Tense, aspect, modality, and evidentiality: crosslinguistic perspectives.* John Benjamins.

Bakhtin, M. M. (1981). *The dialogic imagination: four essays by M. M. Bakhtin* (M. Holquist, Ed.; C. Emerson & M. Holquist, Trans.). University of Texas Press.

Bally, C. (1965). *Linguistique générale et linguistique française* (4th ed.). Francke Berne. (Original work published 1932)

Beeching, K., & Detges, U. (2014). Introduction. In K. Beeching & U. Detges (Eds.), *Discourse functions at the left and right periphery: crosslinguistic investigations of language use and language change* (pp. 1–23). Brill.

Bellert, I. (1977). On semantic and distributional properties of sentential adverbs. *Linguistic Inquiry,* 8(2), 337–351. https://www.jstor.org/stable/4177988

Berbeira Gardón, J. L. (1998). Relevance and modality. *Revista Alicantina de Estudios Ingleses,* 11, 3–22.

Biber, D., & Finegan, E. (1988). Adverbial stance types in English. *Discourse Processes,* 11(1), 1–34.

Böhm, V. (2016). *La imperfectividad en la prensa española y su relación con las categorías semánticas de modalidad y evidencialidad.* Peter Lang.

Bolkestein, A. M. (1980). *Problems in the description of modal verbs: an investigation of Latin.* Van Gorcum.

Boogaart, R. (2011). Imperfective aspect and epistemic modality. In A. Patard & F. Brisard (Eds.), *Cognitive approaches to tense, aspect, and epistemic modality* (pp. 217–248). John Benjamins.

Boogaart, R., & Fortuin, E. (2016). Modality and mood in Cognitive Linguistics and Construction Grammars. In J. Nuyts & J. van der Auwera (Eds.), *The Oxford handbook of modality and mood* (pp. 514–534). Oxford University Press.

Boye, K. (2012). *Epistemic meaning: a crosslinguistic and functional-cognitive study.* De Gruyter Mouton.

Brenes Peña, E. (2011). *Descortesía verbal y tertulia televisiva. Análisis pragmalingüístico.* Peter Lang.

Brisard, F. (2006). Logic, subjectivity, and the semantics/pragmatics distinction. In A. Athanasiadou, C. Canakis, & B. Cornillie (Eds.), *Subjectification: various paths to subjectivity* (pp. 41–74). De Gruyter Mouton.

Briz Gómez, A. (1998). *El español coloquial en la conversación: esbozo de pragmagramática.* Ariel.

Brown, P., & Levinson, S. C. (1987). *Politeness: some universals in language usage.* Cambridge University Press.

Butler, C. S. (2003). *Structure and function: a guide to three major structural-functional theories. Part I: approaches to the simplex clause.* John Benjamins.

Bybee, J., Perkins, R., & Pagliuca, W. (1994). *The evolution of grammar: tense, aspect, and modality in the languages of the world.* University of Chicago Press.

Byloo, P., Kastein, R., & Nuyts, J. (2007). On *certainly* and *zeker.* In M. Hannay & G. J. Steen (Eds.), *Structural-functional studies in English grammar: in honour of Lachlan Mackenzie* (pp. 35–57). John Benjamins.

Caffi, C. (2007). *Mitigation*. Elsevier.

Carballo Calero, R. (1966). *Gramática elemental del gallego común*. Galaxia.

Carnap, R. (1947). *Meaning and necessity: a study in semantics and modal logic*. University of Chicago Press.

Carretero, M., & Zamorano-Mansilla, J. R. (2019). Disentangling epistemic modality, neighbouring categories and pragmatic uses: the case of English epistemic modal adverbs. In *Quinze études de cas sur les modalités linguistiques / Fifteen case studies on types of linguistic modalities* (pp. 131–157). Publications Electroniques de l'ERIAC. http://eriac.univ-rouen.fr/disentangling-epistemic-modality-neighbouring-categories-and-pragmatic-uses-the-case-of-english-epistemic-modal-adverbs/

Centro Ramón Piñeiro para a investigación en humanidades. (2022). *Corpus de Referencia do Galego Actual [4.0]*. http://corpus.cirp.gal/corga/

Chafe, W. (1986). Evidentiality in English conversation and academic writing. In W. Chafe & J. Nichols (Eds.), *Evidentiality: the linguistic coding of epistemology* (pp. 261–273). Ablex.

Chafe, W. (1994). *Discourse, consciousness, and time: the flow and displacement of conscious experience in speaking and writing*. The University of Chicago Press.

Chung, S., & Timberlake, A. (1985). Tense, aspect, mood. In T. Shopen (Ed.), *Language typology and syntactic description. III. Grammatical categories and the lexicon* (pp. 202–258). Cambridge University Press.

Cidrás, F. (2016). Why do they say 'I know' when they mean 'I really don't know'? Semantic change and constructionalization of Galician particle *seica* [Unpublished manuscript].

Cidrás, F., & Dubert-García, F. (2017). A gramática galega, un río de curso curto e sinuoso. Panorama histórico dos estudios gramaticais sobre o galego. *Labor Histórico*, 3(1), 111–125.

Coates, J. (1983). *The semantics of the modal auxiliaries*. Croom Helm.

Comrie, B. (1976). *Aspect: an introduction to the study of verbal aspect and related problems*. Cambridge University Press.

Comrie, B. (1985). *Tense*. Cambridge University Press.

Cornillie, B. (2008). On the grammaticalization and (inter)subjectivity of evidential (semi-)auxiliaries in Spanish. In E. Seoane & M. J. López-Couso (Eds.), *Theoretical and empirical issues in grammaticalization* (pp. 55–76). John Benjamins.

Cornillie, B. (2009). Evidentiality and epistemic modality: on the close relationship between two different categories. *Functions of Language*, 16(1), 44–62.

Cornillie, B. (2010). On conceptual semantics and discourse functions: the case of Spanish modal adverbs in informal conversation. *Review of Cognitive Linguistics*, 8(2), 300–320.

Cornillie, B. (2015). Más allá de la epistemicidad: las funciones discursivas de los adverbios epistémicos y evidenciales en el español conversacional. *Spanish in Context*, 12(1), 120–139.

Cornillie, B. (2016). Acerca de la locución epistémica *tal vez* en el Siglo de las Luces: innovación y especialización. In M. Guzmán & D. Sáez (Eds.), *Márgenes y centros en el español del siglo XVIII* (pp. 183–199). Tirant Humanidades.

Costa Casas, X. X., González Refoxo, M. d. A., Morán Fraga, C. C., & Rábade Castiñeira, X. C. (1988). *Nova gramática para a aprendizaxe da lingua*. Vía Láctea.

Couper-Kuhlen, E., & Thompson, S. A. (2000). Concessive patterns in conversation. In E. Couper-Kuhlen & B. Kortmann (Eds.), *Cause – condition – concession – contrast: cognitive and discourse perspectives* (pp. 381–410). Mouton de Gruyter.

Croissant, Y. (2020). *Mlogit: multinomial logit models [1.1–1]*. R Foundation for Statistical Computing. https://CRAN.R-project.org/package=mlogit

Cruschina, S., & Remberger, E.-M. (2008). Hearsay and reported speech: evidentiality in Romance. *Rivista di grammatica generativa*, 33, 95–116.

Dahl, Ö. (2000). The grammar of future time reference in European languages. In Ö. Dahl (Ed.), *Tense and aspect in the languages of Europe* (pp. 309–328). Mouton de Gruyter.

Davidse, K., Van linden, A., & Brems, L. (2022). A semiotic approach to grammaticalization: modelling representational and interpersonal modality expressed by verbonominal patterns. *Language Sciences*, 91, 101473.

De Wit, A. (2017). *The present perfective paradox across languages*. Oxford University Press.

Declerck, R. (2009). 'Not-yet-factual at time t': a neglected modal concept. In R. Salkie, P. Busuttil, & J. van der Auwera (Eds.), *Modality in English: theory and description* (pp. 31–54). Mouton de Gruyter.

Declerck, R. (2011). The definition of modality. In A. Patard & F. Brisard (Eds.), *Cognitive approaches to tense, aspect and epistemic modality* (pp. 21–44). John Benjamins.

Degand, L. (2014). 'So very fast then' Discourse markers at left and right periphery in spoken French. In K. Beeching & U. Detges (Eds.), *Discourse functions at the left and right periphery: crosslinguistic investigations of language use and language change* (pp. 151–178). Brill.

de Haan, F. (2001). The place of inference within the evidential system. *International Journal of American Linguistics*, 67(2), 193–219.

de Haan, F. (2006). Typological approaches to modality. In W. Frawley (Ed.), *The expression of modality* (pp. 27–69). Mouton de Gruyter.

DeLancey, S. (2001). The mirative and evidentiality. *Journal of Pragmatics*, 33(3), 369–382.

Delbecque, N. (2009). Acerca de la relación entre *cierto* y *seguro*. In M. Veyrat Rigat & E. Serra Alegre (Eds.), *La lingüística como reto epistemológico y como acción social. Estudios dedicados al Profesor Ángel López García con ocasión de su sexagésimo aniversario* (pp. 629–644, Vol. 2). Arco Libros.

Depraetere, I., & Reed, S. (2011). Towards a more explicit taxonomy of root possibility. *English Language and Linguistics*, 15(1), 1–29.

de Saussure, L., Moeschler, J., & Puskas, G. (Eds.). (2007). *Tense, mood and aspect: theoretical and descriptive issues*. Rodopi.

Deshors, S. C., & Waltermire, M. (2019). The indicative vs. subjunctive alternation with expressions of possibility in Spanish: a multifactorial analysis. *International Journal of Corpus Linguistics*, 24(1), 67–97.

Diewald, G. (2002). A model for relevant types of contexts in grammaticalization. In I. Wischer & G. Diewald (Eds.), *New reflections on grammaticalization* (pp. 103–120). John Benjamins.

Dik, S. C. (1997). *The theory of Functional Grammar. Part 1: the structure of the clause* (K. Hengeveld, Ed.; 2nd ed.). Mouton de Gruyter.

Dixon, R. M. W. (2009). The semantics of clause linking in typological perspective. In R. M. W. Dixon & A. Y. Aikhenvald (Eds.), *The semantics of clause linking: a cross-linguistic typology* (pp. 1–55). Oxford University Press.

Downing, A. (2001). "Surely you knew!": *surely* as a marker of evidentiality and stance. *Functions of Language*, 8(2), 251–282.

Dowty, D. (1979). *Word meaning and Montague grammar*. Reidel.

Dryer, M.S., & Haspelmath, M. (Eds.). (2013). *The world atlas of language structures online*. Max Planck Institute for Evolutionary Anthropology. http://wals.info/

Du Bois, J.W. (2007). The stance triangle. In R. Englebretson (Ed.), *Stancetaking in discourse* (pp. 139–182). John Benjamins.

Eckardt, R., & Beltrama, A. (2019). Evidentials and questions. In C. Pinon (Ed.), *Empirical issues in syntax and semantics* 12 (pp. 121–155). CSSP. http://www.cssp.cnrs.fr/eiss12/

Elliot, J.R. (2000). Realis and irrealis: forms and concepts of the grammaticalisation of reality. *Linguistic Typology*, 4(1), 55–90.

Espejo Muriel, M.d.M., & Espinosa Elorza, R.M. (2012). Quiçab, quiçá, quizá. In E. Montero Cartelle & C. Manzano Rovira (Eds.), *Actas del VIII Congreso Internacional de Historia de la Lengua Española: Santiago de Compostela, 14–18 de septiembre de 2009* (pp. 749–760, Vol. 1). Meubook.

Evans, N. (2007). Insubordination and its uses. In I. Nikolaeva (Ed.), *Finiteness: theoretical and empirical foundations* (pp. 366–431). Oxford University Press.

Ferreiro, M. (1999). *Gramática histórica galega. I. Fonética e morfosintaxe* (4th ed.). Laiovento.

Figueras Bates, C. (2018). Atenuación, género discursivo e imagen. *Spanish in Context*, 15(2), 258–280.

Foley, W.A., & Van Valin, R.D.J. (1984). *Functional syntax and Universal Grammar*. Cambridge University Press.

Frawley, W. (1992). *Linguistic semantics*. Erlbaum.

Freixeiro Mato, X.R. (1998–2003). *Gramática da lingua galega*. A Nosa Terra.

Freixeiro Mato, X.R. (2005). *Os marcadores discursivos. Conectores contraargumentativos no galego escrito*. Universidade da Coruña. https://illa.udc.gal/rgf/monografias/

Freixeiro Mato, X.R. (2006a). *Gramática da lingua galega. II. Morfosintaxe* (2nd ed.). A Nosa Terra. (Original work published 2000)

Freixeiro Mato, X.R. (2006b). *Gramática da lingua galega. IV. Gramática do texto* (2nd ed.). A Nosa Terra. (Original work published 2003)

García Murga, F. (2014). *Semántica*. Síntesis.

García Represas, D. (2000). L'expression du doute en galicien. In A. Englebert, M. Pierrard, L. Rosier, & D. Van Raemdonck (Eds.), *Actes du XXIIe Congrès International de Linguistique et de Philologie Romanes (Bruxelles, 23–29 juillet 1998)* (pp. 269–276, Vol. 7). Max Niemeyer.

García Represas, D. (2001). A necesidade e maila obriga en galego. *Cadernos de Lingua*, 23, 89–116.

Garson, J. (2018). Modal Logic. In E.N. Zalta (Ed.), *Stanford encyclopedia of philosophy*. https://plato.stanford.edu/archives/fall2018/entries/logic-modal/

Gavins, J. (2005). (Re)thinking modality: a text-world perspective. *Journal of Literary Semantics*, 34(2), 79–93.

Gerards, D.P., & Kabatek, J. (2018). Grammaticalization, distance, immediacy and discourse traditions: the case of Portuguese *caso*. In S. Pons Bordería & Ó. Loureda Lamas (Eds.), *Beyond grammaticalization and discourse markers: new issues in the study of language change* (pp. 115–159). Brill.

Giannakidou, A., & Mari, A. (2018). A unified analysis of the future as epistemic modality: the view from Greek and Italian. *Natural Language & Linguistic Theory*, 36(1), 85–129.

Gisborne, N. (2007). Dynamic modality. *SKASE Journal of Theoretical Linguistics*, 4(2), 44–61. http://www.skase.sk/Volumes/JTL09/

Givón, T. (1982). Evidentiality and epistemic space. *Studies in Language*, 6(1), 23–45.

Givón, T. (1984). *Syntax: a functional-typological introduction* (Vol. 1). John Benjamins.

Givón, T. (1994). Irrealis and the subjunctive. *Studies in Language*, 18(2), 265–337.

Givón, T. (2001). *Syntax: an introduction* (2nd ed., Vol. 1). John Benjamins.

González Vázquez, M. (2006). *Las fuentes de la información: tipología, semántica y pragmática de la evidencialidad*. Universidade de Vigo.

González Vázquez, M. (2022). Unhas notas sobre o sistema evidencial galego. *Estudos de Lingüística Galega*, 14.

González-Vázquez, M. (2021). The evidentiality system in Galician and the *seica* marker. *Journal of Pragmatics*, 178, 83–92.

Goossens, L. (1985). Modality and the modals: a problem for Functional Grammar. In A.M. Bolkestein, C. de Groot, & J.L. Mackenzie (Eds.), *Predicates and terms in Functional Grammar* (pp. 203–217). Foris.

Grice, H.P. (1975). Logic and conversation. In P. Cole & J.L. Morgan (Eds.), *Speech acts* (pp. 41–58). Academic Press.

Gries, S.T. (2013). *Statistics for linguistics with R: a practical introduction* (2nd ed.). De Gruyter Mouton.

Gumperz, J.J. (1982). *Discourse strategies*. Cambridge University Press.

Halliday, M.A.K. (1970a). Functional diversity in language as seen from a consideration of modality and mood in English. *Foundations of Language*, 6(3), 322–361. https://www.jstor.org/stable/25000463

Halliday, M.A.K. (1970b). Language structure and language function. In J. Lyons (Ed.), *New horizons in linguistics* (pp. 140–165). Penguin.

Halliday, M.A.K. (2004). *An introduction to Functional Grammar* (C.M.I.M. Matthiesen, Ed.; 3rd ed.). Hodder Arnold.

Halliday, M.A.K. (2014). *Halliday's introduction to Functional Grammar* (C.M.I.M. Matthiesen, Ed.; 4th ed.). Routledge.

Harris, A.C., & Campbell, L. (1995). *Historical syntax in cross-linguistic perspective*. Cambridge University Press.

Haßler, G. (Ed.). (2022). *Manuel des modes et modalités*. De Gruyter.

Hatav, G. (1997). *The semantics of aspect and modality: evidence from English and Biblical Hebrew*. John Benjamins.

Haverkate, H. (1994). *La cortesía verbal. Estudio pragmalingüístico*. Gredos.

Hengeveld, K. (1987). Clause structure and modality in Functional Grammar. In J. van der Auwera & L. Goossens (Eds.), *Ins and outs of the predication* (pp. 53–66). Foris.

Hengeveld, K. (1988). Illocution, mood and modality in a functional grammar of Spanish. *Journal of Semantics*, 6, 227–269.

Hengeveld, K. (1989). Layers and operators in Functional Grammar. *Journal of Linguistics*, 25(1), 127–157.

Hengeveld, K. (2004). Illocution, mood and modality. In G. Booij, C. Lehmann, & J. Mugdan (Eds.), *Morphology: an international handbook on inflection and word-formation* (pp. 1190–1201, Vol. 2). Mouton de Gruyter.

Hennemann, A. (2014). The Spanish synthetic future as a means of expression of inference. *Studies in Literature and Language*, 9(1), 11–26.

Hickmann, M., & Bassano, D. (2016). Modality and mood in first language acquisition. In J. Nuyts & J. van der Auwera (Eds.), *The Oxford handbook of modality and mood* (pp. 430–447). Oxford University Press.

Hilpert, M., Cappelle, B., & Depraetere, I. (Eds.). (2021). *Modality and Diachronic Construction Grammar*. John Benjamins.

Hirota, H. (2021). The indicative/subjunctive mood alternation with adverbs of doubt in Spanish. *Journal of Quantitative Linguistics*, 1–15.

Hogeweg, L., de Hoop, H., & Malchukov, A. (Eds.). (2009). *Cross-linguistic semantics of tense, aspect, and modality*. John Benjamins.

Hollebrandse, B., van Hout, A., & Vet, C. (Eds.). (2005). *Crosslinguistic views on tense, aspect and modality*. Rodopi.

Holmes, J. (1984). Modifying illocutionary force. *Journal of Pragmatics*, 8(3), 345–365.

Hopper, P. J. (1991). On some principles of grammaticization. In E. C. Traugott & B. Heine (Eds.), *Approaches to grammaticalization* (pp. 17–35, Vol. 1). John Benjamins.

Hopper, P. J., & Traugott, E. C. (2003). *Grammaticalization* (2nd ed.). Cambridge University Press.

Hosmer, D. W., Lemeshow, S., & Sturdivant, R. X. (2013). *Applied logistic regression* (3rd ed.). Wiley.

Hoye, L. (1997). *Adverbs and modality in English*. Longman.

Hummel, M. (2013). La dimensión intercultural de la expansión diacrónica de los adverbios en -mente. In M. P. Garcés Gómez (Ed.), *Los adverbios con función discursiva: procesos de formación y evolución* (pp. 15–41). Iberoamericana / Vervuert.

Hummel, M. (2018). Romance sentence adverbs in -mente: epistemic mitigation in synchrony and diachrony. *Linguistik online*, 92(5), 111–144.

Iwasaki, S. (1993). *Subjectivity in grammar and discourse: theoretical considerations and a case study of Japanese spoken discourse*. John Benjamins.

Izquierdo Alegría, D. (2019). ¿Qué tipo de información codifica realmente un evidencial? Propuesta de una distinción conceptual entre *fuente, base* y *modo de acceso* para el reconocimiento de unidades evidenciales. *Estudios filológicos*, 63, 211–236.

Izquierdo Alegría, D., González Ruiz, R., & Loureda Lamas, Ó. (2016). Un acercamiento a los fundamentos de la evidencialidad y a su recepción y tratamiento en la lingüística hispánica. In R. González Ruiz, D. Izquierdo Alegría, & Ó. Loureda Lamas (Eds.), *La evidencialidad en español: teoría y descripción* (pp. 9–45). Iberoamericana / Vervuert.

Janda, L. A. (2015). Tense, aspect and mood. In E. Dabrowska & D. Divjak (Eds.), *Handbook of Cognitive Linguistics* (pp. 616–634). De Gruyter Mouton.

Jarrett, D. S. (2022). *Epistemic adverbs of low speaker-commitment in Colombian Spanish* [Doctoral dissertation, Indiana University]. https://iucat.iu.edu/iuk/19776021

Jiménez Juliá, T. (1989). Modalidad, modo verbal y *modus clausal* en español. *Verba*, 16, 175–214. http://hdl.handle.net/10347/2738

Kärkkäinen, E. (2003). *Epistemic stance in English conversation: a description of its interactional functions, with a focus on* I think. John Benjamins.

Kearns, K. (2011). *Semantics* (2nd ed.). Palgrave Macmillan.

Kehayov, P. (2017). *The fate of mood and modality in language death: evidence from minor Finnic.* De Gruyter.
Kiefer, F. (1987). On defining modality. *Folia Linguistica*, 21(1), 67–94.
Kotwica, D. (2020). Mitigation and reinforcement in general knowledge expressions. *Journal of Pragmatics*, 169, 219–230.
Kratzer, A. (1977). What 'must' and 'can' must and can mean. *Linguistics and Philosophy*, 1(3), 337–355.
Kratzer, A. (2002). The notional category of modality. In P. Portner & B. H. Partee (Eds.), *Formal semantics: the essential readings* (pp. 289–323). Blackwell. (Original work published 1981)
Krawczak, K. (2016). Objectivity, subjectivity and intersubjectivity: integrating two Cognitive-Functional theories. *Functions of Language*, 23(2), 179–213.
Kuo, Y. H. (2022). Bidirectionality between modal and conditional constructions in Mandarin Chinese: a constructionalization account. *Diachronica*, 39(1), 88–127.
Kuteva, T. (1998). On identifying an evasive gram: action narrowly averted. *Studies in Language*, 22(1), 113–160.
Labov, W. (1984). Intensity. In D. Schiffrin (Ed.), *Meaning, form, and use in context: linguistic applications* (pp. 43–70). Georgetown University Press. http://hdl.handle.net/10822/555477
Lampert, G., & Lampert, M. (2000). *The conceptual structure(s) of modality: essences and ideologies.* Peter Lang.
Langacker, R. W. (1987). *Foundations of Cognitive Grammar. I. Theoretical prerequisites.* Stanford University Press.
Langacker, R. W. (1990). Subjectification. *Cognitive Linguistics*, 1(1), 5–38.
Langacker, R. W. (1991a). *Concept, image, and symbol: the cognitive basis of grammar.* Mouton de Gruyter.
Langacker, R. W. (1991b). *Foundations of Cognitive Grammar. II. Descriptive application.* Stanford University Press.
Langacker, R. W. (2000). *Grammar and conceptualization.* Mouton de Gruyter.
Langacker, R. W. (2008). *Cognitive Grammar: a basic introduction.* Oxford University Press.
Lassiter, D. (2017). *Graded modality: qualitative and quantitative perspectives.* Oxford University Press.
Lazard, G. (1999). Mirativity, evidentiality, mediativity, or other? *Linguistic Typology*, 3(1), 91–109.
Leech, G. (1970). *Towards a semantic description of English.* Inidiana University Press.
Leech, G. (1981). *Semantics: the study of meaning* (2nd ed.). Penguin.
Leiss, E. (2008). The silent and aspect-driven patterns of deonticity and epistemicity: a chapter in diachronic typology. In W. Abraham & E. Leiss (Eds.), *Modality-aspect interfaces: implications and typological solutions* (pp. 15–41). John Benjamins.
Levshina, N. (2015). *How to do linguistics with R: data exploration and statistical analysis.* John Benjamins.
Littell, P., Matthewson, L., & Peterson, T. (2010). On the semantics of conjectural questions. In T. Peterson & U. Sauerland (Eds.), *Evidence from evidentials* (pp. 89–104). University of British Columbia. http://www.semanticsarchive.net/Archive/WI5NjEzY/EvidenceFromEvidentials.pdf

López-Couso, M. J. (2010). Subjectification and intersubjectification. In A. H. Jucker & I. Taavitsainen (Eds.), *Historical pragmatics* (pp. 127–163). De Gruyter Mouton.

López-Couso, M. J., & Méndez-Naya, B. (2021). From complementizing to modifying status: on the grammaticalization of the complement-taking-predicate-clauses *chances are* and *odds are*. *Language Sciences*, 88, 101422.

López-Couso, M. J., & Méndez-Naya, B. (2023). From chance to epistemic possibility: on the grammaticalization of happenstance expressions in English. In H. De Smet, P. Petré, & B. Szmrecsanyi (Eds.), *Context, intent and variation in grammaticalization* (pp. 109–134). De Gruyter Mouton.

Lorenzo, R. (1977). *La traducción gallega de la Crónica General y de la Crónica de Castilla* (Vol. 2). Instituto de Estudios Orensanos Padre Feijóo.

Loureiro-Porto, L. (2014). Modal necessity and impersonality in English and Galician. In J. I. Marín-Arrese, M. Carretero, J. Arús Hita, & J. van der Auwera (Eds.), *English modality: core, periphery and evidentiality* (pp. 171–200). De Gruyter Mouton.

Lunn, P. V. (1995). The evaluative function of the Spanish subjunctive. In J. Bybee & S. Fleischman (Eds.), *Modality in grammar and discourse* (pp. 429–449). John Benjamins.

Lyons, J. (1977). *Semantics* (Vol. 2). Cambridge University Press.

Malchukov, A., & Xrakovskij, V. S. (2016). The linguistic interaction of mood with modality and other categories. In J. Nuyts & J. van der Auwera (Eds.), *The Oxford handbook of modality and mood* (pp. 196–220). Oxford University Press.

Martin, J. R., & White, P. R. R. (2005). *The language of evaluation: appraisal in English*. Palgrave Macmillan.

Matte Bon, F. (1995). *Gramática Comunicativa del español. II. De la idea a la lengua* (2nd ed.). Edelsa.

Matthews, R. (1991). *Words and worlds: on the linguistic analysis of modality*. Peter Lang.

Mauri, C., & Sansò, A. (2016). The linguistic marking of (ir)realis and subjunctive. In J. Nuyts & J. van der Auwera (Eds.), *The Oxford handbook of modality and mood* (pp. 166–195). Oxford University Press.

Menzel, C. (2016). Possible worlds. In E. N. Zalta (Ed.), *Stanford encyclopedia of Philosophy*. Stanford University Press. https://plato.stanford.edu/archives/fall2021/entries/possible-worlds/

Meyer, D., Zeileis, A., & Hornik, K. (2022). *vcd: visualizing categorical data [1.4–10]*. R Foundation for Statistical Computing. https://CRAN.R-project.org/package=vcd

Míguez, V. (2019). On (un)certainty: the semantic evolution of Galician *seguramente*. In C. Pinon (Ed.), *Empirical issues in syntax and semantics 12* (pp. 217–246). CSSP. http://www.cssp.cnrs.fr/eiss12/

Míguez, V. (2021). The diachrony of Galician *certamente* and *seguramente*: a case of grammatical constructionalization. In M. Hilpert, B. Cappelle, & I. Depraetere (Eds.), *Modality and diachronic construction grammar* (pp. 123–148). John Benjamins.

Míguez, V. (2022). On epistemic modality and discourse strategy: evidence from Galician adverbs. *Journal of Pragmatics*, 201, 32–42.

Míguez, V. (2023). A expresión da incerteza nos textos de *CORTEGAL*: un achegamento paradigmático. In M. Álvarez de la Granja & V. Míguez (Eds.), *Perspectivas sobre a escrita académica en galego. Estudos baseados no corpus CORTEGAL de textos escritos por estudantes* (pp. 325–352). Universidade de Santiago de Compostela.

Montero Küpper, S. (1999). A categoría da modalidade en alemán e galego. In D. Kremer (Ed.), *Actas do V Congreso Internacional de Estudios Galegos* (pp. 727–737, Vol. 1). Centro de Documentación de Galicia da Universidade de Trier.

Mortelmans, T. (2007). Modality in Cognitive Linguistics. In D. Geeraerts & H. Cuyckens (Eds.), *The Oxford hanbook of Cognitive Linguistics* (pp. 869–889). Oxford University Press.

Narrog, H. (2005a). Modality, mood, and change of modal meanings: a new perspective. *Cognitive Linguistics*, 16(4), 677–731.

Narrog, H. (2005b). On defining modality again. *Language Sciences*, 27(2), 165–192.

Narrog, H. (2008). The aspect-modality link in the Japanese verbal complex and beyond. In W. Abraham & E. Leiss (Eds.), *Modality-aspect interfaces: implications and typological solutions* (pp. 279–307). John Benjamins.

Narrog, H. (2009). *Modality in Japanese: the layered structure of the clause and hierarchies of functional categories*. John Benjamins.

Narrog, H. (2012). *Modality, subjectivity, and semantic change: a crosslinguistic perspective*. Oxford University Press.

Narrog, H. (2016). Three types of subjectivity, three types of intersubjectivity, their dynamicization and a synthesis. In D. Olmen, H. Cuyckens, & L. Ghesquière (Eds.), *Aspects of grammaticalization: (inter)subjectification and directionality* (pp. 19–46). De Gruyter.

Nauze, F. D. (2008). *Modality in typological perspective*. Institute for Logic, Language and Computation. https://eprints.illc.uva.nl/id/eprint/2068

Nikolaeva, I. (2016). Analyses of the semantics of mood. In J. Nuyts & J. van der Auwera (Eds.), *The Oxford handbook of modality and mood* (pp. 68–85). Oxford University Press.

Nolan, B. (2008). Modality in RRG: towards a characterisation using Irish data. In R. D. J. Van Valin (Ed.), *Investigations of the syntax–semantics–pragmatics interface* (pp. 147–159). John Benjamins.

Nuyts, J. (1992). *Aspects of a cognitive-pragmatic theory of language: on cognition, functionalism and grammar*. John Benjamins.

Nuyts, J. (2001a). *Epistemic modality, language, and conceptualization: a cognitive-pragmatic perspective*. John Benjamins.

Nuyts, J. (2001b). Subjectivity as an evidential dimension in epistemic modal expressions. *Journal of Pragmatics*, 33(3), 383–400.

Nuyts, J. (2005). The modal confusion: on terminology and the concepts behind it. In A. Klinge & H. Høeg Müller (Eds.), *Modality: studies in form and function* (pp. 5–38). Equinox.

Nuyts, J. (2006). Modality: overview and linguistic issues. In W. Frawley (Ed.), *The expression of modality* (pp. 1–26). Mouton de Gruyter.

Nuyts, J. (2009). The "one-commitment-per-clause" principle and the cognitive status of qualificational categories. *Linguistics*, 47, 141–171.

Nuyts, J. (2012). Notions of (inter)subjectivity. *English Text Construction*, 5(1), 53–76.

Nuyts, J. (2014). Subjectivity in modality, and beyond. In A. Zuczkowski, R. Bongelli, I. Riccioni, & C. Canestrari (Eds.), *Communicating certainty and uncertainty in medical, supportive and scientific contexts* (pp. 13–30). John Benjamins.

Nuyts, J. (2015). Subjectivity: between discourse and conceptualization. *Journal of Pragmatics*, 86, 106–110.

Nuyts, J. (2016). Analyses of the modal meanings. In J. Nuyts & J. van der Auwera (Eds.), *The Oxford handbook of modality and mood* (pp. 31–49). Oxford University Press.

Nuyts, J. (2017). Evidentiality reconsidered. In J. I. Marín Arrese, G. Haßler, & M. Carretero (Eds.), *Evidentiality revisited: cognitive grammar, functional and discourse-pragmatic perspectives* (pp. 57–83). John Benjamins.

Nuyts, J., & Byloo, P. (2015). Competing modals: beyond (inter)subjectification. *Diachronica*, 32(1), 34–68.

Nuyts, J., Byloo, P., & Diepeveen, J. (2010). On deontic modality, directivity, and mood: the case of Dutch *mogen* and *moeten*. *Journal of Pragmatics*, 42(1), 16–34.

Nuyts, J., & van der Auwera, J. (Eds.). (2016). *The Oxford handbook of modality and mood*. Oxford University Press.

Ochs, E. (1996). Linguistic resources for socializing humanity. In J. J. Gumperz & S. C. Levinson (Eds.), *Rethinking linguistic relativity* (pp. 407–437). Cambridge University Press.

Olbertz, H., & Dall'Aglio Hattnher, M. M. (2018). On objective and subjective epistemic modality again: evidence from Portuguese and Spanish modal auxiliaries. In E. Keizer & H. Olbertz (Eds.), *Recent developments in Functional Discourse Grammar* (pp. 132–168). John Benjamins.

Oliveira, T. (2015). Between evidentiality and epistemic modality: the case of the future and the conditional in European Portuguese. *Belgian Journal of Linguistics*, 29, 101–122.

Palmer, F. R. (1979). *Modality and the English modals*. Longman.

Palmer, F. R. (1986). *Mood and modality*. Cambridge University Press.

Palmer, F. R. (1990). *Modality and the English modals* (2nd ed.). Longman.

Palmer, F. R. (2001). *Mood and modality* (2nd ed.). Cambridge University Press.

Paolillo, J. C. (2002). *Analyzing linguistic variation: statistical models and methods*. CSLI.

Papafragou, A. (2000). *Modality: issues in the semantics-pragmatics interface*. Elsevier.

Patard, A., & Brisard, F. (Eds.). (2011). *Cognitive approaches to tense, aspect, and epistemic modality*. John Benjamins.

Pic, E., & Furmaniak, G. (2012). A study of epistemic modality in academic and popularised discourse: the case of possibility adverbs *perhaps*, *maybe* and *possibly*. *Revista de Lenguas para Fines Específicos*, 18, 13–44. https://ojsspdc.ulpgc.es/ojs/index.php/LFE/article/view/35

Pietrandrea, P. (2005). *Epistemic modality: functional properties and the Italian system*. John Benjamins.

Pietrandrea, P. (2008). *Certamente* and *sicuramente*: encoding dynamic and discursive aspects of commitment in Italian. *Belgian Journal of Linguistics*, 22(1), 221–246.

Pinto de Lima, J. (2008). Ongoing lexicalization and grammaticalization: a case from European Portuguese. In M.C. Almeida, B. Sieberg, & A.M. Bernardo (Eds.), *Questions on language change* (pp. 49–67). Colibri.

Portner, P. (2009). *Modality*. Oxford University Press.

Portner, P. (2018). *Mood*. Oxford University Press.

Przyjemski, K. (2017). Strong epistemic possibility and evidentiality. *Topoi*, 36(1), 183–195.

R Core Team. (2022). *R: a language and environment for statistical computing [4.2.1]*. R Foundation for Statistical Computing. https://www.R-project.org

Regueira, X.L. (2022). Language as object of research versus language as political object: old and new horizons in the study of Galician. In O. Castro, D. Baena, M.A.R. López, & M. Sánchez Moreiras (Eds.), *Gender, displacement, and cultural networks of Galicia: 1800s to present* (pp. 27–61). Palgrave Macmillan.

Rivas, J., & Sánchez-Ayala, I. (2012). Procesos de gramaticalización en el desarrollo de las aportaciones reactivas: el caso de *efectivamente*. In E. Montero Cartelle & C. Manzano Rovira (Eds.), *Actas del VIII Congreso Internacional de Historia de la Lengua Española* (pp. 2363–2374, Vol. 2). Meubook.

Robins, R.H. (2000). *Breve historia de la lingüística* (M. Condor, Trans.). Cátedra.

Rodríguez Rosique, S. (2017). The future of necessity in Spanish: modality, evidentiality and deictic projection at the crossroads. In J.I. Marín-Arrese, J. Lavid-López, M. Carretero, E. Domínguez Romero, M.V. Martín de la Rosa, & M. Pérez Blanco (Eds.), *Evidentiality and modality in European languages: discourse-pragmatic perspectives*. Peter Lang.

Rodríguez-Espiñeira, M.J. (2010). Modalidad, gramática y discurso: *posible*, *probable* y sus antónimos. In M.J. Rodríguez-Espiñeira (Ed.), *Adjetivos en discurso. Emociones, certezas, posibilidades y evidencias* (pp. 181–253). Universidade de Santiago de Compostela.

Rodríguez-Espiñeira, M.J. (2019). La expresión epistémica *si cuadra* en español de Galicia. *Estudos de Lingüística Galega*, 11, 197–231.

Rojo, G. (1974). *Perífrasis verbales en el gallego actual*. Universidade de Santiago de Compostela.

Rosales Sequeiros, X. (2000). Uso interpretativo de la lengua: *disque* y *seica* en lengua gallega. In F.J. Ruiz de Mendoza Ibáñez (Coord.), *Panorama actual de la lingüística aplicada* (pp. 375–386, Vol. 1). Universidad de La Rioja.

Saco Arce, J.A. (1868). *Gramática gallega*. Imprenta de Soto Freire.

Sadock, J.M. (1971). Queclaratives. *Chicago Linguistic Society*, 7, 223–231.

San Roque, L., Floyd, S., & Norcliffe, E. (2017). Evidentiality and interrogativity. *Lingua*, 186, 120–143.

Santamarina, A., González Seoane, E., & Álvarez de la Granja, M. (2018). *Tesouro Informatizado da Lingua Galega [4.1]*. Instituto da Lingua Galega. http://ilg.usc.gal/TILG/

Schneider, S. (2017). Las dimensiones de la intensificación y de la atenuación. In M. Albelda Marco & W. Mihatsch (Eds.), *Atenuación e intensificación en géneros discursivos* (pp. 23–42). Iberoamericana / Vervuert.

Schoonjans, S. (2019). Modal particle meanings: new insights from gesture research. *Review of Cognitive Linguistics*, 17(2), 303–330.

Simon-Vandenbergen, A.-M. (2000). The functions of *I think* in political discourse. *International Journal of Applied Linguistics*, 10(1), 41–63.

Simon-Vandenbergen, A.-M., & Aijmer, K. (2007). *The semantic field of modal certainty: a corpus-based study of English adverbs*. Mouton de Gruyter.

Sousa, X. (2012). Estrategias evidenciales y expresión de la fuente de información en gallego: los marcadores gramaticalizados. In X. Viejo Fernández (Ed.), *Estudios sobre variación sintáctica peninsular* (pp. 75–98). Trabe.

Sperber, D., & Wilson, D. (1995). *Relevance: communication and cognition* (2nd ed.). Blackwell.

Squartini, M. (2001). The internal structure of evidentiality in Romance. *Studies in Language*, 25(2), 297–334.

Squartini, M. (2004). Disentangling evidentiality and epistemic modality in Romance. *Lingua*, 114(7), 873–895.

Squartini, M. (2008). Lexical vs. grammatical evidentiality in French and Italian. *Linguistics*, 46(5), 917–947.

Squartini, M. (2016). Interaction between modality and other semantic categories. In J. Nuyts & J. van der Auwera (Eds.), *The Oxford handbook of modality and mood* (pp. 50–67). Oxford University Press.

Stein, D., & Wright, S. (1995). *Subjectivity and subjectivisation: linguistic perspectives*. Cambridge University Press.

Stubbs, M. (1986). A matter of prolonged field work: notes towards a modal grammar of English. *Applied Linguistics*, 7(1), 1–25.

Suárez Hernández, A. (2018). *Análisis diacrónico de adverbios con función discursiva: hacia una descripción lexicográfica*. Cilengua. https://www.cilengua.es/tienda/historia-de-la-lengua

Sučić, L. (2019). El caso de *acaso*: una partícula modal. *Verba*, 46, 279–312.

Suzuki, D. (2018). The semantics and pragmatics of modal adverbs: grammaticalization and (inter)subjectification of *perhaps*. *Lingua*, 205, 40–53.

Sweetser, E. (1990). *From etymology to pragmatics: metaphorical and cultural aspects of semantic structure*. Cambridge University Press.

Talmy, L. (1988). Force dynamics in language and cognition. *Cognitive Science*, 12(1), 49–100.

Talmy, L. (2000). *Toward a cognitive semantics. I. Concept structuring systems*. MIT Press.

Thieroff, R. (2010). Moods, moods, moods. In B. Rothstein & R. Thieroff (Eds.), *Mood in the languages of Europe* (pp. 1–29). John Benjamins.

Traugott, E. C. (1989). On the rise of epistemic meanings in English: an example of subjectification in semantic change. *Language*, 65(1), 31–55.

Traugott, E. C. (2003a). Approaching modality from the perspective of Relevance Theory. *Language Sciences*, 25(6), 657–669.

Traugott, E. C. (2003b). From subjectification to intersubjectification. In R. Hickey (Ed.), *Motives for language change* (pp. 124–139). Cambridge University Press.

Traugott, E. C. (2006). Historical aspects of modality. In W. Frawley (Ed.), *The expression of modality* (pp. 107–139). Mouton de Gruyter.

Traugott, E. C. (2007). (Inter)subjectification and unidirectionality. *Journal of Historical Pragmatics*, 8(2), 295–309.

Traugott, E. C. (2010). (Inter)subjectivity and (inter)subjectification: a reassessment. In K. Davidse, L. Vandelanotte, & H. Cuyckens (Eds.), *Subjectification, intersubjectification and grammaticalization* (pp. 29–71). De Gruyter Mouton.

Traugott, E. C., & Dasher, R. B. (2002). *Regularity in semantic change*. Cambridge University Press.

Traugott, E. C., & Trousdale, G. (2013). *Constructionalization and constructional changes*. Oxford University Press.

Tucker, G. H. (2001). Possibly alternative modality. *Functions of Language*, 8(2), 183–215.

van der Auwera, J., & Ammann, A. (2013a). Epistemic possibility. In M. S. Dryer & M. Haspelmath (Eds.), *The world atlas of language structures online*. Max Planck Institute for Evolutionary Anthropology. http://wals.info/chapter/75

van der Auwera, J., & Ammann, A. (2013b). Overlap between situational and epistemic modal marking. In M. S. Dryer & M. Haspelmath (Eds.), *The world atlas of language structures online*. Max Planck Institute for Evolutionary Anthropology. http://wals.info/chapter/76

van der Auwera, J., & Ammann, A. (2013c). Situational possibility. In M. S. Dryer & M. Haspelmath (Eds.), *The world atlas of language structures online*. Max Planck Institute for Evolutionary Anthropology. http://wals.info/chapter/74

van der Auwera, J., & Plungian, V. A. (1998). Modality's semantic map. *Linguistic Typology*, 2(1), 79–124.

van der Auwera, J., & Zamorano Aguilar, A. (2016). The history of modality and mood. In J. Nuyts & J. van der Auwera (Eds.), *The Oxford handbook of modality and mood* (pp. 9–29). Oxford University Press.

Van linden, A. (2012). *Modal adjectives: English deontic and evaluative constructions in synchrony and diachrony*. De Gruyter Mouton.

Van linden, A., & Verstraete, J.-C. (2011). Revisiting deontic modality and related categories: a conceptual map based on the study of English modal adjectives. *Journal of Pragmatics*, 43(1), 150–163.

Van Olmen, D., & van der Auwera, J. (2016). Modality and mood in Standard Average European. In J. Nuyts & J. van der Auwera (Eds.), *The Oxford handbook of modality and mood* (pp. 362–384). Oxford University Press.

Van Valin, R. D. J. (2005). *Exploring the syntax-semantics interface*. Cambridge University Press.

Van Valin, R. D. J., & LaPolla, R. J. (1997). *Syntax: structure, meaning and function*. Cambridge University Press.

Varela Barreiro, X. (Dir.). (2007). *Tesouro Medieval Informatizado da Lingua Galega*. Instituto da Lingua Galega. http://ilg.usc.es/tmilg

Veiga, A. (1991). Sobre a decadencia do subxuntivo en prótases condicionais en galego e español e a subxuntivación da forma *cantara*. In M. Brea & F. Fernández Rei (Eds.), *Homenaxe ó Profesor Constantino García* (pp. 497–539, Vol. 1). Universidade de Santiago de Compostela. http://hdl.handle.net/10347/12474

Veiga, A. (1992). Sobre a reorganización das oposicións temporais en subxuntivo e subxuntivo irreal na diacronía do verbo hispánico. In R. Lorenzo (Ed.), *Actas do XIX Congreso Internacional de Lingüística e Filoloxía Románicas. V. Gramática Histórica e Historia da Lingua* (pp. 435–466). Universidade de Santiago de Compostela.

Verhagen, A. (1986). *Linguistic theory and the function of word order in Dutch*. Foris.

Verstraete, J.-C. (2001). Subjective and objective modality: interpersonal and ideational functions in the English modal auxiliary system. *Journal of Pragmatics*, 33(10), 1505–1528.

Verstraete, J.-C. (2005). The semantics and pragmatics of composite mood marking: the non-Pama-Nyungan languages of northern Australia. *Linguistic Typology*, 9(2), 223–268.

von Fintel, K., & Gillies, A. S. (2008). CIA Leaks. *Philosophical Review*, 117(1), 77–98.

von Wright, G. H. (1951). *An essay in modal logic*. North-Holland.

White, P. R. R. (2003). Beyond modality and hedging: a dialogic view of the language of intersubjective stance. *Text & Talk*, 23(2), 259–284.

Willett, T. (1988). A cross-linguistic survey of the grammaticization of evidentiality. *Studies in Language*, 12(1), 51–97.

Wittgenstein, L. (1969). *On certainty* (G. E. M. Anscombe & G. H. von Wright, Eds.; D. Paul & G. E. M. Anscombe, Trans.). Basil Blackwell.

Woehr, R. (1972). "Acaso," "quizá(s)," "tal vez": free variants? *Hispania*, 55(2), 320–327.

Wright, S. (1995). Subjectivity and experiential syntax. In D. Stein & S. Wright (Eds.), *Subjectivity and subjectivisation* (pp. 151–172). Cambridge University Press.

Appendixes

APPENDIX A

Appendix of tables

Table A.1 Frequency of verb lemmas in the dataset

Lemma	Freq.	Lemma	Freq.
abondar	4	*gustar*	3
abranguer	1	*haber*	67
abrir	2	*idealizar*	1
acabar	6	*identificar*	1
acender	1	*ignorar*	4
aceptar	2	*impedir*	1
acontecer	2	*implicar*	2
acordarse	1	*impoñer*	1
actuar	3	*importar*	1
adiar	1	*impulsar*	1
adoitar	1	*incidir*	1
adoptar	1	*indicar*	1
adormecer	1	*influír*	5
adquirir	1	*informar*	1
afastar	2	*inspirar*	1
afinar	1	*inspirarse*	1
afortalar	2	*interesar*	4
agardar	2	*interpretar*	1
agradar	1	*intuír*	3
agradecer	1	*ir*	36
agromar	1	*irromper*	1
albiscar	1	*irse*	1
alcanzar	1	*lanzar*	1
alegrarse	1	*latexar*	1
aliviar	2	*lembrar*	2
amar	1	*ler*	3
amolar	2	*levar*	12
amosar	2	*limitar*	1
amparar	1	*manter*	3
andar	2	*manterse*	1
apadriñar	1	*marchar*	2
aparecer	4	*matinar*	1
aportar	1	*mellorar*	1
apostar	1	*merecer*	3
apreciar	1	*mermar*	1

Table A.1 *(continued)*

Lemma	Freq.	Lemma	Freq.
aproveitar	4	*minar*	1
aproveitarse	1	*minguar*	1
apuntar	1	*mirar*	1
arrastrar	1	*modificar*	1
arrefriar	1	*morrer*	1
asistir	2	*mover*	1
aspirar	1	*nacer*	4
atacar	1	*naufragar*	2
atender	1	*necesitar*	2
atinar	1	*notar*	1
atopar	6	*obedecer*	4
atoparse	2	*obrigar*	1
atrapar	1	*obstruír*	1
aturar	1	*ocorrer*	4
aumentar	3	*ocorrerse*	1
aveciñarse	1	*odiar*	1
axudar	1	*oír*	2
baixar	1	*ollar*	1
basearse	1	*olvidarse*	1
bastar	1	*operar*	1
beber	2	*padecer*	1
bocexar	1	*pagar*	1
botar	1	*parecer*	4
botarse	1	*pasar*	7
buscar	3	*pedir*	2
cabalgar	1	*pelexar*	1
caer	1	*pendurar*	1
calibrar	1	*pensar*	14
cambiar	1	*percorrer*	1
carecer	1	*perder*	4
causar	1	*perdoar*	1
chamar	1	*permanecer*	3
chegar	11	*permitir*	5
cheirar	1	*persistir*	1
chover	1	*pesar*	1
cobrar	1	*pintar*	1
coincidir	2	*poder*	83
coller	1	*poñer*	3
comer	2	*poñerse*	1
comezar	9	*posibilitar*	1
compensar	3	*posuír*	4

Table A.1 *(continued)*

Lemma	Freq.	Lemma	Freq.
competir	1	precisar	4
comprar	2	predominar	1
comprender	1	preferir	1
comprobar	2	pregar	1
concorrer	1	prender	1
conducir	1	preservar	1
confiar	1	presumir	1
confundir	1	pretender	1
confundirse	1	prever	1
conlevar	1	proceder	6
conmover	1	prodigar	1
conseguir	6	producir	2
considerar	2	producirse	2
consistir	3	provir	1
consolidar	1	provocar	3
constituír	6	quedar	8
contar	3	quedarse	1
continuar	3	querer	12
contrastar	1	radicar	3
contribuír	2	recibir	2
controlar	1	recitar	1
converter	1	reclamar	1
convidar	1	recoller	4
convir	7	recoñecer	1
coñecer	8	recuperar	2
corresponder	3	reducir	2
crer	3	referirse	3
cubrir	1	reflectir	2
cumprir	2	reflexar	1
custar	2	regalar	1
dar	13	regresar	3
darse	3	rematar	5
deber	17	rememorar	1
deberse	7	remitir	1
decatarse	2	remontar	1
decidir	1	reparar	1
declarar	1	requirir	1
dedicar	2	residir	1
deixar	5	resistir	2
demostrar	2	responder	2
depender	2	resultar	8

Table A.1 (continued)

Lemma	Freq.	Lemma	Freq.
derivar	1	retirar	1
desagradar	1	retornar	1
desaparecer	1	rexeitar	1
desaproveitar	1	rir	1
desconcertar	1	roubar	1
descoñecer	2	saber	19
descubrir	3	sacar	1
desembocar	1	saír	6
desencadear	1	salvar	1
desexar	1	seguir	8
desilusionar	1	semellar	2
despreciar	1	sentir	4
destacar	1	sentirse	2
desvelar	1	ser	570
detectar	1	servir	5
dicir	7	significar	1
diferir	1	sinalar	1
dilatarse	1	soar	1
disfrutar	1	sobrar	1
distar	1	sobreestimar	1
doer	2	soltar	1
dubidar	1	someter	1
durar	1	soñar	2
durmir	1	soportar	1
eclosionar	1	soprar	1
elixir	1	sospeitar	3
empezar	2	soterrar	1
encerrar	1	subsistir	2
encontrar	2	substituír	1
engadir	1	subxacer	1
enganchar	1	suceder	6
enteirarse	1	sufrir	2
entender	3	superar	1
entorpecer	1	supoñer	2
entrañar	1	suscitar	1
entrar	2	tardar	4
entreter	1	temer	2
envasar	1	tender	3
escapar	2	tentar	1
escoitar	4	ter	112
escribir	2	tinguir	1

Table A.1 *(continued)*

Lemma	Freq.	Lemma	Freq.
esixir	2	*tomar*	3
esmorecer	1	*tornar*	1
esperar	3	*tornarse*	1
espoldrear	1	*traballar*	1
esquecer	1	*traer*	1
estar	93	*transcorrer*	2
evidenciar	1	*transmitir*	1
evitar	1	*trasladar*	1
excitar	1	*tratar*	1
existir	13	*tratarse*	11
experimentar	1	*tropezar*	1
explicar	5	*turbar*	1
extremar	1	*ulir*	2
fabricar	1	*uliscar*	1
facer	35	*usar*	2
facerse	1	*utilizar*	1
facilitar	2	*valer*	1
falar	3	*ver*	10
faltar	3	*viaxar*	1
ficar	1	*vir*	11
figurar	1	*visitar*	1
fixarse	1	*vivir*	5
formar	3	*voltar*	1
formular	1	*volver*	11
fraquear	1	*xantar*	1
gañar	2	*xerar*	1
gardar	3	*xogar*	1
gastar	2	*xulgar*	1
gozar	2	*zoupar*	1

Table A.2 Mood share by adverb

	ind N	ind %	sbjv N	sbjv %
cert	300	100.00	0	0.00
segu	288	96.00	12	4.00
prob	221	73.67	79	26.33
posi	185	61.67	115	38.33
quiz	147	49.00	153	51.00
seca	290	96.67	10	3.33

Table A.3 Mood share by adverb. Pre-verbal position only

	ind N	ind %	sbjv N	sbjv %
cert	213	100.00	0	0.00
segu	245	95.33	12	4.67
prob	163	67.36	79	32.64
posi	137	54.58	114	45.42
quiz	113	42.48	153	57.52
seca	250	96.15	10	3.85

Table A.4 *p*-values for the MLR model (one vs. rest approach)

	cert	segu	prob	posi	quiz	seca
(Intercept)	0.00000	0.00000	0.00000	0.00000	0.00000	0.00000
CLAUSEsubord	0.00106	0.72874	0.00369	0.05142	0.07756	0.71785
POLARITYneg	0.00000	0.01395	0.82253	0.41843	0.33464	0.52975
POSITIONpre-v	0.02933	0.41068	0.47746	0.11291	0.00268	0.00450
POSITIONpost-v	0.00099	0.30009	0.11030	0.46278	0.00891	0.04072
POSITIONfin	0.00000	0.61609	0.11030	0.10772	0.23185	0.16643
TIMEfut	0.00002	0.02612	0.00577	0.00058	0.00440	0.89046
TIMEfutpast	0.00863	0.00077	0.90287	0.00178	0.39686	0.00616
TIMEindet	0.10343	0.97565	0.03121	0.54099	0.71728	0.82692
TIMEpast	0.84296	0.00417	0.63931	0.15101	0.02798	0.01917
MEDIUMoral	0.00000	0.73825	0.97533	0.56355	0.65399	0.00000

APPENDIX B

Appendix of listings (R output)

Listing B.1 Summary of the morpho-syntactic MLR model. Pairwise approach (`mlogit` package)

```
Call:
mlogit(formula = ADVERB ~ 1 | CLAUSE + POSITION + DISTANCE + MEDIUM,
    data = mlr.data, reflevel = 3, method = "nr")
Frequencies of alternatives:
    prob         cert         posi         quiz         seca         segu
  0.16667      0.16667      0.16667      0.16667      0.16667      0.16667
nr method
6 iterations, 0h:0m:1s
g'(-H)^-1g = 9E-06
successive function values within tolerance limits
Coefficients :
                          Estimate     Std. Error    z-value    Pr(>|z|)
cert:(intercept)         -0.1503467    0.1739415     -0.8644    0.3873945
posi:(intercept)         -0.0731691    0.1641393     -0.4458    0.6557600
quiz:(intercept)          0.0850476    0.1627905      0.5224    0.6013666
seca:(intercept)          0.1376180    0.1606528      0.8566    0.3916566
segu:(intercept)          0.1701764    0.1593351      1.0680    0.2855021
cert:CLAUSEsubord        -0.7267124    0.2042933     -3.5572    0.0003748   ***
posi:CLAUSEsubord        -0.0155609    0.1798087     -0.0865    0.9310359
quiz:CLAUSEsubord        -0.5801190    0.1940277     -2.9899    0.0027909   **
seca:CLAUSEsubord        -0.4766409    0.1909139     -2.4966    0.0125380   *
segu:CLAUSEsubord        -0.2725655    0.1835939     -1.4846    0.1376469
cert:POSITIONpre-v       -0.2972062    0.2957753     -1.0048    0.3149750
posi:POSITIONpre-v        0.3608028    0.2446051      1.4750    0.1402013
quiz:POSITIONpre-v        0.5108826    0.2394990      2.1331    0.0329140   *
seca:POSITIONpre-v       -0.5062935    0.2796422     -1.8105    0.0702175   .
segu:POSITIONpre-v        0.1293044    0.2471717      0.5231    0.6008797
cert:POSITIONpost-v       0.4516772    0.2288820      1.9734    0.0484493   *
posi:POSITIONpost-v      -0.1000155    0.2345059     -0.4265    0.6697476
quiz:POSITIONpost-v      -0.5632653    0.2590186     -2.1746    0.0296591   *
seca:POSITIONpost-v      -0.5622178    0.2464663     -2.2811    0.0225417   *
segu:POSITIONpost-v      -0.4788116    0.2430649     -1.9699    0.0488507   *
cert:POSITIONfin          2.9257547    1.0385845      2.8171    0.0048465   **
posi:POSITIONfin         -0.0099026    1.4200736     -0.0070    0.9944362
quiz:POSITIONfin          1.1070439    1.1628507      0.9520    0.3410926
```

Listing B.1 *(continued)*

```
seca:POSITIONfin           0.8649919    1.1653078    0.7423    0.4579140
segu:POSITIONfin           1.3579616    1.1255542    1.2065    0.2276314
cert:DISTANCEnear-adj      0.4935434    0.2191566    2.2520    0.0243215   *
posi:DISTANCEnear-adj      0.0477355    0.2112759    0.2259    0.8212487
quiz:DISTANCEnear-adj      0.0691465    0.2120153    0.3261    0.7443190
seca:DISTANCEnear-adj      0.1256977    0.2076083    0.6055    0.5448759
segu:DISTANCEnear-adj      0.0589616    0.2063598    0.2857    0.7750908
cert:DISTANCEnon-adj       0.5274097    0.2442155    2.1596    0.0308030   *
posi:DISTANCEnon-adj       0.1489085    0.2402132    0.6199    0.5353228
quiz:DISTANCEnon-adj      -0.0815147    0.2476963   -0.3291    0.7420867
seca:DISTANCEnon-adj      -0.1674861    0.2434046   -0.6881    0.4913915
segu:DISTANCEnon-adj      -0.2051366    0.2451485   -0.8368    0.4027135
cert:DISTANCEdistant       0.8472906    0.3251395    2.6059    0.0091625   **
posi:DISTANCEdistant       0.2044832    0.3385968    0.6039    0.5459011
quiz:DISTANCEdistant       0.6329374    0.3119219    2.0292    0.0424426   *
seca:DISTANCEdistant      -0.2090388    0.3519233   -0.5940    0.5525190
segu:DISTANCEdistant      -0.3627705    0.3643413   -0.9957    0.3194014
cert:MEDIUMoral           -1.2363479    0.3305251   -3.7406    0.0001836   ***
posi:MEDIUMoral           -0.0590099    0.2443354   -0.2415    0.8091585
quiz:MEDIUMoral           -0.0428110    0.2431080   -0.1761    0.8602163
seca:MEDIUMoral            0.7192533    0.2174876    3.3071    0.0009427   ***
segu:MEDIUMoral           -0.0083876    0.2396696   -0.0350    0.9720825
---
Signif. codes:  0 '***' 0.001 '**' 0.01 '*' 0.05 '.' 0.1 ' ' 1
Log-Likelihood: -3124.6
McFadden R^2:  0.031189
Likelihood ratio test : chisq = 201.18 (p.value = < 2.22e-16)
```

Listing B.2 Summary of the morpho-syntactic MLR model. One vs. rest approach (polytomous package). Not stastically significant coefficients are in brackets

```
Formula:
ADVERB ~ CLAUSE + POSITION + DISTANCE + MEDIUM

Heuristic:
one.vs.rest


Log-odds:
                    cert      segu        prob       posi       quiz        seca
CLAUSEsubord       -0.478    (0.0604)    0.3943     0.3741    (-0.3082)   (-0.1897)
DISTANCEdistant     0.7414   -0.6867    (-0.2624)  (-0.02139)  0.5157     (-0.5088)
DISTANCEnear-adj    0.4311  (-0.07882)  (-0.1491)  (-0.08843) (-0.06547)   (0.006564)
```

Listing B.2 *(continued)*

```
DISTANCEnon-adj        0.5886      (-0.2795)    (-0.03516)    (0.1459)     (-0.1301)    (-0.2289)
(Intercept)           -1.826       -1.458        -1.663       -1.752       -1.562       -1.497
MEDIUMoral            -1.4         (-0.03039)   (-0.01963)   (-0.0885)    (-0.06566)    0.9105
POSITIONfin            2.105       (-0.2621)    (-1.714)     (-1.736)     (-0.5667)    (-0.7786)
POSITIONpost-v         0.7722      (-0.3494)     (0.2291)     (0.1021)    -0.4375      -0.4417
POSITIONpre-v         (-0.442)     (0.05557)    (-0.1037)     (0.3374)     0.5361      -0.6995


Null deviance:                         6450    on    10800    degrees of freedom
Residual (model) deviance:             6250    on    10746    degrees of freedom
R2.likelihood:                                 0.0311
AIC:                                           6358
BIC:                                           6655
```

Listing B.3 Summary of the lexico-semantic MLR model. Pairwise approach (mlogit package)

```
Call:
mlogit(formula = ADVERB ~ 1 | VERB + POLARITY + TIME + CONTROL + DYNAM + PERFORM, data = mlr.data,
reflevel = 3, method = "nr")

Frequencies of alternatives:
prob            cert            posi            quiz            seca            segu
0.16667         0.16667         0.16667         0.16667         0.16667         0.16667

nr method
7 iterations, 0h:0m:1s
g'(-H)^-1g = 3.48E-06
successive function values within tolerance limits

Coefficients :
                      Estimate       Std. Error     z-value        Pr(>|z|)
cert:(intercept)     -0.217151       0.472786      -0.4593         0.646018
posi:(intercept)      0.246243       0.391662       0.6287         0.529536
quiz:(intercept)      0.155244       0.420138       0.3695         0.711749
seca:(intercept)     -0.036229       0.455755      -0.0795         0.936641
segu:(intercept)     -0.145036       0.423439      -0.3425         0.731960
cert:VERBestar       -0.190942       0.418429      -0.4563         0.648152
posi:VERBestar        0.261567       0.399950       0.6540         0.513112
quiz:VERBestar        0.197654       0.405988       0.4868         0.626366
seca:VERBestar       -0.034362       0.411084      -0.0836         0.933384
segu:VERBestar        0.434611       0.377481       1.1513         0.249589
cert:VERBhaber        1.015267       0.481704       2.1077         0.035061      *
```

Listing B.3 *(continued)*

posi:VERBhaber	0.163961	0.537249	0.3052	0.760225	
quiz:VERBhaber	0.234505	0.539412	0.4347	0.663750	
seca:VERBhaber	0.617479	0.492507	1.2537	0.209934	
segu:VERBhaber	0.692601	0.485431	1.4268	0.153645	
cert:VERBpoder	0.643083	0.415707	1.5470	0.121873	
posi:VERBpoder	-0.190683	0.471760	-0.4042	0.686069	
quiz:VERBpoder	0.663765	0.405807	1.6357	0.101909	
seca:VERBpoder	0.487495	0.409022	1.1919	0.233318	
segu:VERBpoder	-0.414776	0.485370	-0.8546	0.392797	
cert:VERBser	-0.040783	0.213583	-0.1909	0.848568	
posi:VERBser	0.021255	0.218033	0.0975	0.922342	
quiz:VERBser	0.293310	0.212876	1.3778	0.168251	
seca:VERBser	-0.022218	0.215964	-0.1029	0.918058	
segu:VERBser	-0.399692	0.227135	-1.7597	0.078458	.
cert:VERBter	-0.461830	0.385137	-1.1991	0.230477	
posi:VERBter	-0.075929	0.340316	-0.2231	0.823447	
quiz:VERBter	0.043360	0.347437	0.1248	0.900682	
seca:VERBter	-0.244593	0.353585	-0.6918	0.489093	
segu:VERBter	-0.048624	0.336352	-0.1446	0.885057	
cert:POLARITYneg	0.460345	0.216088	2.1304	0.033142	*
posi:POLARITYneg	-0.148572	0.231222	-0.6426	0.520515	
quiz:POLARITYneg	-0.119946	0.233982	-0.5126	0.608211	
seca:POLARITYneg	-0.076960	0.231396	-0.3326	0.739444	
segu:POLARITYneg	-0.433423	0.244746	-1.7709	0.076576	.
cert:TIMEfut	-3.460330	0.745190	-4.6436	3.425e-06	***
posi:TIMEfut	0.086474	0.277412	0.3117	0.755255	
quiz:TIMEfut	-0.877718	0.315777	-2.7795	0.005443	**
seca:TIMEfut	-0.605116	0.282110	-2.1450	0.031956	*
segu:TIMEfut	-0.285034	0.287483	-0.9915	0.321451	
cert:TIMEfutpast	-1.257834	0.566016	-2.2223	0.026266	*
posi:TIMEfutpast	0.580198	0.406765	1.4264	0.153761	
quiz:TIMEfutpast	-0.289122	0.456757	-0.6330	0.526741	
seca:TIMEfutpast	-1.838250	0.670894	-2.7400	0.006144	**
segu:TIMEfutpast	0.440331	0.410429	1.0729	0.283336	
cert:TIMEindet	-0.611406	0.257628	-2.3732	0.017634	*
posi:TIMEindet	-0.433066	0.274522	-1.5775	0.114673	
quiz:TIMEindet	-0.274404	0.244145	-1.1239	0.261038	
seca:TIMEindet	-0.615598	0.254450	-2.4193	0.015549	*
segu:TIMEindet	-0.377359	0.275061	-1.3719	0.170091	
cert:TIMEpast	-0.045147	0.201379	-0.2242	0.822609	
posi:TIMEpast	0.096998	0.211303	0.4590	0.646201	
quiz:TIMEpast	-0.287696	0.207139	-1.3889	0.164863	

Listing B.3 *(continued)*

```
seca:TIMEpast       -0.482599    0.208773    -2.3116    0.020800    *
segu:TIMEpast        0.199513    0.211586     0.9429    0.345712
cert:CONTROLctrl    -0.896105    0.346379    -2.5871    0.009680    **
posi:CONTROLctrl     0.157429    0.281315     0.5596    0.575740
quiz:CONTROLctrl     0.383273    0.306232     1.2516    0.210724
seca:CONTROLctrl    -0.030934    0.291148    -0.1062    0.915385
segu:CONTROLctrl     0.189255    0.272208     0.6953    0.486892
cert:DYNAMdyn        0.241171    0.243699     0.9896    0.322358
posi:DYNAMdyn        0.053318    0.241411     0.2209    0.825202
quiz:DYNAMdyn       -0.194666    0.261033    -0.7458    0.455818
seca:DYNAMdyn        0.232219    0.243381     0.9541    0.340016
segu:DYNAMdyn        0.251634    0.236441     1.0643    0.287211
cert:PERFORMperf     0.451930    0.436225     1.0360    0.300202
posi:PERFORMperf    -0.320987    0.339738    -0.9448    0.344756
quiz:PERFORMperf    -0.044171    0.376165    -0.1174    0.906524
seca:PERFORMperf     0.340788    0.417501     0.8163    0.414354
segu:PERFORMperf     0.151426    0.376783     0.4019    0.687763
---
Signif. codes:  0 '***' 0.001 '**' 0.01 '*' 0.05 '.' 0.1 ' ' 1
Log-Likelihood: -3110.9
McFadden R^2: 0.035433
Likelihood ratio test : chisq = 228.56 (p.value = < 2.22e-16)
```

Listing B.4 Summary of the lexico-semantic MLR model. One vs. rest approach (polytomous package). Not stastically significant coefficients are in brackets

```
Formula:
ADVERB ~ VERB + POLARITY + TIME + CONTROL + DYNAM + PERFORM

Heuristic:
one.vs.rest

Log-odds:
                 cert        segu        prob         posi        quiz        seca
CONTROLctrl     -1.033      (0.2156)   (-0.02723)   (0.155)     (0.4376)    (-0.04275)
DYNAMdyn        (0.1569)    (0.1844)   (-0.1274)    (-0.06053)  (-0.3456)   (0.1526)
(Intercept)     -1.913      -1.873     -1.688       -1.358      -1.492      -1.707
PERFORMperf     (0.4512)    (0.1354)   (-0.05779)   (-0.4768)   (-0.1205)   (0.3277)
POLARITYneg      0.6088     -0.4694    (0.04335)    (-0.1244)   (-0.1165)   (-0.06739)
TIMEfut         -3.141      (0.2702)    0.6393       0.744      (-0.4256)   (-0.09776)
TIMEfutpast     -1.199       0.7847    (0.2233)      0.9618     (-0.1225)   -1.836
TIMEindet       (-0.2746)   (0.006177)  0.462       (-0.06053)  (0.1329)    (-0.2838)
```

Listing B.4 *(continued)*

TIMEpast	(0.06285)	0.3495	(0.1108)	(0.225)	(-0.2325)	-0.4699
VERBestar	(-0.3728)	(0.3927)	(-0.1404)	(0.167)	(0.09204)	(-0.1803)
VERBhaber	0.6367	(0.2544)	(-0.5737)	(-0.3778)	(-0.3165)	(0.1376)
VERBpoder	(0.4519)	-0.7624	(-0.3007)	(-0.4905)	(0.4987)	(0.2749)
VERBser	(-0.03803)	-0.4466	(0.01406)	(0.04155)	0.374	(-0.01099)
VERBter	(-0.3959)	(0.07978)	(0.1397)	(0.0418)	(0.1956)	(-0.1505)

```
Null deviance:               6450  on  10800  degrees of freedom
Residual (model) deviance:   6224  on  10716  degrees of freedom
R2.likelihood:               0.03516
AIC:                         6392
BIC:                         6853
```

Listing B.5 Summary of the final MLR model (`mlogit` package)

```
Call:
mlogit(formula = ADVERB ~ 1 | POLARITY + CLAUSE + POSITION + DISTANCE + TIME + MEDIUM,
data = mlr.data, reflevel = 3, method = "nr")

Frequencies of alternatives:
prob       cert       posi       quiz       seca       segu
0.16667    0.16667    0.16667    0.16667    0.16667    0.16667

nr method
7 iterations, 0h:0m:1s
g'(-H)^-1g = 5.98E-06
successive function values within tolerance limits

Coefficients :
```

	Estimate	Std. Error	z-value	Pr(>|z|)	
cert:(intercept)	0.118899	0.206126	0.5768	0.5640574	
posi:(intercept)	-0.083120	0.201572	-0.4124	0.6800777	
quiz:(intercept)	0.344753	0.194500	1.7725	0.0763106	.
seca:(intercept)	0.388331	0.192150	2.0210	0.0432822	*
segu:(intercept)	0.078241	0.200059	0.3911	0.6957297	
cert:POLARITYneg	0.525296	0.244986	2.1442	0.0320179	*
posi:POLARITYneg	-0.202290	0.258847	-0.7815	0.4345058	
quiz:POLARITYneg	-0.253397	0.264255	-0.9589	0.3376032	
seca:POLARITYneg	-0.270764	0.261431	-1.0357	0.3003421	
segu:POLARITYneg	-0.574729	0.271726	-2.1151	0.0344209	*
cert:CLAUSEsubord	-0.720700	0.209689	-3.4370	0.0005882	***
posi:CLAUSEsubord	-0.072654	0.182653	-0.3978	0.6908000	

Listing B.5 *(continued)*

```
quiz:CLAUSEsubord         -0.524538    0.196987    -2.6628    0.0077494    **
seca:CLAUSEsubord         -0.406723    0.193243    -2.1047    0.0353155    *
segu:CLAUSEsubord         -0.313279    0.186719    -1.6778    0.0933840    .
cert:POSITIONpre-v        -0.174409    0.301776    -0.5779    0.5633023
posi:POSITIONpre-v         0.396641    0.246873     1.6067    0.1081291
quiz:POSITIONpre-v         0.581909    0.242778     2.3969    0.0165354    *
seca:POSITIONpre-v        -0.459786    0.281980    -1.6306    0.1029829
segu:POSITIONpre-v         0.197941    0.249892     0.7921    0.4282987
cert:POSITIONpost-v        0.479662    0.235366     2.0379    0.0415560    *
posi:POSITIONpost-v       -0.040385    0.235530    -0.1715    0.8638586
quiz:POSITIONpost-v       -0.561406    0.260552    -2.1547    0.0311868    *
seca:POSITIONpost-v       -0.563344    0.247592    -2.2753    0.0228883    *
segu:POSITIONpost-v       -0.414071    0.244189    -1.6957    0.0899426    .
cert:POSITIONfin           2.854368    1.045758     2.7295    0.0063436    **
posi:POSITIONfin          -0.054518    1.421729    -0.0383    0.9694115
quiz:POSITIONfin           0.961715    1.166127     0.8247    0.4095369
seca:POSITIONfin           0.736595    1.168561     0.6303    0.5284696
segu:POSITIONfin           1.249002    1.128806     1.1065    0.2685186
cert:DISTANCEnear-adj      0.342206    0.249725     1.3703    0.1705838
posi:DISTANCEnear-adj      0.092894    0.236731     0.3924    0.6947608
quiz:DISTANCEnear-adj      0.225096    0.239034     0.9417    0.3463529
seca:DISTANCEnear-adj      0.281343    0.233080     1.2071    0.2274067
segu:DISTANCEnear-adj      0.239832    0.230314     1.0413    0.2977238
cert:DISTANCEnon-adj       0.524269    0.253785     2.0658    0.0388473    *
posi:DISTANCEnon-adj       0.176826    0.244619     0.7229    0.4697638
quiz:DISTANCEnon-adj       0.020900    0.252642     0.0827    0.9340713
seca:DISTANCEnon-adj      -0.094108    0.247970    -0.3795    0.7043077
segu:DISTANCEnon-adj      -0.117569    0.249330    -0.4715    0.6372553
cert:DISTANCEdistant       0.784249    0.331649     2.3647    0.0180449    *
posi:DISTANCEdistant       0.236689    0.340870     0.6944    0.4874527
quiz:DISTANCEdistant       0.673900    0.315132     2.1385    0.0324788    *
seca:DISTANCEdistant      -0.149332    0.354392    -0.4214    0.6734819
segu:DISTANCEdistant      -0.324745    0.366444    -0.8862    0.3755067
cert:TIMEfut              -3.345097    0.738166    -4.5316    5.853e-06    ***
posi:TIMEfut               0.090277    0.255512     0.3533    0.7238502
quiz:TIMEfut              -1.055600    0.297932    -3.5431    0.0003955    ***
seca:TIMEfut              -0.477542    0.261661    -1.8250    0.0679949    .
segu:TIMEfut              -0.071081    0.266654    -0.2666    0.7898013
cert:TIMEfutpast          -1.169794    0.562308    -2.0803    0.0374941    *
posi:TIMEfutpast           0.658714    0.394955     1.6678    0.0953514    .
quiz:TIMEfutpast          -0.292877    0.448101    -0.6536    0.5133712
seca:TIMEfutpast          -1.541215    0.664979    -2.3177    0.0204662    *
```

Listing B.5 *(continued)*

```
segu:TIMEfutpast            0.714021    0.399685    1.7865   0.0740246    .
cert:TIMEindet             -0.671295    0.262073   -2.5615   0.0104227    *
posi:TIMEindet             -0.478738    0.276923   -1.7288   0.0838492    .
quiz:TIMEindet             -0.323704    0.249384   -1.2980   0.1942831
seca:TIMEindet             -0.366480    0.258878   -1.4156   0.1568789
segu:TIMEindet             -0.342864    0.277039   -1.2376   0.2158633
cert:TIMEpast              -0.120991    0.198639   -0.6091   0.5424564
posi:TIMEpast               0.116304    0.206605    0.5629   0.5734817
quiz:TIMEpast              -0.372006    0.203964   -1.8239   0.0681698    .
seca:TIMEpast              -0.370334    0.204670   -1.8094   0.0703859    .
segu:TIMEpast               0.307793    0.205867    1.4951   0.1348870
cert:MEDIUMoral            -1.259688    0.335779   -3.7515   0.0001758    ***
posi:MEDIUMoral            -0.077584    0.248366   -0.3124   0.7547534
quiz:MEDIUMoral            -0.056064    0.248141   -0.2259   0.8212520
seca:MEDIUMoral             0.649146    0.222535    2.9170   0.0035336    **
segu:MEDIUMoral             0.036450    0.244457    0.1491   0.8814713
---
Signif. codes:  0 '***' 0.001 '**' 0.01 '*' 0.05 '.' 0.1 ' ' 1
Log-Likelihood: -3053.5
McFadden R^2:  0.053237
Likelihood ratio test : chisq = 343.39 (p.value = < 2.22e-16)
```

Listing B.6 Summary of the final MLR model One vs. rest approach (`polytomous` package). Not stastically significant coefficients are in brackets

```
Formula:
ADVERB ~ POLARITY + CLAUSE + POSITION + TIME + MEDIUM

Heuristic:
one.vs.rest

Log-odds:
               cert        segu       prob       posi       quiz       seca
CLAUSEsubord  -0.5684   (0.05094)    0.4096   (0.2773)   (-0.2794)  (-0.05601)
(Intercept)   -1.385    -1.828      -1.902    -1.897    -1.323     -1.425
MEDIUMoral    -1.442   (0.06274)   (-0.005901) (-0.1123) (-0.08558)  0.8739
POLARITYneg    0.8281   -0.4852    (0.03963)  (-0.1477) (-0.1784)  (-0.1156)
POSITIONfin    2.2     (-0.2734)   (-1.628)   (-1.641)  (-0.7344)  (-0.8589)
POSITIONpost-v 0.5543  (-0.1979)   (0.2715)   (0.1318)   -0.5426    -0.3977
POSITIONpre-v -0.5309  (0.1507)    (-0.1396)  (0.2847)    0.5128    -0.635
TIMEfut       -3.044    0.4748      0.5649    0.694     -0.7119   (-0.02872)
TIMEfutpast   -1.278    0.9716     (0.04155)  0.8903    (-0.2948)  -1.649
```

Listing B.6 *(continued)*

```
TIMEindet       (-0.3397)    (-0.006893)    0.4271        (-0.1387)    (0.06944)    (-0.04471)
TIMEpast        (-0.02923)   0.4477         (0.0746)      (0.2268)     -0.3369      -0.3631

Null deviance:                              6450   on    10800    degrees of freedom
Residual (model) deviance:                  6138   on    10734    degrees of freedom

R2.likelihood:                              0.04847
AIC:                                        6270
BIC:                                        6632
```

Index

A
affective modality, 87, 90–93, 96–98. *See also* boulomaic modality
alethic modality, 12–13, 16
ambiguities, 147–148, 154–156, 160–162, 164–167, 177, 180–181, 183, 185–190

B
boulomaic modality, 18–20, 47, 90. *See also* affective modality

C
certainty paradox. *See* epistemic modality: and strengthening; maxim of quantity
challenging, 161–162, 186–187
co-occurrence of modal expressions, 50–51, 71–72, 125, 167–176, 184–185, 198
cómpre, 10, 16, 27–28
concession. *See under* epistemic modality
conditionality, 9, 106, 109, 143–144, 149, 165–166, 183, 190–191, 198. See also *se cadra*
conjectural questions, 172–173
cooperative principle, 152
critical contexts. *See* ambiguities

D
deber (de), 2, 8, 13- 15, 21–24, 26–28, 30, 63–64, 69, 71–74, 76, 88–89, 95, 97, 112, 155, 168–169, 172–173, 184–185, 198
deontic modality, 12–19, 21–31, 36–37, 39–42, 45–47, 50–51, 55, 63–64, 82, 85–86, 88–92, 96–98, 154, 162, 167–168, 188–189
descriptivity. *See* performativity
direct evidentiality. *See* evidentiality: experiential
directive meaning, 14, 16–18, 24–27, 63–64, 76, 88, 155

disque, 9, 104
Dutch, 51, 71, 78–79, 83, 122, 141, 143, 148, 186–187, 198
dynamic modality, 13–19, 23–28, 36–37, 39–42, 46–47, 86–87, 108, 149, 164–166, 176, 183, 188–189, 195

E
emphasis. *See* strengthening
English, 6, 9–10, 14–15, 17–20, 27–28, 35, 45, 51, 56–58, 71, 75, 79, 83, 87, 90, 102, 107–109, 122, 139–140, 148, 158, 186–187, 197–198
epistemic adverbs in questions. *See* tendency
epistemic modality: and concession, 77–79, 160
and inferential evidentiality, 14–15, 18, 23, 28, 61–63, 68–74, 104, 150, 168–174, 184–185, 195, 198
and mitigation, 52–53, 57, 67, 74–77, 154–156, 166, 177–178, 183–186, 195, 197
and strengthening, 74–75, 79–81, 104–105, 107, 147, 157–162, 166, 174–176, 180, 182–184, 189, 197–198
and time, 49–50, 60–63, 85–86, 97–98, 134–138, 142, 144–145, 196–197
definition of, 12–15, 18–19, 30–31, 35–38, 50, 92–94
evidentiality: definition of, 67–68, 87–88
experiential, 47, 68, 87
inferential, 9, 17–18, 46–47, 50–51, 68, 86–88, 95–96 (*see also under* epistemic modality);
quotative, 9, 47
reportative, 9, 26–27, 47, 68–71, 87, 104

exemplification, 164–165

F
factuality, 6, 17, 20, 29–30, 33–36, 41, 60, 85, 88, 194. *See also* reality status
facultative modality, 18, 45, 47. *See also* dynamic modality
force dynamics, 29–30, 36–38, 41–42, 194
French, 109, 173
futurity, 20–21, 26–27, 60–61, 63 *See also* modal future; time reference

G
German, 8, 51, 122, 141, 143
grammaticalization, 9, 20, 28, 38, 109, 130, 144, 190, 198
Greek, 7, 67

H
haber (de), 8, 20–24, 26, 28, 61, 69–70, 74, 88, 95, 112, 169–173, 184, 198
haber que, 21–24, 28, 88
happenstance, 9, 109, 165–166, 190, 198

I
illocutionary mood. *See* sentence type
imperative. *See* sentence type; verbal mood
implicature, 74, 112–113, 188 *See also* maxim of quantity
indicative. *See* verbal mood
indirect evidentiality. *See* evidentiality: inferential; evidentiality: reportative
inferential modality. *See* evidentiality: inferential
insubordination, 113–114, 118
intensity. *See* strengthening
interrogative flip, 188

(inter)subjectification, 83–84, 188–189. *See also* unidirectionality
intersubjectivity, 18, 51–53, 58, 81–84, 143, 157–160, 174–176, 183
irony, 153
irrealis. *See* reality status
isolating contexts, 190–191
Italian, 28, 61, 71–72, 75, 104, 158, 172–173

L
language contact, 22, 130
Latin, 7, 45, 67, 107–109, 170
left periphery. *See* peripheries of the clause

M
manner adverb, 107–108, 144, 189
maxim of quantity, 143, 147, 149, 184, 198. *See also* epistemic modality: and strengthening
mitigation, 46, 55, 66–67, 77–79, 148, 161. *See also under* epistemic modality
modal future, 61–62, 69–74, 95, 112, 125, 156, 161, 171–174. *See also* futurity; time reference
modal theme, 140, 176, 197
mood alternation, 103, 106, 122, 125, 128–130, 142–143, 190–191, 196–197, 200. *See also* verbal mood

N
negation, 37–38, 45, 49, 89–91, 111, 125, 133–137, 143–144, 159–160, 163, 183. *See also* negative raising
negative raising, 36, 92–93, 96

newness of the hypothesis, 105–106, 122, 151–152

O
objective modality, 36, 45–48, 81–82
one-commitment-per-clause principle. *See* co-occurrence of modal expressions
orality, 117, 122, 126, 134–138, 145, 147, 177–179, 181–182, 185

P
performativity, 16, 24–25, 27, 51–53, 86–87, 97–98, 116–117, 126, 139, 141–142, 162, 167–169, 188, 196
peripheries of the clause, 143, 176–181, 185
poder, 2, 8, 13–14, 16, 21–25, 28, 88–89, 92–93, 104, 108, 112, 118, 174–176, 184, 188
polarity. *See* negation
polyphony. *See* intersubjectivity
Portuguese, 9, 61, 70, 109, 113, 144, 163, 190
public face, 57–58, 76–78, 154–156, 161–163, 182, 184–185, 195, 198

R
realis. *See* reality status
reality status, 49, 62, 64–67, 75, 112, 142. *See also* factuality
reinforcement. *See* strengthening
right periphery. *See* peripheries of the clause

S
scope, 13, 18–19, 26–27, 44–50, 85–87, 96–98, 108, 167
seica, 9, 57, 104

sentence type, 5–6, 55, 64–67, 76–77, 113–114, 125, 139, 141, 172–173, 196–197. *See also* tendency
Sherpa, 69
Sicilian, 9
situational modality. *See* dynamic modality
Spanish, 7, 9, 22, 57, 61, 71, 76, 84, 103–109, 113, 128, 130, 145, 163, 190, 199–200
spoken language. *See* orality
strengthening, 46, 58, 148, 168–169, 177–178. *See also under* epistemic modality
subjectivity, 18, 29, 34, 46–48, 51–53, 64, 81–84, 103–104, 107–109, 143
subjunctive. *See* verbal mood

T
tendency, 147, 162–163, 183–184, 186–188, 197
ter de, 21–23
ter que, 8, 20–24, 28, 88, 95, 112
time reference, 20, 112–113, 126, 170–171, 190. *See also* epistemic modality: and time; futurity

U
unidirectionality, 83–84, 145, 189–190

V
verbal mood, 5–6, 8, 16, 55, 64–67, 76, 112–113. *See also* mood alternation
volitive modality, 14, 18, 47